From
Miss Helen Mc Manus
Feb. 3rd. 1956.

B
AnTHoNy/DF
QUE

SAINT ANTHONY OF THE DESERT

By Henri Quefférec

ISLAND PRIEST

SAINT ANTHONY OF THE DESERT

E·P·DUTTON & CO. INC
1852 1954
CREATIVE·102 YEARS·PUBLISHING

SAINT ANTHONY
OF THE DESERT

By Henri Queffélec

Translated from the French by
JAMES WHITALL

E. P. DUTTON & CO., INC.
NEW YORK, 1954

CONTENTS

INTRODUCTION

How does it happen that Saint Anthony the Great, also called Saint Anthony the Hermit, Abbot Anthony, Saint Anthony of the Desert, and Father of Monks, has fascinated writers and painters so deeply? Have they, perhaps, been victims of an illusion? Why, for example, was a man like Gustave Flaubert — a writer inimical to empty ideas and high-sounding intellectual systems—haunted throughout his whole life by this figure whose existence is surrounded by such obscurity that he might almost be consigned to the realm of the mythical? Why were there, in Flaubert's work, a first, a second, and a third Anthony, as in Goethe's, a first and a second Faust?

Is the theme of the temptation of Saint Anthony, with which the imagination can play indefinitely, each outdoing the next in monstrous and wanton details, enough to account for this enthusiasm? Was Saint Anthony what André Gide called a "pretext," and was not the clamor roused by his name in great part a huge exaggeration? Were Hieronymus Bosch and Flaubert, whose original intention was merely to frighten others and stir them to thought, caught in their own trap, and did they find themselves promoting Saint Anthony as though he were a seaside resort or a spa?

I shall not throw stones. The subject of the temptation has been responsible for some magnificent works of art upon which it is profitable to meditate. I shall be happy indeed if the pages that follow make it possible for some readers to draw nearer to the true Anthony, who was a sturdy man, and, above all, a man of this earth, and not that victim of diabolical torments, that Christian fakir, who has been created for our entertainment. It is true that Saint Anthony fought until his last day against the diabolical spirits, but his fight was a joyful and passionate one.

7

Introduction

The book that follows is not a novel. My wish has been to write insofar as possible, an accurate book. I am aware that the words "insofar as possible" do not usually mean very much, and that it has often been necessary to resort to speculation. I shall offer my speculations as such.

History, especially that of the distant past, is no enemy of greatness. The biographer of Saint Anthony, who lacks first-hand documentation as much as his chief character could have lacked physical comforts, derives a stubborn pleasure from this deprivation. At this stage, the most faithful account is little more than invention. It is no use wanting to increase the stature of the chief character upon our stage. Flaubert felt that he should present the philosophical side of Anthony, and portray him at grips with intellectual temptations, with all the heresies of the period swooping down upon his poor hut like a band of robbers. He thus fell into the error with which he reproached the middle classes: that of gilding the truth, and of valuing the case more than the clock inside it. The real temptation of Saint Anthony was more commonplace. Let us not confuse matters. Anthony had nothing of the armchair intellectual about him, or of the dialectician; he was not in any sense a man of books. During the first half of his life, at least, there was something a little slow and heavy about him. And, be it said parenthetically, what did it matter? Saint Anthony was himself and managed to get along in his own way. The intensity and continuity of his meditation enabled him to accomplish just as much as the greatest. He did not employ subtle refinements of speech, and there was a blunt awkwardness in everything he said, but his final reward was the very deepest wisdom.

This book is not an apologia. Although my intention has been to adhere as faithfully as might be to historical facts, this has not prevented me from regarding my subject as one of the greatest of the Saints. And that is precisely where I differ from Amélineau, that learned man whose intelligent and detailed research has done so much to increase our knowledge of Egypt in the early centuries of Christianity, and whose estimate of Saint Anthony on essential points is more discerning than Flaubert's. For Amélineau, Anthony was no more than an ordinary man, a "poor wretched monk," if I can put it in that way without distorting his opinion.

It is to be regretted that Rousseau, *"le douanier,"* never wanted to paint Saint Anthony. He seems to me the very painter for the task, with his understanding, sincerity, imagination and meticulousness. His naively theatrical beasts would have been more like hallucinatory illusions than Bosch's admirable but too sophisticated caricatures. They would have smelled less of sulphur, but they would have better suggested the desert silence. And we should have believed that Anthony could finally have confounded, and yet respected his enemies; whereas the secret of his victory is completely lost sight of in the amazing turmoil of shapes which unfolds its frightening bacchanal upon the reredos at Lisbon.

But Rousseau's would have been merely another interpretation, and not an authentic documentation. Almost all the essential knowledge we have about Anthony is contained in the *Vita Antonii* of Saint Athanasius, who knew him and was very probably initiated by him into the ways of asceticism. But Athanasius cannot be said to have overloaded his biography with tangible details. He wrote for monks, intending his book to be one of edification. Strict exactitude was not important to him, and, though there is no cause to complain of this, it is reasonable to challenge him, if not step by step, at least on many occasions. Apart from this, we can have nothing but praise for him. He was a sincere man and a clever psychologist. He wrote of Christian asceticism and its struggles with the pen of a master. Besides this unique and fundamental document, there are certain other sources scattered through the *Lausiac History*, the *Vitae Patrum*, the *Apophtegmata Patrum*, etc., and passages in the writings of Eusebius, Sozomen, and other historians. All of these borrow frequently from the *Vita Antonii* and are open to the same criticisms.

Introduction

Nevertheless, we are much more fortunate today than the researchers of former years. Many Coptic texts have been published during the last few years; only rarely do they throw light on Anthony's life itself, but they clarify the general history of the period, and that is of considerable importance. Sensational finds have occurred, of which the Gnostic Writings, discovered in 1949, are by far the most valuable. These texts refresh the knowledge already in our possession regarding the epoch of Anthony and the evolution of its ideas; they also lead us to a better understanding of Anthony's personality and the role he played.

I must acknowledge my deep gratitude to Father Louis Bouyer, of the Oratory, who has made available to me his thesis, *Vita Antonii et la Spiritualité du Monachisme Primitif*, a remarkable piece of work, solidly constructed upon dynamic ideas and full of original material. I must admit that, at first, the brilliance of the work discouraged me. This master theologian is at home with Saint Anthony. And who am I to disturb this lofty conversation?

Having said this, I can only thank Father Bouyer again heartily. I am saturated with his book and, though I have not as far as I know done any too direct or obvious borrowing, my debt to him is considerable.

Moderns are, in all modesty, in a position to pass judgment on Saint Anthony more objectively and with more assurance than was possible in Flaubert's day. It is not only that they have access to more Coptic material, but also, and perhaps especially, that Peguy and Claudel have come and gone, and because they and a few others have restored the sense of history.

Then let Saint Anthony appear—or rather, Anthony. I should be indeed happy if this book, which I have wanted to make objective and impartial, were to help explain the singular radiance of my chief character and show that he was a man in his own right and not a creation of ecclesiastical contrivance or of excessive artistic passion.

SAINT ANTHONY OF THE DESERT

Chapter 1

THE BIRTH OF ANTHONY –
A GLANCE AT EGYPT

WE cannot be certain of the place or time of Anthony's birth. Lacking exact dates and easily recognizable topography, our verifications must be undertaken with caution. If we state that he was born about 251 A.D. in a village of Heptanomis, or Middle Egypt (capital: Memphis), we closely approximate the truth, and if we go a little further—the Jacobite Arabic Synaxary and other official documents indicate Koma or Qiman as Anthony's birthplace—we find a village still in existence called Qeman-el-Arous, about sixty miles south of Cairo. Thus Anthony can be regarded as a citizen of the monarchy of Lower Nohuit (capital: Medum).

An Egyptian infant saw the light of day; another human being was born in a house of bricks made of Nile mud—a boy who was to learn gradually to walk, feed himself, and be different from other children. What would become of him? Behind his large eyes and in the humid smile upon his lips, a purpose seemed to be hidden. On the threshold of all the vocations he appeared to hesitate, unwilling to say which one he had already chosen.

13

The grace and charm of children convey a false impression of freedom. No horoscope of Anthony is intended — in any case, we have no data, even if astral influences were being considered —but what is meant is that this infant was closely bound, invisibly but surely, to his own soil, his own family, and his own epoch. From the hour of his birth he was definitely a part of that world. Being an Egyptian, he had a hard skull; "the Persians," says Herodotus, "have such soft skulls that you can break them even with a little pebble, but the Egyptians' heads are so hard that you can scarcely crack them with a stone." He was "a cubit in length," according to the normal Egyptian pattern, and he was robust at birth; his parents were strong and healthy, and his mother's breasts swelled with milk for him because she did not tire herself like so many of the village women. This does not mean that she lay upon a soft mat for the accouchement. Like others, she sat, gritting her teeth, while the midwives firmly grasped her clutching hands.

In 251 A.D. men remembered that for a very long time there had been human beings on the earth—especially the men of Egypt, whose enormous monuments almost everywhere riveted the gaze. Tradition told of empires with humble beginnings which had spread slowly out to the edges of the world and then one day collapsed. Glittering armies had fought terrible battles and men were annihilated; rivers flowed red with blood. Silence fell upon cities at which for hundreds of years the greatest poets had gazed in wonder, praising them as if they had been matchless pearls, dimming the sun with their beauty. Then at last the cities were nothing but heaps of rubble shrouded in layers of sand.

The long valley of the Nile stretches down into the wildest region of Africa, where men born of men had never been able to penetrate. (Nero was puzzled by this failure and sent navigators up the Nile, but they were forced to return because of the impenetrable jungle and the mosquitoes.) Here and there in this valley, and over the surface of the delta, opening out like a duck's webbed foot, human ants, so astonishing to the Greek travelers because of their numbers and their energy, hurried this way and that over the land of Egypt. Like a good cow producing her annual calf, the Nile overflowed its banks and fertilized the soil with silt.

For two centuries and a half Egypt had been deprived of her independence. Rome had overthrown the dynasty of the Ptolemies, who, while supporting their Greek compatriots, had passed for native kings. Their downfall had not greatly troubled the people. Wasn't it merely one dynasty yielding to another? When Rome's turn came to lead the world, it suited them well; they would belong to this Empire which intended at least to give them peace. When necessary these Emperors knew how to say the right things, and these things were always carefully repeated to the people of even the smallest market towns. "A good shepherd shears his sheep; he does not skin them." Thus Tiberius—the man we now know for a cruel tyrant—expressed himself when speaking of his Egypt.

There was perhaps a certain melancholy pleasure in being dominated by the nation which ruled lands and sea, and in going through life as a subject of the sovereign named in the *Acts of the Martyrs* of the Coptic Church by the titles *Cosmocrat of the Realm; Beautiful Youth, Worthy of Love; King of Upper and Lower Egypt and Master of Both Countries, Chosen by Ptah and by Noun; Child of the Sun, Born of Kings*—in these terms the local poets addressed the Emperor. Despite these doubtful satisfactions, however, the humble people of Anthony's time discovered that their material situation was worsening. The good shepherd had turned into an unscrupulous tax-farmer who tore off pieces of skin while shearing the wool from his flock.

When Anthony was born, the Roman world had long been suffering from a serious trade depression. This was particularly the case in Egypt, whose prosperity was rapidly waning because of the necessity of feeding the Roman multitudes as well as its own numerous population, and where the system of canals, wonderful but difficult to maintain, had fallen into disuse owing to the lack of regular upkeep. Discouragement and worry possessed what one might call the aristocracy; that is, the people whose rotating duty it was to undertake the various offices—the "liturgies"—and who were responsible to the agents of the central authority, out of their own possessions, for any inadequate deliveries in money or grain on the part of those whom they administered.

The precision of Saint Athanasius' style, in his *Vita Antonii*, does not extend to the use of many figures. We are the more prone to believe him accurate, therefore, when he writes that Anthony's parents owned "three hundred *aroures* of fine fertile land." Three hundred *aroures* would be more than two hundred and fifty acres—a sizable property in the valley of the Nile. If one compares Koma with the existing Qeman-el-Arous, which has about 4500 acres and a population of 3000—and the parallel is fair in a land where so many traditions still persist—Anthony's parents must have belonged to the prosperous upper level. His father was, if not the most, at least one of the most substantial farmers in the community, especially since the words "fine fertile land" were probably used accurately.

"Anthony was Egyptian by birth". . . . Some have pretended to believe that Athanasius, willfully or not, erred in so writing and that Anthony was of Greek stock. We cannot prove positively that this view is erroneous, and we can understand its fascination. But we must refuse to accept it. To link Anthony with the Greek minority, or even to place him in the Egypto-Greek category, which was small for a long time, but later numerous, would seem to be a grave error. According to every tradition, Anthony knew no Greek. He needed interpreters in order to converse, if not with Athanasius, at least with those Alexandrians who did not speak or understand Coptic. It would have been strange indeed if one of those Greek families, so deeply imbued with a sense of their own superiority—a superiority evidenced first of all by their use and precise knowledge of that richly conjugated language, of eel-like flexibility, that sings in the works of Homer and Sophocles—strange indeed if such a family had voluntarily decided to deny its origins and to pool its interests with those of the native people.

Far from being able to regard Anthony as a Greek, we find that his Egyptian family appears to have been quite ostentatiously national. Anthony was the only son of the man who was perhaps the chief citizen of his village, and yet, instead of going to school along with the other sons of the rich, he stayed at home. Anthony himself made this decision, declares Athanasius, and his action was prompted by his natural piety and a determination not to endanger his youthful Christian faith. But even saints must not be credited with too much! We should be surprised if a youngster belonging to an Egyptian family of that period could have come of his own accord to such a decision regarding his education. It is not at all impossible, but indeed easily believable, that Anthony's parents kept him at home for religious reasons, but for this measure they themselves would have been responsible. They must have wished above all to avoid the taint of Hellenism, which they may have confused in some way with paganism. Only the Greek language was taught in the village school. What would a little Egyptian boy gain by getting to know the tricks and the subtleties of a language which came from across the seas and was not spoken in his father's house?

This suspicious withdrawal on the part of Anthony's parents from worldly things, represented by a somewhat dilapidated village school, a somewhat driveling old scribe, and the most elementary exercises—learning the alphabet and the proverbs, reading and writing out fine poetry, studying simple arithmetic—throws an invaluable light upon the psychological future of the saint.

Christianity had by no means completely triumphed in Egypt, but it had become widely and firmly rooted there. The

Christian minority was important and energetic. The Egyptian Church was not recognized by the authorities, but its role in the national life was considerable because of its discipline and its unity. Its head, the patriarch of Alexandria, ranked second in the church hierarchy, coming directly after the Pope of Rome, and one can reasonably give his church the highest rating for enlightenment among all those in Christendom. Alexandria, where the fine flower of the world's thought was concentrated and where occurred the loftiest contests in philosophical doctrine, possessed a Christian "school" whose masters excelled in knowledge and eloquence. The most celebrated of these had been Origen, sometimes under suspicion but possessed of a force and a severity that was clearly shown by the austerity of his life—a beacon light for all.

In different localities and on several occasions the blood of martyrs was shed: a sowing by neophytes, and, said the Christians, indisputable proof of the divinity of Christ. In certain regions, immediately afterwards, Christianity began gradually to gain ground. And one of the beliefs of this Christianity, which grew secretly in men's minds—a belief that was not dogma, although it could be linked with actual texts—was a singularly consoling one: the Saviour would soon come again. Doubtless several generations had passed, believing themselves to be the privileged ones, those who would see the end of the world—but the Lord would not continue to keep his people waiting. What had been a dream to Saint Paul would become reality for the men of this century. In a little while the surface of the earth, stupidly reverenced by the heathens, would vanish. Once again, and for the last time, He Who Is would send His Son. Even people of mature years would live to see Him descend upon the earth.

After centuries of Christianity this early belief, which is still a part of human consciousness, sobered down. Great saints discovered serene formulas. Such a one was Saint Aloysius Gonzaga, who refused to take an artificial attitude of piety and contrition in the presence of death. Had he been warned of the imminent approach of his own end in the midst of a game of court tennis, he would have kept on playing.

This sovereign calmness, enlightened by intelligence and trust in God, would have been—in the early Church—the last refinement of Hellenic wisdom purified by the new religion. But in the little village where Anthony was born, we are in the very heart of native territory. There everything was taken literally; life was a serious matter, and people dreaded the repercussions of their words and actions. Christianity had not been completely assimilated.

To these simple people, Egypt was receiving special treatment according to the divine plan. Egypt represented, in time, the first of those foreign nations chosen by Christ to replace the Jews. She may not have been the first to be converted to Christianity, but the nation privileged to shelter Mary, Joseph, and the Holy Infant in the days of the wicked King Herod would not want to change her lot. Wonderful legends circulated, gratifying to self-esteem and imagination. Almost everywhere idols had fallen before the Holy Family; trees bent over them to offer their shade or their fruits. Joseph's staff took root in the sand and from it grew a balsam tree which cured blindness and leprosy. At Memphis, on the left bank of the Nile, huge pyramids rose towards the skies: and what were all these stones but useless heaps, compared with the little spring at Heliopolis, on the right bank, where the Virgin, Jesus, and Joseph drank; compared with the little marble basin where the Virgin had washed her son's swaddling clothes? Several years later, it was not known exactly how many, the Holy Family went up or down the Nile, mingling with the caravans, sleeping under the sky, always miraculously safe from sickness, brigands, hunger, storms; and making themselves known everywhere by the working of wonders—proof that the land they traveled was being secretly watched from on high.

It was not, moreover, impossible that their forefathers—

those who lived in early darkness and watched the pyramids slowly rising while laborers and overseers shouted—should have had a revelation. Did not most of their gods: Isis with a cow's horns, Horus with a hawk's head, or Anubis with a jackal's, frequently hold a curved cross in their right hand? The heathens said that this emblem—a cross whose vertical member was looped at the top—symbolized the key to the Nile canals; but the Christians, always clear-sighted, knew the right explanation: that cross was an adumbration of the Cross of Calvary, like the Old Law and the New. In tracing that symbol, the men of long before and those of more recent years showed a foreknowledge of their submission to Christ. Moreover, the Jews had played a role hard to describe, but clearly very important, in the ancient history of the country. The name of Egypt resounds a thousand times in the Holy Writ. Though the prophets cursed Egypt, the "chosen people" of old yearned just the same, during their long desert journey, for the leeks and cabbages that grew in abundance in the favored soil where every sowing yielded a hundredfold. When the wise men talked of the "promised land," the people groaned and recalled, gloomily, the "lost land." From cover to cover of the Bible, Egypt figures at one and the same time as the hateful land where the Holy People were held in captivity, and as a sort of composite of Bresse and Beauce, astoundingly rich and fertile.

The Christians in Egypt did not have inferiority troubles and they wished to live their religion to the fullest extent. Orders came from Alexandria, where the heads of the Church were quarreling, and the country people obeyed. They did not always understand the situation, but the need for loyalty was greater than the need for understanding. Whether the Christians in the village of Koma were a minority or a majority, they felt themselves to be a happy, fiercely compact group, and definitely united with all the Christian communities of Egypt, in fact of the world.

The Birth of Anthony — A Glance at Egypt

Athanasius speaks of the "church," of "God's house" which Anthony attended and where the Christians gathered. We are justified in believing that there were in existence, in much more important localities such as the capitals of neighboring *nomes* or *toparchies*, little true churches, but not in the humble village of Koma. Its quota of Christians probably gathered in a large or comparatively large second-floor room belonging to one of the faithful. They met there at least once a week—probably on Sunday morning. Crowded together in an oppressive and fervent atmosphere, they recited prayers, listened to readings from the Gospels or the Old Testament, sang a few psalms, and took Communion. On fairly rare occasions a priest or a bishop came among them and celebrated Mass. Priests were not numerous, and this was the case throughout the entire Roman world as well as in Egypt; no parish organization, strictly speaking, was possible. It was the business of each Christian group to maintain its own faith and zeal. Priests made inspections, changes, provided an impetus and a helping hand, consecrated the Hosts which the faithful could then offer one another at Communion. They did not remain, but left to the various village congregations the details of their daily existence. Koma, however, possessed a "minor cleric," a reader who, up to a certain point, could pass for the bishop's representative. He had a fine voice and possessed a certain moral authority.

It may be easily guessed that this situation was favorable to schisms, but such a danger, at the dawn of Christianity, was largely canceled out by the great good will of everyone. There was a competitive holiness in the hearts of all Christians and of all Christian groups. In contemporary documents, whether Greek or Coptic, there was a constantly recurring metaphor: that of the stadium. Each author attempted to vary his presentation, but the substance of it never changed. Christians were Christ's athletes, and Christ was the Champion of them all—in a class by Himself. Life was a difficult race to run. The martyrs, "the Fathers," were "the powerful athletes of the faith." Exercises in piety were like the oil with which a runner rubbed his limbs, or the training which was needed to keep him in form.

The persecutions gave point to these metaphors. In 251 A.D. Christian Egypt, having just experienced a few peaceful years, was suddenly shattered by a violent unheaval. During the two decades just passed, a series of Emperors had, as it were, marched by without having much effect upon Egypt—always in awe of authority and willing to bow down to new masters—and then Decius inaugurated his terrible persecutions. Eusebius, the Christian historian, declared this first attack on the Egyptian Church as a whole to have been the result of Decius's hatred of his predecessor, Philip, who was converted to Christianity. Up to that time, those in power had tried to strike only at the leaders: philosophers or members of the clergy. The magistrates now exacted from each man his *libellus*, a written declaration of his fidelity to the heathen divinities; and to further guarantee this loyalty they succeeded in forcing the people to make public sacrifices.

The pure Christianity of these early centuries took fright at such coercive treatment and the faithful were forbidden to compromise with their religion. If a man sent in a *libellus* or made a sacrifice to the gods, he was expelled from his group. But "weakness was universal," wrote Dionysius, Bishop of Alexandria and Primate of Egypt. Though energetic and possessing great gifts for proselytism, the Christian minority felt itself unequal to its tasks. For more than a year it had been a prey to "pogroms" which were tolerated by the magistrates. The Imperial edict seemed like the finishing blow. Against the minority, suddenly picked out as the scapegoat, there were armed demonstrations, and from that moment it became clear who was responsible. Perhaps without suspecting it, Decius had done a politic thing. Away with the Christians! In Alexandria there was murder and destruction. The city abounded in evil characters, idle and excitable, who welcomed the chance to make trouble legally: theft, violation, burning, destruction of property, and killing.

In other cities also, and in the country, the Christians were hunted; the less courageous ones (who, if we are to believe the Church historians themselves, were in the majority) denied their faith and tried to pass for honest, peaceful heathens, while certain others escaped and attempted to hide themselves. Families and whole groups reached the neighboring desert; individuals took refuge in the woods, in reedy marshes, in tombs and caves, perhaps in the houses of heathens. But in the end, persecution—and this is the reason for its failure—was powerless to incite unanimous zeal against the new religion.

Alexandria set the fashion for Egypt, yet Egypt was reluctant to imitate slavishly a city just as famous for its debauchery as for its libraries and just as notorious for its pimps as for its learned men. Alexandria was not Egypt, of which, strictly speaking, the city was not a part: *Alexandria ad Aegyptum* (Alexandria near Egypt). Facing away from Egypt towards the sea and Italy, the city lived only on the edge of the inundations of the Nile. The atmosphere of the rest of the country was less rarefied; ideas changed more slowly. Here and there the inmates of a temple, magistrates in search of advancement, fanatics, were able to inaugurate and continue persecutions, but on the whole the zeal of the populace died down as quickly as a fire made of straw; it had other fish to fry.

Thus we see the Church, disorganized by imprisonments, by the deaths or the scattering of her leaders and the defection of many of her members, collecting herself little by little and facing up to her difficulties. Dionysius, the bishop, was safe and sound; before the Imperial edict, while the bloodthirsty populace was indulging in new kinds of circus games, stripping Christians of their goods and then burning them, he had preferred to escape into the country to assist in the formation of a Christian *maquis*, which, while biding its time, fought with the weapons of the mind: speech and the written word. Dionysius was seized; then the peasants snatched him from the soldiers, and, though he begged them to leave him to his fate, carried him off by force.

It appeared that the dividing line between Christians and heathens, despite the official demarcation, still wavered. When persecutions began, Christianity was in a fair way to converting the souls of a great many people, and it was largely because of this that the new religion was thought dangerous. In that so-called heathen throng which was present at the lootings without actually taking part, or which listened silently to the public questioning of those denounced as Christians, many varied feelings emerged.

The number of martyrs, set against that of persons who repudiated their faith at once or after a few well-chosen tortures in prison, was perhaps not very great, but their ability to withstand suffering, their unshakable belief in the existence of a just God who would help them in all ways, the brave exactitude of their replies, which embarrassed their judges more than subtle quibblings, amply compensated for the weakness and the opportunism of their fellows. On this matter, one can believe the statement of Eusebius, who had not previously sought to conceal weaknesses: "The sturdy, righteous pillars of the Lord, strengthened by Him, acquiring dignity from faith in Him and a proportionate force and power, provided admirable witnesses to His Kingdom." One man let himself be burned alive; two others were sprayed with quicklime. In the case of one saintly woman, a judge set in motion the arsenal of tortures—and let no one think, in spite of the frightfulness of modern police practices, that there was anything picturesque or naive about them—and that judge did not obtain a disavowal. In exasperation and shame, he ordered the immediate death of two other Christian women.

Since Antigone, the idea of justice had made headway in the world, and it was becoming more and more difficult to condemn a man to death for his beliefs alone. We have no reason to think that the magistrates of the time were excessively cruel. Their relative callousness as judges and their fear of losing their jobs, if not their lives, must have combined with common sense and a sort of basic honesty. Frequently they made use of artifice in trying to prove that they were within their rights in condemning Christians. What they wanted above all was to avoid having to invoke the cruelties of the law. They delighted in Christians who abjured their faith, because that gave them a clear conscience. But how far would one who refused to give way lead them? In witnessing his painfully assumed cheerfulness when tortured, and the losing of his courage when confronted with whips, racks, pincers, chains, quicklime, pitch, boiling oil, would not the magistrates have the feeling that they were in the presence of a witness for the truth? It was impossible to treat him as a fanatic if they themselves became fanatical.

The service done to Christianity by the martyrs was greater than the disservice done by those who abjured their faith, and the populace, sneering when they saw the apostates turn green and tremble with fear, knew well enough that their denials were in part excusable. And as for the apostates themselves, they secretly and shamefully admired the martyrs. They hoped that the persecutions would cease and that they could be cleansed of their sins.

In many cases, public persecution clearly led to setbacks. To one judge were brought as Christians three men and a young boy, Dioscorus. None of them would abjure his faith. The magistrate, having some humanity and some prudence, turned over the three men to the executioners, but not the boy. The men were cleverly and barbarously tortured before the eyes of their young companion. Dioscorus did not weaken. He was shocked by the blood, the cries, and the huge clanging instruments of torture, but he was even more affected by the tenacity of the three martyrs. He would not be unworthy of their example. The judge would have liked to win him over, trip him up, lead him astray or frighten him, but his cleverness was no match for the passionate sincerity of the fifteen-year-old boy who scoffed at his questioning. The judge was greatly perplexed: to torture Dioscorus would be to give him the martyrdom he coveted and to demonstrate again, in a very spectacular manner, the impotence of that procedure in the face of such a firm belief. So he granted the boy a reprieve, which was merely a makeshift. Time would perhaps break the spirit of this youngster, exalted now by the sight of three martyrdoms.

Dioscorus was inevitably considered to have achieved a victory and people wondered, when they saw him, how this victory had been won. Some of them, with sadistic serenity, had looked forward to further tortures and were disappointed and perplexed.

Equal disappointment and perplexity possessed the governor and his assistants on another day. A Christian, not of the martyr breed, was about to abjure his faith. After trying in vain to attract attention to themselves and encourage their brother, some soldiers ascended the tribunal in a group and declared themselves to be Christians too. The authorities were taken by surprise and ordered them from the court, frightened by this little collective demonstration that resembled a mystical conspiracy and could have been a sign of the future triumph of such an ardent religion. Put them to death? That would have been an easy and a dangerous solution. There was something tremendously contagious in their heroism. More than a few would have been in danger of being won over to the new faith if they had seen such men dying so courageously.

A few impressive petty victories were all Christianity needed to recover and increase a prestige that the weaknesses of the body of the faithful must have tainted. Those who had escaped and were secretly bearing upon their shoulders the burden of the Church's resurrection strove jealously to rescue the remains of their martyred brothers, and to gather together the accounts of their martyrdom—perhaps without enough critical sense, as

The Birth of Anthony — A Glance at Egypt

is suggested by the contents of the *Acts of the Martyrs*[1] of the Coptic Church, which have the flavor of the *chanson de geste.* Embroidery and embellishment . . . but at least this elite loyally safeguarded the assurance of ultimate triumph.

[1] Though these accounts deal with a later period, the state of mind under which they were set down existed long before, and in a more pronounced degree.

Chapter II

CHILDHOOD

A BIOGRAPHER always looks for early indications of the triumphant future of his subject. Especially when his book concerns a saint, he desires that infantile actions should have a special significance. He should beware of this desire because it leads, even with the best intentions, to the easy stringing together of a chain of errors. "It is said that, during his infancy" . . . . Too frequently, writers of the lives of saints endeavor to begin their golden legends with little stories of the boyish exploits of their heroes. It is a pleasant custom, but one that a contemporary satirist was justified in caricaturing in the portrait he paints of a saint who, at the age of one year, refused to take milk from his mother's breast because it was Friday.

Psychoanalysis has been a great help to the colored print industry at Epinal, in the sense that it shows how all the events of a man's life may be controlled by a kind of subconscious logic. God forbid that we should speak ill of it, or deny that the first little happenings in life can appreciably influence the whole long extent of it. But biographers have a determined habit of excluding all but the conditioning actions.

Saint Athanasius is usually free from this failing. In his extremely short account of Saint Anthony's childhood there is not a single sensational incident or picture of "sainthood in embryo." The author complacently points out that his hero was not greedy, and that this was creditable, for his family's easy circumstances would have permitted him to satisfy his appetite. But why should this not be true? We believe him the more willingly because he does not ask the reader to regard this spurning of pigeon breast and figs as an auspicious sign.

But let us beware lest the barren rapidity of Athanasius' account dispose us to clothe Anthony's childhood with an undeviating piety; or to regard him merely as a model child — cleansed and sterilized, as it were, to whom nothing happened at all. We should remember that Athanasius' book conforms to the requirements of his day for a work of the sort. There is in it something of special pleading, of eulogy. We would say today that it is "vigorously focused" upon its purpose: to tell monks about the saintly life of the father of all monks, to make known to ascetics the education and training in asceticism of an enthusiast for the desert. Athanasius writes: "Since you have questioned me about the sort of life led by our blessed Anthony and are desirous of learning how he began his asceticism, and who he was before that" . . . but it is obvious that the account of Anthony's first years was of secondary importance for his readers. In any case, Athanasius was not writing history, and it is likely that his knowledge of the childhood of his hero was limited.

In its day, Alain-Fournier's novel *Le Grand Meaulnes* restored certain valuable elements scorned by intellectuals: childhood, elementary school, life in the provinces and in the real country; it also proved in a way how strongly and with what flexible outgiving the mind of a child can probe the depths of his seemingly commonplace life. There never was a childhood without its story.

We have every reason to think that, from childhood to early manhood, Anthony knew nothing of Egypt except a village and its near surroundings. This was sufficient. There was ample room for contemplation and careful thought. The outward appearance of Koma was similar to that of all the other villages of the region: a group of houses slightly raised above the encircling land. The sunlight was bright and warm. The calm glow of evening came down like a benediction upon it. There lived the children of men; there, those who worked the fertile fields crept into bed at the end of each day. No walls, no towers, no gates — the top of a pigeon house barely cut the sky above the roofs where storks seemed, by their absolute immobility, to play at imitating primitive hieroglyphic figures: a stork standing, a stork sitting on its nest of sticks. The great, dark-green branches of the woolly-trunked palms rose up in clusters like huge ostrich plumes, while here and there a fat sycamore spread its heavy leaves and branches closer to the earth.

On all sides, rich meadows lay in the sun. It was a landscape of the sort often painted by Van Gogh: tidy, perhaps too finished, divided into a series of plots and pieces, each one glowing with a different color. And there were stone bounds everywhere, meaning "Here begins Ammon's land," "Here begins Chreas' land" . . . and suggesting a peasantry jealous of its property and hostile to all encroachments. A broad canal flowed down slowly and lazily from a point sixty miles up the Nile, edged by willow and tamarisk, then with reeds that seemed to be pricked into the mud where crocodiles lay watching. Here and there were quiet blackish pools left by the flood, natural stretches of watery picturesqueness where herons and ibises glided among the blue and white lotus flowers. Irrigation canals were to be seen almost everywhere: wide, medium, and narrow ones, twisting their courses over the land and promising fertility.

Not in the memory of man had the water ever risen above a certain point, well below the level of the houses, nor had any-one save the rash or the clumsy been drowned. During the period of the inundation, Koma simply withdrew to its flood quarters and provided a refuge, as though by tacit agreement, for many little reptiles and rodents from the fields. To the north, south, east, and west, the neighboring villages rose above the floodwaters like big flat cakes or clumps of bushes. The villagers waited. The waters would recede in their own good time, and meanwhile they were benefiting the land. Upon the elevated roads, built and many times repaired by previous generations, caravans and flocks made their leisurely way.

Seen at close range during a flood Koma was far from an idyllic spot, and its daily existence taught the children at an early age how harsh and severe life could be. Dirt, poverty, and wretchedness were to be encountered everywhere in the narrow streets and in the houses. The village was smeared in the collective misery of Egypt, a fact which did not disgust the children or make them curse their fate. They simply took things as they came.

The Egyptian farmer, in the days of the pharaohs or the Ptolemies, was, generally speaking, in the grip of the country's poor economic condition; nevertheless, there was usually plenty for him to eat — good peasants cared little for meat — and he had a house, a wife, and children who were by no means starving. A strict and unrelenting supervision was maintained over the grain, eggs, buffaloes, vineyard products, everything that could be weighed or counted; but the internal revenue taxing was far harder on the rich than the poor. The government strove, by means of levies and curtailed allotments, to redistribute the wealth of the people, and to insure to all a moderate and respectable way of living. Thus several famous pharaohs were socialists before their time.

In the middle of the third century of the Christian era, the Romans bore down heavily upon the country. Their legions quartered in Egypt represented actually a very small number of mouths to feed, and their exigencies should have been complied with willingly, considering that their first duty was to keep off the barbarians: Blemmyes, Arabs, Nubians, and Ethiopians, all of whom were jealous of the people who lived securely in the beautiful valley of the Nile. The Egyptians were not interested in the Imperial bickerings in Rome, but their repercussions upon the troops were severe; frequently for the slightest of reasons, and sometimes for no reason at all, they marched from Alexandria to Babylon, from Babylon to Thebes, and vice versa. Whenever they passed through a town or village, preparations had to be made for satisfying the hungry and thirsty soldiers. Provisions and money were thus wasted; the men were stuffed with food so that they might have the strength to fold up their tents and leave the villages in peace.

This was no more than a visibly violent and, to a certain degree, picturesque aspect of foreign domination. The carousing of the soldiery did not vitally affect Egypt. A hundred times, a thousand times more serious were the levies imposed by the Governor for the greater good of his native Italy. Grain and varied merchandise, sent by local authority, moved steadily from the farthest corners of the province, over the roads, the canals, and the Nile itself, to far-off Alexandria, from whence the ships with their holds full of good Egyptian grain swept out around Pharos and into the open sea. Egypt labored to enable the Roman aristocrats to relieve their stomachs in vomitoria, and to make it possible for millions of semiemployed Romans to digest happily on the benches of the Colosseum. *Panem Aegyptium et circenses.*

Actually more was told than was true; cunning Jews, clever Greeks from Alexandria, serious-minded and gullible Egyptians from distant villages—all these knew how to exaggerate rumors. Whether huge or not, however, the Roman levies ruined Egypt, which thought them huge; the peasant world was disheartened by them. The heathen gods, or Providence, had imposed a duty upon the Nile to maintain the population of its valley, in no sense to support a distant and lazy country. Every year the flood was more or less satisfactory. Just as in Joseph's time there were stretches of fat and lean years. The Governor pretended to take into account the crop records in fixing the size of the levies, but the levies continued and, as though at fixed intervals, there were riots, burnings, and lootings which transgressed the rules of the game.

The fertility of Egyptian soil was due less to the Nile floods, which assured the fundamental goodness of the soil, than to a watchful collaboration by the men and the river. Human effort and skill doubled, perhaps tripled the natural effect of the willing waters. The dredging of the canals and the innumerable irrigation ditches, the straightening of their courses, the unremitting care of the primitive devices (wisely thought out and of sufficient strength) which carried the water up to the arable fields that were beyond the reach of the flooding river — all these labors may never have been placed under the protection of a special god: Anubis of the greenish silt, or Osiris, controller of the beneficent waters. Without such labors, however, the Nile mud and the work of harvesting would never, in those days, have succeeded in securing the existence of a powerful Egyptian kingdom. Hundreds of makeshifts and a kind of odd-jobbery on a large scale assured, in detail, the success of the operations involved in the simple but mighty seizure by the ancient Nile of its surrounding lands during three months out of every year.

The Egyptian peasantry were discouraged by the extortions of foreigners who kept off the barbarians but ate too much, and by the agricultural inexperience of prefects who followed the rule of looking out for themselves and intended to fill a given number of ships with grain without bothering about the methods employed by the growers. Would a prefect be unaware that inferiors, by definition, always try to cheat and waste time? This explained why the area of cultivation grew smaller and smaller. The desert widened and drew nearer to the river. Along the edges of the valley, in the zone not reached by the floodwaters, where earth and rocks fought for supremacy, it would be absurd to suppose that a piece of land could be neglected with impunity and still be used for pasture. The sun's rays would do to it what a hyena's teeth did to the carcass of a donkey: devour it down to the bone. If it was not manured with pigeon droppings, spread with crushed rubbish, and watered regularly, the arid dryness of the great red desert would take it over for good and all.

At the same time the population decreased. This occurred both in Alexandria, where mad riots destroyed whole districts, and in the country, where infant mortality, already considerable, rose still higher. In happier times, Egypt had bewildered the visiting Greeks: the Egyptians were actually raising all the children born in this country! Was it some mad wager? Now, though Egypt was still prolific, underfeeding and general poverty were diminishing the number of the populace.

Anthony's first years coincided with a violent epidemic of the plague, which began immediately following the persecutions of Decius. It spread from Egypt throughout the Roman world. The plague was no stranger to Egypt, where it had long been like a flame turned low but always burning. In Alexandria its ravages were terrible. Stifling heat, the odor of corpses and filthy canals, clouds of flies and mosquitoes, silence instead of laughter in the streets, mourning and anguish everywhere. Its curse was a heavy one. The Nile was full of dead fish; buffaloes died in the fields.

As for Koma, despite the silence of Athanasius on the subject it is hard to believe that it escaped the ravages of this plague. The sanitary arrangements of the little village, pleasantly situated on its gentle elevation, were just as inadequate as everywhere else, and from one end of Egypt to the other, the purely formal precautions taken by the people could not prevent the plague from spreading alarmingly. Contemporary religious anxiety perceived conflicting reasons for this spreading. In the heathen version, the subversive talk of the Christians had greatly reduced the number of sacrifices to the gods, and these deities had let loose their anger. In the Christian version, God struck down human beings who gave themselves up to the most degrading vices rather than be converted. Consequently, in either view, moral revolution was a necessity. Disinfection and prophylaxis were like poultices on a wooden leg.

Men got very involved in their reasoning, for the sadness and dejection of some and the anguish of others, did not create an atmosphere favorable to moral revolution. In certain towns, however, Christians set a good example by nursing both fellow Christians and heathens, sitting beside them in their agony and burying them afterwards. Modern medicine would find much to criticize in the noble madness of these men who exposed themselves without protection and ran the risk of becoming carriers of infection, but against this rational criticism must be placed the beneficent effect of a courageous action among people who had lost all hope.

We should like to know the reaction of the Christian minority in Koma: did they practice the charitable principles they taught, or were they content to submit to the evil and await the coming of the Lord? We should like to know this out of sympathy for those peasants and those humble people of long ago, whose troubles and anxieties were not quite like ours, but were just as numerous and just as serious, and because their conduct, in a measure, was going to influence that of our hero—a child who looked at them with wide-open eyes.

It seems that Athanasius was right—actually he devotes several sentences of an extremely short introductory passage to the matter—when he insisted that Anthony was taught at home and did not attend school. In keeping him with them in a Christian atmosphere, his parents made a decision which was to have important consequences. Let us examine the situation more closely.

Is it not significant that, in Athanasius' biography and in passages devoted to Anthony among the writings of the Church Fathers, we find no allusion to any childhood memory, to any vision out of the distant past which might have come to the monk in middle age? "They were themselves Christians and they brought him up as a Christian," says Athanasius; and after mentioning the filial obedience of his hero it must have seemed to him that he had told all when he wrote: "As he grew older he did not look down upon [his parents], but was a dutiful son." Only once did an incident take Anthony back to the days when he lived under his family's roof. It occurred late in his life, at least several years after he had taken refuge as a hermit on Mount Qolzum. Complying with the earnest prayers of some monks who were his disciples and had established themselves near the Nile, he left his solitary abode and paid them a visit; and it was during this journey that he encountered his sister, whom he had perhaps not seen since the days of his adolescence. "Anthony rejoiced . . . at this meeting with his sister, who in her old age was still a virgin, and head of a group of other virgins." This sentence is completely lacking in human warmth. It would have been pleasant to read that he had been made happy in this meeting, first of all and quite simply, because she was his sister, and not because of her religious garb.

All who talked with Anthony said that he lived his life with eyes turned toward the future. He experienced something like nostalgia for the hereafter. He thought that men, restored by the blood of Christ, should strive to fill the first Adam's place and to recover the happy years before the fall. To use Proustian words, the subject which filled his soul was "Heaven's Way," or perhaps "Christ's Way."

But if it is true that even the greatest saint sins seven times a day, may we not take it that he recalls his childhood at least once? And since, in the case of Anthony, contemporary writing does not allow us this, could we not fall back on a more modest supposition and say that at least seven times a day visions of his young days explained the actions and the thoughts of perhaps the greatest saint of them all?

How many floors did Anthony's house have? Was it built of fired or unfired bricks? Was it situated in the heart of the village or on its outskirts? Did it have its cat and its dog? Was the family living opposite, supposing there was such a family, a discreet one or not? Heathen or Christian? If we are not to know the answers to these questions, or to hundreds of similar ones, we can at least offer a few surmises.

"As he grew older he did not look down upon [his parents], but was a dutiful son." Obedience is a virtue. But being modern and sentimental, we should like to think of Anthony as more spontaneously affectionate. His attitude seems to have been excellent but cold. "Despite his family's considerable fortune," Athanasius writes further on, "the boy did not pester them for food in greater quantity and variety." In other words, it rested with him whether to become a spoiled child or not. By pestering his parents he would not have gotten a clout over the head or a tongue-lashing, but every kind of tasty food. We had thought that the fathers and mothers of antiquity were readier to chastise.

Anthony's parents seem to have loved him better than he loved them, and it would be easy to put this down to a quite considerable difference in age. Both parents died when he was still in his teens. They must have been people of good stock to have produced a son like Anthony who died at the age of one hundred without having lost a single one of his teeth, whereas his unbelievable fastings would have loosened those of any normal man a thousand times over. "His gums were slightly shrunken on account of his great age," writes Athanasius with discreet precision, as though asking us to tolerate this detail. The vigorous good health of Anthony seems like the final culmination of a race of men with iron constitutions.

When Anthony was an adolescent he had "an infant sister," and this cuts down the difference in age which might have existed between him and his mother. But we find in several Italian legends—not historically authenticated, we hasten to add—that Anthony's mother was barren for some time, as if the good sense of the people could not otherwise be made to comprehend his coldness towards his doting parents.

I speak of coldness a second time, for it would appear that much more than a difference in age existed between Anthony and his parents. There was a difference in religious intensity. While they were alive he had a frightening capacity for concentration and silence. They had no sooner died—had not been buried six months—when, on the score of human compassion, he relinquished everything they had left him. All that they had worked for and guarded with such care he distributed among the poor, which is to say that he threw his inheritance out the window.

Saint Augustine, who admired Saint Anthony, called him a "theodidactic" in an attempt to indicate in one word the mystery of this illiterate man who could converse with scholars and disconcert them. Would not "auto-didactic" do just as well? God taught those who deserved to be taught. Briefly, Saint Augustine, who knew all about parental influence, seems to deny that Anthony's father and mother had a profound influence upon their son.

A woman need not be a Saint Monica to qualify as an excellent mother, a good Christian, and a competent teacher. Anthony's renunciation of his inheritance may have amounted to a declaration of independence as far as family ties were concerned, and freedom from all compromise and restraint, but it does not follow that his father and mother were not admirable people. Athanasius' account is short and a little vague, and we are therefore cautious. But it furnishes no facts in support of the suspicions that arise out of its perusal. For instance, we might easily imagine a skeleton in the family closet. It would not surprise us to learn that, during the persecutions, Anthony's parents had knuckled under and given the magistrates all the *libelli* they required. Then, when the danger was passed, back to the fold and much giving of alms. If ever the authorities considered cleansing Koma of its Christians, would they not have started with Anthony's father and mother? And what of those fine paternal *aroures*, which Athanasius numbered at three hundred? They might not have had a very catholic origin. In the third century, money and land changed hands a good deal. Many small farmers were ruined and had to farm on shares or do ordinary farm labor. And a peasant middle class sprang up here and there, over the remnants of their prosperity. It would not be too extravagant to suppose that Anthony's father enlarged his holdings by means of a series of small speculative transactions at the expense of neighbors who did not possess his shrewdness.

Even the smallest piece of precise information would indeed be welcome. We have no idea whether the persecutions of Decius affected the village or not. Elsewhere, in the larger towns and the cities, things happened differently. Perhaps Anthony's parents were well thought of and it might have been considered unwise to arrest these village leaders who took such good care of their land and facilitated the collection of taxes. Koma was two day's march from Memphis and one from Arsinoë or Heracleopolis Magna; thus the police would not have far to go if matters there were ever deemed serious. And if we set one rational guess against another, and clear the parents of the suspicion of weakness, we might find simply that the Christian minority in Kôma was badly frightened. Perhaps they had long expected arrests, imprisonments, and tortures; and while splendid tales were whispered about Christians who had silenced the magistrates and converted the executioners, who were bewildered when they sang during the tearing off of nails or the breaking of teeth, each one wondered if perhaps he did not belong to a less distinguished category, and, rather than attempt the impossible, ought not, in case of arrest, to yield at once to superior strength. But then, perhaps the persecutions spared the village, and the little Christian group never had to shed its blood for its beliefs, nor was put in the position of refusing to do so.

So we concede that Anthony's parents were probably worthy people, according to current standards. But Anthony believed that there were better things for a Christian to do than carry on the paternal occupation and play at being the little peasant aristocrat, proud of his many bags of grain and head of cattle; so he made a clean break. Like a widower, waiting just long enough to satisfy the conventions before remarrying, he let a few months go by and then the rupture was final.

The child who did not go to school and sit with the bad boys of the village to learn "sigma, tau, phi" and "a self-respecting man does not tell lies," before going out of doors to hunt for crickets and frogs; who stayed at home when the sky was blue, listening with wide, softly gleaming eyes while his mother told him for the hundredth time about the Passion of our Lord, was not a dull child. Since he preferred listening to talking, and had no interest in what there was for lunch or in knowing why he didn't have duck or eggs to eat more often, his father and mother believed him to be a sensible boy. If asked to get a few cakes of cow dung from the shed to throw them on the fire over which the bread was baking, he would obey. If told to move his sleeping mat so that a visitor could be more comfortable on his, or to get the jug and pour water on his father's hands and feet, he would do so. His thought processes were deliberate and serious, in the fashion of the peasant. He was continually turning over in his mind—under the hot sun and perhaps even at night in his dreams—things people had said to him, things he had seen, and formulas he had just learned. He had not been taught literature, and the characters on a papyrus were still unintelligible scrawls, so he trained his memory eagerly. He devoured chapters from the Gospels, and the Psalms, sentence by sentence. There is no reason to think that he was less persistent than the martyred Coptic saint named John, whose parents were also rich and did not send him to school, and who knew by heart before he was twelve years old "the whole Book of Psalms, the fourteen Epistles of Paul, and the letters of our fathers, the Apostles." A secret joy rewarded him for his labors whenever an object, a scene, or a word suddenly recalled some beautiful passage he had just learned, and he could make the whole procession of words pass slowly through his mind: a lamb bleating in the street—the parable of the Good Shepherd; a coin on the dusty floor—the Lost Drachma.

Every word, he reflected, possessed a deep significance; also everything he saw around him. Meditation was not for animals; it was for men. In a little familiar universe, bounded by a few houses, several narrow streets, surrounding fields and hills, other villages, ruins and always the wide-flowing river, there was room for a thousand and one problems. And these problems were so many aspects and symbols of the only real problem: how best to follow Christ's teachings.

It is written: "Judge not . . ." and "Honor thy father and thy mother," and also "First be reconciled to thy brother," but these declarations do not contradict the exalted and convincing enunciations with which Christ attacked and destroyed the empty wisdom of this world. In the light of those enunciations, Anthony perceived—alas, frequently—reasons for criticising the behavior of his father and mother. He held his peace. Christ provided an example of filial submission all through his youth. Anthony suffered for their mistakes and prayed unceasingly.

What was this broad domain which made his father so proud, with its fields of wheat, millet, corn, barley or fenugreek? What were these fields where cabbages and onions grew, or where buffaloes grazed? What were these fine acres which the Nile covered with its silt every year, as a host fills the bowl of his guest? It was the owner's men who sowed those acres when the river's waters receded, wallowing up to their knees in the fertile slime. What were all these plows and donkeys and scows, these spears and ropes? Were goods and chattels real possessions? Not at all! Man was but the usufructuary of his own fortune, and God would demand an accounting.

Childhood

"It is easier for a camel to go through the eye of a needle, than for a rich man to enter into the kingdom of God."

Anthony became aware that he was one of the privileged and that his parents were also of that class. He sniffed, nosed about, and gathered his facts. In most families, fuel for the fire where bread was baked was rationed, but in Anthony's household the buffalo manure was not scarce—indeed it was sometimes wasted. And what was more serious, neither Anthony's parents nor Anthony himself walked behind the beasts to catch it in baskets before mixing it with mud and shaping it into cakes to dry in the sun; men and women were paid to do this. The house resembled the others where there was no poverty. No special luxury was noticeable. There was a garden full of melons and cucumbers. A room contained discarded furniture, and, during the flood periods, the livestock. On the second floor the family ate and slept, and the roof was a sort of terrace. Nevertheless, for no particular reason, the house had an atmosphere of wealth. The people and the things in it were clean, and this was not the case with the other houses. The mats and covers, the chests and the stool of honor were all in perfect order—no rents, spots, or blemishes anywhere. Dogs and chickens came in; also flies and mosquitoes, but their entry was, as it were, respectful. It was the dwelling of a well-to-do man—one who had better things to do than to master Greek and its conjugations, which were as complicated as the Nile's delta. Life had given him experience in other things.

Was it their Christianity and not their stinginess which caused the father and mother to eat the same food as that consumed by their servants? Did they eat turnips and raw onions and cheese made from curdled buffalo's milk, day after day, so that they could take more chickens and ducks to market? They would willingly have pampered their son, for they loved the silent boy. But Anthony gently avoided taking their gifts. He didn't want to eat food that was different from theirs or

that of the other villagers. He filled himself with bread, food
sanctified by Christ, noble product of the earth. He bitterly
reproached himself for his indiscretions in eating: a handful of
broadbeans nibbled at; a piece of meat (a wounded buffalo had
had to be killed) gobbled up in a flash, with his stomach cry-
ing "More! More!"

These small sacrifices, this childish remorse and contrition
should be carefully described; affectation can quickly creep in
when a writer allows himself to be too much moved. In the picture of Anthony as a small child, fighting against greed, there
is something of the colored prints of Epinal, and we run the
risk of deserving the reproaches we directed at certain chroniclers of saints' lives.

It is important, however to realize the great underlying significance of the somewhat solemn and banal gesture of a child
resisting the desire to eat an egg or a piece of fruit, which was
actually a refusal to share in the world's injustice, and reflected
a desire for perfection. The eating of a piece of fruit or an egg
could not be an innocent pleasure for him so long as there
were wretched people alive who could not do likewise. There
was poverty in his own village. Beggars clamored at his father's
door, their sacks empty and their beards dirty, asking for
bread. Among them were Kôma's professional unemployed:
blind, one-armed, luckless, and lazy; also vagrants from the
Delta and Upper Egypt who had deserted their wives and
children, youngsters who had deserted father and mother. To
anyone listening to their tales of woe Egypt seemed an ancient,
once prosperous country which could no longer feed its sons.
One man had had his house, land, and cattle sold for taxes. Two
others had suffered similarly. A fourth had been able to escape
with two donkeys, his wife, and his daughters, but desert brigands took donkeys, wife, and daughters and sent him off after
beating him black and blue. A fifth had lost his land because
the river had changed its course during a flood, and the authorities had replaced it with a stony field which shattered all his

plowshares; then the plague took his sons and his buffaloes, and his wife went mad. A sixth was mistaken for someone else and wrongly accused of counterfeiting; he then found it better to clear out. A seventh . . .

Anthony's father said that these stories had to be taken with a grain of salt; these chaps could work with their tongues and their legs but not with their arms, except to plunder and steal. But that did not interfere with his efforts to give each of them some bread, an egg, or an old coat. He agreed that times were hard, and Anthony might have heard him muttering to one of them: "Tomorrow we ourselves will have to . . ." The Christians of Koma tried to help the village poor, but the task overwhelmed them—there were too many "deserving cases." Young women who could not get goat's or buffalo's milk suckled wretched brats for years and risked ruining their own health. Families, evicted by their creditors, huddled in rooms only a few yards square, without light or ventilation, and full of vermin. An old woman's buffalo, her only possession apart from her rags and the hole in the ground she called her house, was strangled by its tethering rope. A cripple, in despair at the sight of his family dying of hunger, sent his daughters out into the streets to sell themselves as soon as it was dark.

Yes, the beloved native village, proud, mellow Koma, glowing under the sun like a many-colored scarf, offering its refuge from the gray floodwater, presented an epitome of the epoch's poverty. A peasant might be peacefully baking bread within the walls of his large room in the thick smoke of his fire of dung cakes, and, perhaps the next day, find himself a beggar along with the rest—a little less good than they at putting out his hand and telling of his troubles. Anthony observed and inquired, and his heart was heavy in his breast. He was reluctant to condemn his parents, because he was no more than a child; he knew that he lacked judgment in many ways and he pitied his father and mother because they were involved in this succession of misfortunes and injustices. His father seemed to be a man who was neither prudently satisfied with himself nor sure of the future, constantly pestered by technical worries and some moral ones too. He was afraid that the next flood would be too high, or that it would not be high enough. He was afraid that he would not be able to pay the village taxes, and he was afraid that he would be able to pay them. The position of the rich, he groaned, was not as happy as people thought. And besides, was he rich? He owned three hundred *aroures* but perhaps he would not have more than two hundred and eight-seven to leave Anthony, or even two hundred and sixty-nine! Times were so hard! The currency of the Roman Emperor had already gone down one third in value, and in financial circles at the capital there were rumors that there was still worse to come.

Chapter III

"IF THOU WILT BE PERFECT . . ."

Not one of the documents we have offers any illumination of the features that we would like to believe were attractive: those of Anthony's sister. "A good little soul" she must have been, with just the faint touch of disparagement implied by the words. Her brother must have frightened her with his silences and the imposing regularity of his life. A great difference in age undoubtedly existed between her and her parents, so that she must have felt much closer to him and probably obeyed him.

Visits of priests or bishops to the little group of Christians were rare and this fact made their presence in Koma the more august. On these occasions Anthony's religion was all-engrossing. He did not miss a single spoken sentence, a single inflection of the voice or the slightest quivering of the features of the man who stood in the place of, who imitated Christ. A glamorous aura surrounded the veterans of religious struggles, those hunted men, those outlaws who bore and would always bear the scars of their tortures.

The Church of Mark, the apostle evangelist, marched onward. Rumors of persecutions were heard continually, but the number of Christians increased with satisfying constancy. Truth, as well as death, came like a thief in the night.

*   *   *

47

Almost everywhere in the world the Christian religion was gaining adherents. Relatives of the Emperor were mentioned; also several important functionaries, and some ladies of high degree. As for the Emperor, no one seemed certain that he had not become a Christian himself, and, when he instituted a persecution, most of the well-informed declared that this was not entirely his fault: he had been badly advised; Satan had prodded him; when he feared that he was almost converted, he tried vainly to put off the evil moment by beginning the persecution.

Although what might be called the right-thinking party of those days drifted into optimism and rejoiced at the "return to faith" of the "masses" or the "intellectuals," Anthony was full of suspicions. The number of the faithful was one thing, but the sincerity of their religion was quite another, and far more important. The victory of Christianity, supposing it was called upon to win a material triumph before the coming of the Kingdom of God, would be hopeless bungling if it did not mean, for each Christian, the triumph of good over evil, of the mind over the flesh, and of God over the world. To try to make a Christian of the Emperor by converting his cook, his mother-in-law, and his wife, and by proving to him that Christians who respected Caesar were the natural supporters of his regime, was like putting the cart before the horse. Self-conversion first; then self-renewal and setting an example to others.

The worm was in the fruit. Egypt still had the Pharaohs' taste for statistics: take any six men and there will be one Christian among them; and of the other five I'll wager that more than one is vacillating, and perhaps tomorrow. . . . But the chart showing the increase of Christianity took no account of the disquieting progress of heresy.

In the room where the Christians of Koma worshiped, the faithful sat close together. They sang and prayed and listened to the reader; they were huddled so close that they couldn't cross themselves without touching elbows. A flagstone, well bedded in mortar, a palm tree with a straight trunk, a powerful buffalo—to such could the religion of the Christians of Koma be likened. It was not possible to speak thus of the Church as a whole.

Sanguis martyrum semen Christianorum. But also *semen haeresium.* Novatian, a Roman priest, made use of the heroism of the martyrs for purposes of revenge, and he maintained that the renegades had lost their places in the community of the faithful. Ceaseless penance for them; and they could neither have absolution nor be allowed to take Communion.

As if Saint Peter had not set an example to the renegades in other, more serious circumstances! As if the martyrs, who deserved to be heard, had not declared that their blood was shed to wipe out the sins of their fellow men! A council quickly condemned such mistaken proceedings, but did not stamp them out. Recently converted Christians were fascinated by a new doctrine which allowed them to become righters of wrongs; and the disguised persecutions which were going to last for ten years or more seemed to justify them in believing that the council had not been firm enough.

In Egypt particularly, Dionysius, the patriarch, was obliged to fight hard, by means of writing and speaking, in order to win the intelligent people over to indulgence. The controversy excited Koma, a few of the villagers took it as an insult to Christ himself. Let the renegades burn in Hell fire! It was the patriarch who wanted reconciliation and permission for the misguided to take Communion; and it was rumored that all over Egypt bishops and priests were being much stricter.

When the great majority of the Churches came out for reconciliation, the controversy flared up again. Wasn't it fitting that all the heathens and the children of Christians who had been baptized by heretical priests should be baptized again? The Churches argued endlessly, most of the Eastern bishops leaning towards the necessity for rebaptism, and the Western bishops declaring against it and basing their declaration on tradition and the authority of Pope Stephen. The persecutions and the natural wisdom of the principal contenders kept the dispute from becoming bitter except in certain places.

An unusual doctrine flourished in the neighboring province of Arsinoë. Nepos the bishop, saying that he understood the Revelation of Saint John and seeming rather to have been inspired by the disastrous example of Paul of Samosate, declared that righteous people were summoned back to earth for a thousand years of bodily pleasures. Such affirmations were scarcely in harmony with the point of view of the epoch, one which took satisfaction in being gloomy—the heresies erred on the score of dolefulness and misanthropy. The great local success of Nepos was undoubtedly due to a revival of the former high spirits of the people of El Faiyum, where, in the days when farming was profitable, there had been a sort of Egyptian Burgundy. The prospect of an afterlife in which they could drink the best vintages without the limitation of an empty purse, would not have frightened those people. In any case, if the proportion of Christians was larger in El Faiyum than elsewhere, the new religion—whatever the sincerity of its adherents—won their hearts rather than their minds; and all sorts of heathen ideas continued to haunt them. This promise of an afterlife from which the fleshpots were not excluded brought the country's old beliefs to the fore again.

The doctrine of Nepos, which made a stir in Arsinoë, also stirred Koma, about a day's march from the neighboring province, from whence it must have imported gossip along with grapes. Athanasius says not a word about this, but the matter was nevertheless serious. Despite the patriarch's entreaties, many of the priests in El Faiyum refused to acknowledge their mistakes and were pronounced guilty of schism and apostasy. We can imagine young Anthony's despair. There was still talk of persecutions; the plague lurked everywhere, and Christians were wasting their time in arguments and factionalism, when all they needed to do was to follow the patriarch.

Anthony's passing from childhood into adolescence was not accomplished in a day; the transition took a long time. The silent, stubborn boy had to take himself in hand and pay heed to the shaping of his ideal. Obstacles strengthened his spirit tenfold. Faced by the disunion which was disturbing the Churches, he came more and more to believe that obedience was the most important of all duties. In principle, heresy was not without its uses, for the problems elicited occasioned a deeper grasp of the content of revealed truth under the guidance of the Divinely guided magisterium. But if only God would stop men's pride from leading them into further palavering and hairsplitting! Men were like children who fell down and were so cross at everything that they beat the ground and would not get up; and they would never mend their ways.

Perhaps the spectacle of the extractors of quintessences and unconscious gazers at their own navels should have been regarded as the first heralding of the end of time. Did not those who cried out, "I am right and will not give in," foreshadow the false prophets who, according to the Gospel, were to cause men to say, "God is here" or "God is there?"

Anthony's father taught him more and more each year about the care of the family property. An important landowner had to be as familiar with soil, seeds, the sicknesses of animals, the whims of the Nile, and so forth, as did the lesser ones. He had to know how to handle his laborers as well as the revenue officers. And it was not easy! Always on call for emergencies! Father and son made long tours of inspection of the family acres. "Watch carefully over the land when I am gone, and then leave it to your son. This system of canals and the pumping apparatus will take a long time to complete. The high taxes and the complaints of the poor—rich men are always thought to be better off than they actually are—have often made me feel like leaving it all unfinished. But that would be impossible. I must do it for the sake of my name and my land. And I have faith in you, for I know you hate waste and are not greedy."

Anthony listened in silence. Would he be a temperate and a just master? Yes, but a Christian first . . . . But these days spent in rambling over his father's property delighted him: the air, the sunlight, the swinging along beneath the trees and beside the streams. He was too innocent, too full of instinctive longing for the lost paradise, not to experience a keen and ingenuous joy at being in the country. Without going so far as to make a Francis of Assisi out of him, we must admit that he was fond of being alone in quiet places and at one with animals and green things. Opportunity for such pleasure was not lacking in that fertile valley, which, though it no longer secured its people against poverty, none the less kept on adorning itself with many-colored harvests. Countless flowers bloomed as close to one another as the very drops of water in a river, waving and flashing in the meadows for months at a time. The north wind, by far the most frequent, kept the sky a tender blue. Dawn and twilight, bringing the sun up from its hiding place behind the hills and then letting it slide down again, had a luminous clarity. In the marshes, the lotus flowers slept. . . .

It was impossible not to love the Nile floods, their laws, their peculiarities, and their caprices; times when the earth took its ease in a bath of brown water like a weary hippopotamus. How could one not love its rising from the flooding river, rich and streaming with silt, anxious to exhibit its potency and to lift up its plateau of ripening grain and blossoming flowers towards the sun?

Though the face of the earth was destined to be destroyed, the hand of God could be seen in all things of nature. Each landscape was a fresco of divine origin. The course of the Nile, its majestic floods, shutting off the whole valley as easily as a herd of buffaloes might close a village street; towns risings up like the backs of crocodiles; mountains to the east and west, with their gray ruins and their rocks that looked like ruins; the sun drawing an arch of flame across the sky beneath which gently flowed the Nile—none of these things was left to chance. Not a single blade of grass withered, not a single stream dried up in all the millions and millions of *aroures* that made up the world, without the event being foreseen and at least allowed to occur.

During his preadolescent years, Anthony, like the first man in the new world, heard the call of the desert and meditated upon the terms of the friendly agreement that was to bind him to it. His father, a man of the fertile earth, told him of his contempt for the desert's huge sterility, its dominion of desolation and malediction, where travelers died of thirst after losing their way among the rubble and the nameless dunes and meeting desert monsters which they could not kill. And he lowered his voice to say, "The heathens tell lies about the desert, but just the same it is better not to go there. It is Satan's country. . . ." Memory recalled several passages in the Bible which spoke of the desert as nature's dregs, as the vitriol thrown by the Eternal in the faces of defiant people. But to no purpose. Nowhere was it written: "Thou shalt not walk in the desert." The Jews had journeyed through it for forty years. Christ fasted there for forty days. The idea of a reconciliation between God and the whole earth began to captivate Anthony. Satan's privileged domain had to be recovered. Though the desert was hot all day like the ashes of a house after a conflagration; though its sterility, its monotonous topography dented by rocks, its steaming dunes, were proofs of the Creator's angry gesture, everywhere could be heard the spontaneous and violent panting of a world awaiting the coming of the Lord. On all sides of the valley of the Nile, it was audible in the overwhelming dryness of these lands, a groaning like that of the bedridden of the Gospels: "Christ have mercy; Christ have mercy upon me!"

The lands of the villagers of Koma did not reach as far as

the desert, and the tiny mountain range to the west was no more than a suggestion of the desert which made a thin screen between El Faiyum and the Nile valley. To the east only, when there was leisure to cross the river, could be seen stretching away above a seemingly formal edging of rich soil and greenery, the steep, barren plateau of the Arabian desert. To the north, the valley of the Nile narrowed on the left bank, becoming a sort of esplanade; but to the south, immediately below the village, it widened perceptibly. A little farther below it reached a width of about twelve miles. There, in the heart of the rich lowland, rose up Heracleopolis, which assumed the role of a capital city —Crocodilopolis and Aphroditopolis were also centers of attraction for the people of Koma, but Aphroditopolis was on the right bank and Crocodilopolis near El Faiyum behind the little mountain range.

Living in almost any other village of the Nile valley, from Aswan to Memphis, Anthony would have been more likely to feel drawn to the desert; in Koma there were a hundred pleasing country scenes to take his attention away from its melancholy charm. Though near, the desert was not immediately accessible; the lands belonging to another village, or the Nile itself, had to be crossed in order to reach it. In the beginning, Anthony had, inevitably, the curiosity of the river-dweller, but perhaps religious reasons came first. He regarded the desert not as one of two predominant aspects of the natural world, but first of all as the symbol and the proof of a Divine act.

The monuments that rose up, in varying states of ruin, to the northward, on the left bank of the river, all the way from Memphis to Koma, made it easier for Anthony to get to the desert. In his youth, the little villager probably did not go down the Nile as far as the Delta, but he had no need of a personal expedition to know of the great burial places that all the world talked about. Some of these were very near his own village, with others beyond them, and still others beyond those. Near Memphis were the most famous of all the pyramids—that is to say, the most insane of all human extravagances. The kingdom of the dead, reaching to the very ends of the desert, was like the field of battle on which Satan defeated the heathens. To wander there, in the ragged underbrush and among the stones where snakes were coiled, was to hear again the world's lament and to be one with its longing for the return of the Saviour.

Anthony's father tried to keep this youthful devourer of psalms occupied with agricultural affairs, and with the leadership, rights, and duties of a rich man, passively resistant to the tax collectors, and attentive to the deficiencies and excesses of the Nile. But the youngster was unconsciously preparing methods for establishing his independence. Up to that time, though he had found things to criticize in his father's behavior, he had not visualized any future for himself but that of taking the older man's place. This was as preordained as a Nile flood or the gestation period of a female buffalo. And had not Christ said to His disciples: "The poor always ye have with you," which seemed to imply the existence of rich men. Well. . . .

It is very probable that, from early childhood, Anthony had had his ears filled with accounts of those who condemned themselves to poverty in order to live in authentic Christianity and to be able to spur on their brothers in Christ to repentance—the ascetics. There were several of these in the neighboring villages. Dirty, ragged, and miserable, they lived apart from other people, completely given over to praying and fasting. They were not beggars but wove mats and baskets out of esparto grass, selling them and then buying the nourishment they required. They were ridiculed, admired, loved, and feared, depending on the mood of the person accosting them. They were thought to be miracle-workers and prophets.

Rich or poor, all you need do is submit to the hardships that life contrives, said Anthony's father. To seek the Kingdom of God and His justice does not mean that you must eat peelings and cut down on your sleep. Christ himself would not ask that much of you.

Now that Anthony's personality had begun to develop, the world's wisdom seemed a hollow thing to him; and he thought with longing of the asceticism regarded by certain people as unachievable because they had never tried to achieve it. An ascetic could enter into the kingdom of God more easily than a rich man.

He chose this hero. There were no ascetics close to him. Neither his family nor the Christians of Koma could provide him with one to suit his primitive purity. Elias seems to have been the man of his heart; Elias was loved by him as a Mermoz or a Saint-Exupéry is loved by an adolescent of our own day. And Anthony repeated to himself the words spoken by King Ochozias and his messengers: "What appearance had the man who came up to meet you and spoke thus to you?" "He was a hairy man with a leathern belt round his loins." "It is Elias, the Thesbite."

Elias, the gruff prophet, who did not leave us the complete text of his maledictions, interests us less than some. But, in his role of desert Robinson Crusoe, he may be ranked among the most representative figures of the Old Testament. With Moses, he witnessed the Transfiguration. In their controversies with Christ, the Jews mentioned his name, and several of those who went up to Golgotha imagined without surprise that they had heard Jesus call him. Anthony was not an intellectual and was enchanted by this hairy man who spoke his mind to kings and queens and defied all laws from his caves in the wilderness where angels parachuted food down to him. Anthony carried about with him a whole pouch full of discontent and longing to grumble and fulminate, which never burst open. He was glad that others had had the power, which he lacked, to speak out with boldness.

Anthony secretly recognized himself as being of the lineage of Elias. In the absorbed daydreaming of this illiterate boy, several civilizations fluctuated. Ancient Egypt, Rome, and Greece he discarded. He lived in an earthly dependency of the Christian realm whose parent country was Heaven; his countrymen were all those who did penance in Christ's name.

During the flood months, an atmosphere of easy intimacy existed between boys and girls, and men and women. It was then that the village cut itself off, as it were, from its arable fields which were more or less under the floodwaters, drew itself up and waited in the muddy water like a comfortable old fishing boat without masts—a crowded ark. From morning till night, and from night till morning, all the villagers lived in the same lazily watchful atmosphere—a dangerously long period of leisure for dreaming.

Koma was such a small village and its people knew each other so well. When the time came round for getting in the harvest, every available person would be in the fields, wearing a minimum of clothing. A primitive, healthy custom? Perhaps. But nature's demands assumed the first importance; they were in the Middle East, the land of Cleopatra and early lovemaking. There was no young girl whose eyes had not been gazed into by those of an adolescent boy, not a single girl who had not exchanged glances with the youngster she preferred.

In Church, the half light and the tendency to reverie heightened the charm of people's features. The words "love" and "desire," so often encountered in religious readings, were likely to soften young hearts and produce tender feelings among those in whom kinship and propinquity had already established an intimacy. The house of the Lord sheltered many innocent youthful meetings. Is it possible that the young Anthony could have reached the age of "eighteen or twenty" (with scorn for such things, Athanasius leaves us free to decide for ourselves) without feeling the pangs of love? Would not that be an insult to a future centenarian and international champion of fasting and abstinence? We are too apt to picture him in later life when he had entered the stadium and when his long strides were more and more balanced. Though we have no text at our disposal to support these statements, we surely have the right to base them on psychology.

But if, as is entirely possible, Anthony did experience the pangs of love, it was not for long. He had no time to turn aside from the task he had set himself: to follow God. When he chose freedom, which meant for him renunciation and repentance, no unhappy love affair, however insignificant, was needed to clarify his decision. He had assimilated everything, had left every worldly thing behind. He seemed to himself like a bundle of varied energies and there was no longer room in his mind for anything but thoughts of dry sand, stretching away before him, upon which he would journey forth in the morning of his life.

Anthony's parents departed this life. Athanasius does not go into detail, but hints that death carried them off together. Anthony received their blessings, promised them that he would take good care of his still very young sister, and assumed the management of the family lands. He was eighteen or twenty years old, and that places the event in 269 or 271 A.D.

Knowing nothing of Anthony's youth and burning to tell of the beginnings of his asceticism, Athanasius skips several months and presents his hero in the limelight. With wrinkled brow, Anthony walked towards the house of God, dreaming of the days when the early Christians, both rich and poor, lived in a wonderful atmosphere of solidarity. What changes had taken place since then! He entered the church to find the service just beginning; he sang and prayed absentmindedly. The reader read out a passage which seemed like a marvelous coincidence: the verses concerning the rich young man from the nineteenth chapter of Saint Matthew. He listened with passionate attention now, having not the slightest doubt that he was the rich young man and that the voice he heard was Christ's own voice. Every word went straight to his heart: "If thou wilt be perfect, go and sell what thou hast, and give to the poor, and thou shalt have treasure in heaven: and come and follow me."

Christ had spoken. At the risk of scandalizing the others in the church he left immediately, his expression calm and his step rapid. On reaching his house he began at once to give away the rich young man's property. The poor of Koma crowded to his door, and a smile played about his lips at the happiness he was giving, all in one day. How wonderful to have the burden slip from his shoulders! He was like a woman at the end of her labor, an exhausted well-digger raising his eyes to the light of day, a farmhand watching the Nile mud close like a mouth over the grain he has sown. The crowd at his door thought him half-crazy, and old men muttered that in their time nothing like this had ever been known, but they hailed him as their benefactor and would have fallen on their knees and kissed the edge of his coat.

When no more land remained to distribute, Anthony sold his furniture. The few middle-class villagers who were buying grumbled that they needed nothing, but had come to help him out; Anthony was pressed for time and did not argue with them. He intended to give the larger part of the proceeds to the poor, reserving but a small sum for the support of his sister. That night he and the little girl slept in an empty house.

Though the scene reported by Athanasius was spectacular, it does not seem improbable. The fact that it was scarcely referred to later puts the seal of authenticity upon it for us. Even the small sum Anthony had set apart for himself he gave to the poor, for he remembered the parable of the lilies of the field. The words, "Take therefore no thought for the morrow; for the morrow shall take thought for the things of itself" struck him again with great force. He had no doubt that this was another personal message for him from Christ. One might say that all this sounded somewhat theatrical and that too many passages from the Gospel came into that thoughtful head at the right moment, but if Athanasius was merely indulging himself by putting in a purple patch, a smartly contrived touch, he would not have taken the trouble to differentiate between the two occasions.

The young man had promised his parents that he would care for his sister, and they doubtless took it for granted that he would share his house with her, and would clothe and feed her properly, until she married a good Christian. But Anthony considered that his true obligations were moral. What he had promised his parents was that, insofar as it lay in his power, he would see to it that she remained a respectable girl. In Koma there was a home—part *pension*, part school, if not actually convent—managed by several women of excellent reputation. Where could he find a better place for the little girl? He went to see them and left her in their care. At last he had rid himself, cleansed himself of his riches! He was released from all family obligations. He undertook now to make himself an ascetic. If he ever burst into laughter, it must surely have been on that day. He was happy at last—so very, very happy! Money no longer bothered him; the financial pinnacle where he scarcely dared step to right or left for fear of falling, had collapsed, and there he was at last—firmly on the comfortable earth, the good sandy track that led to perfection. For the first time since his birth he could call himself really alive and a Christian. Until then he had lain there, surrounded by his sacks of grain and his buffaloes, like a wretched mummy all covered with wax. Hallelujah! Anthony risen from the dead! One of Christ's tears would fall no longer! One of the manifold insults endured by Him had been obliterated. The rich young man had obeyed Christ's second request that he sell what he possessed and follow Him. Instead of showing a melancholy face to those about him, he was like the very personification of the world's joy when Jahveh's eyes first rested upon it.

*　　　*　　　*

"If Thou Wilt Be Perfect..."

The speed of the scenario, with no time lost between re-flection and decision, or between decision and execution, is somewhat disconcerting, but the illiterate Anthony was no dramatic critic. He was wonderfully, awesomely ingenuous. For him, a buffalo was a buffalo, a house a house, giving up one's money an actual and not a sham stripping. It is not enough to say that he was approaching perfection; he jumped, he plunged, he rushed into it. In two snaps of a finger, Anthony the rich became Anthony the poor, and he stayed poor until his dying day.

The modern philanthropist may shed tears over the young fanatic's sister. Wasn't it his sacred duty to attend personally to her upbringing and not to break away from the social order until she had the protection of a husband? It seems like intol-erance not only to have chosen poverty for himself but also to have forced it upon a human being who was unable to stand up for herself. But we are not going to settle that problem, and we should at least not reproach him with having acted like a cad. There is no analogy between his action and that of Jean-Jacques Rousseau, who made public charges of his offspring, or that of certain contemporaries who put their aged parents in the poor-house. Anthony lived in a very different psychological atmos-phere from ours. It is true that he rid himself of a sister who interfered with his asceticism, but we can credit him with hav-ing the highest opinion of those respectable women, and, above all, a firm belief in the eminent virtue of poverty. In his youth he burned with a desire that could not be expressed in a phrase like "If I were king..." but in one like "If I were poor...." He persuaded himself that he was acting for the best, for the true happiness of the little girl who had been left in his care. Strange, perhaps, but we must accept his point of view. And, since the name of Jean-Jacques Rousseau has been spoken, let us observe that the famous, "If I were rich, I would have a white house with green shutters on some pleasant hillside..." is the exact opposite of Anthony's thinking. If he had possessed the gift of words in his youth, he would have declared: "If I were poor, I would have no house built of fired bricks of Nile mud; I would have no buffaloes with long horns; I would have no surfeit of bread and cheese". . . and his voice would have trembled at the thought of that unattainable happiness, and the thousand luxuries of such poverty.

Having said this, and even if Anthony acted, as we believe he did, with surprising rapidity when the moment arrived, we must elaborate Athanasius' pages. Before the death of his parents, Anthony, in our opinion, had not decided to give up his worldly goods; but he already regarded them as a burden, a hindrance to his following the Lord. When still very young and inexperienced he had been called upon to manage a large agricultural enterprise, and he must have been bewildered by the power his new rank gave him. It probably frightened him to discover that his father's property was even larger than he had thought, and to realize what disagreeable consequences a stupid order of his might have for hundreds of men. It was unthinkable that he should play the role of a rich man—disguised, made-up, smirking. . . .

In his desire for holiness everything was grist to his mill. If the harvest was a rich one, he felt that no one man had the right to so much grain. If it was a bad one, he suffered too much at the sight of men like him, his equals, his brothers, dying of hunger. The sound of their laments was intolerable to him.

Saint Matthew's verses did not catch a rash youngster off balance. Between the death of his parents and the day when he gave their property to the poor, Anthony had broken the ties that bound him to a rich man's existence: tradition, love of occupation, the carrying on of the family name. He walked out of the church for two reasons of equal importance: to proclaim his independence and to acquire the means to assert it.

In principle, Christian asceticism may have been an individual and a spiritual practice, above the rough-and-tumble of rewards and prices, but Anthony, in order to attain it, did not rely upon God's love alone. His disillusioned thoughts regarding the daily existence of his times contributed in great part to that attainment. He was neither an economist nor a social theorist, nor did he have any background of learning; with the weathered complexion and broad shoulders of a peasant, he was first and last a Christian, fully aware of the manner in which his century lived. When he turned his back upon his fellow men to take refuge in silence and solitude, he was not going to betray the Anthony who suffered for others and for the wrongs of the world; up to the very end of his life, his asceticism was to represent an immolation. Christ, his master, had not died in order to establish a record for individual suffering. In mystical language we can say that Anthony's true cell was built less of boards and stones than of the tears of men.

When Anthony walked towards the house of the Lord, he was unaware of his imminent decision. He muttered to himself, thinking aloud. What were his thoughts? Did they concern the death of his parents less than six months before? "He was wondering . . . how the Apostles had left everything and followed Christ; how, according to the *Acts of the Apostles*, the faithful had sold their property and brought the proceeds to lay at the feet of the Apostles, giving up their possessions for the benefit of the needy: and how great was their reward in Heaven." Anthony knew that he was rich, and in a moment or two he was to hear for himself the Master's words to the rich young man; he began to consider with longing those early groups of Christians, with their communal social organization. Naturally the fair distribution of this world's goods did not seem to him an end in itself, but merely a way of following Christ; and, on the other hand, renunciation of wealth would be an enormous benefit to a rich man, for it would free him of a thousand anxieties. Nevertheless, however this passage is interpreted, we cannot help concluding that Anthony's asceticism was in great part the result of his brooding on the miseries and the wrongs of a day when they were countless.

Let us go back from those years—268 to 270 A.D.—to the beginning of the century. Let us leave Middle Egypt, heavily burdened with taxes and but recently freed from the plague, for a glance at Alexandria at the height of its power and gaiety, its philosophical discussions, and its commercial prosperity. Let us listen to Clement, the master of the famous school of Alexandria and the patriarch of the moment, setting an example of austere living and thus increasing the impact of his reproaches. For he was continually inveighing against the depravity of Alexandrian society. He denounced the use of perfumes, jewelry, bust supports and bustles: "Their hips and their thighs are flat and without grace; they build out their garments with added materials . . . so that those who visit them go into raptures over the elegance of their figures. . . ." He condemned also depilatory preparations: "God gave men beards as He gave lions their manes, and He covered their chests with thick hair as a sign of strength and pre-eminence. . . . It is an unholy thing and a crime against nature to destroy these distinctive marks of man's superiority." Perhaps this last quotation recalls a certain hairy prophet? And does it not seem that this Father of the Church was extremely rigid?

However, when it is a question of going back to the origin of evil, a new discretion overlies Clement's ideas here and there. He was a Greek; he knew the Greeks and was always on the lookout for their exaggerations. Among the writings from his pen that have come down to us is a short treatise called *What Rich Man Can Be Saved?*, in which the style of a quibbler already twists and turns. First: "Those who praise the rich . . . are godless people and traitors." But life had to go on; there had to be great commercial activity in Alexandria, with big bankers, big shipowners, big merchants dealing in warehoused goods. Second: "It is not our riches we must destroy; it is our vices." Yes, Christ had given the rich young man an extremely severe program to follow, but it had to be understood. One might decide, on the basis of one's own experience, that beggars were not the best of men, which should have been the case if the Gospel were taken literally. One should not sell one's possessions. Moreover, in order to acquire "an empty fame," certain pagan philosophers like Anaxagoras, Democritus, and Crates, had not been afraid to be the first to beg in the streets.

So when the assembled faithful shall hear the Gospel story of the rich young man, let no one leave the church to give away his possessions like so much rubbish. But that was exactly what Anthony did. Whether or not he was familiar with Clement's reticences does not matter to us. He was not a Greek, but an Egyptian, and he was not expecting to find malice in what he read. And in the meantime, the economic situation had altered; Egypt was deep in her material difficulties.

Should we be tempted to tax Anthony with holding extravagant ideas, to find him too uncompromising, and to maintain that he acted in contradiction to his later mature opinions on "discretion," the most important of all virtues, we must remember the personal and mystical character of his decision. This man who distributed his land because of a kind of youthful response to the great feverish lament that has too frequently risen from people's lips—from the Russia of the Tzars to the Hungary of 1939, or certain parts of Portugal and Spain—was not familiar with the words *"Latifundia Italiam perdiderunt:* great estates were the downfall of Italy." Though he had suffered at the spectacle of a wronged world, he did not actually follow his own impulse when he renounced the world; he obeyed the summons of the Master Himself, that voice which had called, one after the other, Abraham, Jacob, Moses, and Elias, and on that day spoke just as urgently and tenderly to Anthony of Koma, a rich young man who was already dreaming about the simple garments of poverty.

Chapter IV

EARLY ASCETICISM AND FIRST TEMPTATIONS

A CHILD's first act is frequently that of giving; the second, that of taking back. What must be admired in Anthony is not his spectacular first gesture, but his perseverance.

Anthony was alone. His day, in fact his whole life, unrolled before him like a papyrus upon which he had to write. He prayed. The Lord who commanded people to follow Him could not fail to send His instructions.

Anthony was in his garden, kneeling upon the earth. Not a sound came from the house, empty now of its furniture and its people. Confused noises came from the rest of the village: lowing, cackling, cooing, chirping, crowing, and barking. Someone calling . . . someone singing. . . .

Athanasius is as mute as a carp when it comes to the physical appearance of this man who knelt in prayer. In writing of Anthony in middle age, he declares that he had hardly changed at all since his young days; but this observation does not get us very far, since he did not describe him as a youth. Lacking actual documentation, historians must follow the example of painters: rely upon ethnology and psychology, and imagine their subject.

Anthony belonged to the Egyptian race whose characteristics were as a rule simple and clear-cut: more than average height; slightly curly black hair; dark almond-shaped eyes with thick lashes and narrow eyebrows. Complexion flat and usually tanned — lightening as we come down the Nile valley; large mouth; low forehead; prominent cheekbones. Square shoulders and narrow hips. Long legs . . . . Can we manage with this anthropometric chart? If we adopt the distinctions of several writers, there were at least two main types of Egyptians, patrician and plebeian, with, obviously, many individual differences. If we chose the patrician, Anthony would resent it.

Each one of us is free to imagine Anthony, with the foregoing data as a starting point. He was undoubtedly tall and powerfully built (and he certainly never turned into the bent and gnarled old man, with a tired look on his expressionless face, who crouches in some bacchanal painted by Hieronymus Bosch). Almond-shaped eyes. Thick eyelashes. . . . But more than these classic traits, more than the broad shoulders of a circus wrestler and the long legs of an athlete, we must visualize the mighty brow of the mystic, burning with faith and determination; and we must try to see the eagerness and joy in his far gazing eyes, and the calm depths of them. With these intangible characteristics the years invest innocent Christian shyness. We must imagine too, that other-worldly manner, carrying him above and beyond, which no objective description takes note of and which counts more than all the rest of it.

Anthony's perseverance was "perseverance in surpassing himself." From the moment when he chose God, he was careful not to form lazy habits, and in this manner he maintained his carefulness. If he selected a pattern for his life, it was one of small daily increases in the effective austerity of it. The progress of Christ's athlete could not be slowed down; his stride had constantly to be lengthened and his lung capacity to become greater.

He knew himself to be a beginner and acted accordingly. He went to see an old man of whom he had surely heard people talk when he was merely his father's son. Athanasius passes over that event far too quickly. How is the man whom Anthony considered his master to be distinguished from other ascetics? Athanasius describes him as "an old man who lived a solitary life from youth onward." This tells us very little. He no doubt impressed Anthony greatly because he was the first ascetic the young man had ever seen, the first of that rare company to whom he unhesitatingly desired to belong, and whose members, whatever his respect for old men, he was to examine minutely and carefully for behavior, physical appearance, and garments — the size of the beard, the number of signs of the cross to be made, the daily ration of water, the look of ecstasy to be seen sometimes on the wide, wrinkled brow.

Everything points to a minimum of words between apprentice and master as we read of similar cases in "the literature of the desert." Formalities were got through with in the simplest manner. After names and salutations were exchanged and acknowledged, the old man asked, "Do you wish to become one of Jesus Christ's athletes?" Then the young man nodded his head or spoke a brief word of assent. After a silence, the old man, not entirely without hesitation, said he would accept him and the initiation began without preamble. The old man did not actually give advice unless he was asked a direct question (and the young one blushed at his own curiosity); he went about his occupations as serenely as if he had been alone and his pupil had only to watch and take inspiration from his conduct. When the old man wove baskets the young one got some willow shoots and did likewise. When the master sang hymns the pupil sang with him. It frequently occurred to the old man to set tests in asceticism: indefinite postponement of the time for eating; the saying of endless prayers before eating bread; the placing of a piece of bread before each pupil and eating but half of his own; the interrupting of sleep every three hours to chant a psalm nine times over. The young man had to be on his guard and never let himself weaken under the serene but watchful eye of his piously crafty master. For instance, it was necessary to realize that if the old man ate but half of his bread, no matter how impatient his pupils — "You are young; you've got all your teeth; but I am approaching the tomb"—he was still required to imitate him and eat but half of his own. In one sense Anthony and his master were antagonists; the old man played the role of the Devil and invented temptations, which the young one had to know, with God's help, how to resist.

These were only the first stages of asceticism — its husk, its outside covering. But these procedures were indispensable. The new life would permit of no quibbling. This tunnel of privations and varied exhaustions would lead inevitably to the light. Then came a day when the old man unbent; a few beautiful and pious phrases emerged between mustache and beard; only a few, but they were weighted with the experience of a whole lifetime of wisdom. The young man endorsed them and added several personal remarks. There followed a long silence. Each one assimilated the words of the other — a sort of spiritual digestion which could not be hurried. Then they parted company. . . . Years later, when the old man had long since "rejoined the Fathers," the young man, himself old now, would be instructing, with the selfsame simple methods, some other young man who had come to him because of his reputation for piety. And he would not fail to tell this pupil that he had begun his asceticism with an old man named so-and-so, who had been a great athlete.

Anthony's sojourn with the old man did not perhaps resemble in all its details those of later candidates for the monastic life with their famous elders. It was short and he seems to have been a half-time, rather than a full-time pupil. Apparently he returned almost every evening to his village.

The pattern of his life underwent other changes. After building a little hut in his garden, he abandoned it for another, which, according to the rules of asceticism, he had erected some distance from human dwellings. He refrained from begging. Athanasius says that he accepted the opinion of Saint Paul, whose words, "If any would not work, neither should he eat," formed one of the most famous slogans in desert literature. So he worked. He wove mats and made baskets, and this occupation did not interfere with his thinking or his praying.

It appears that he sold his mats and baskets profitably, since, according to Athanasius, "with part of his earnings he bought bread; he gave the rest to the poor." It is true that he needed very little bread, but all the same, one wonders if the village really needed an extra artisan, and if people did not buy merely out of charity. We can imagine them going to him for small repairs — for odd jobs, to speak frankly. When he gave away his property he had shown too much generosity for people to refuse their help now. Curiosity also played its part, and admiration. The village was moving with the times: it had its pigeon house, its Virgins' Home, its ascetic!

But the villagers could not have suspected that this delightful eccentric with his still meager beard and the manner, not of a simpleton, but of someone seeking, seriously and trustingly, the solution of a problem, would ever set the world's greatest painters dreaming. And it was better so, for the village children might have felt that they should bother him oftener — creeping stealthily to his door and giving it a push to see if he were not asleep instead of praying.

Occasionally the documentation is fuller. The old man's restrictions on eating and other pious recommendations had not completely satisfied Anthony's own requirements. Possibly the old man had suspected him of possessing unusual mystical qualities and had, of his own accord, told him the names of other local ascetics he should visit. However this may have been, Anthony saw them all. Athanasius likens him to a zealous bee. He makes one think also of a young painter of long ago, going from studio to studio and examining the masters' work in order to decide upon an original manner for himself.

Anthony profited enormously by these pious pilgrimages, for, in going from one ascetic's hut to another, he familiarized himself with many different ways of living: and these varied not only in small changes of schedule, in the choice of psalms, or in the size of the water ration. All the ascetics led lives of privation and solitude, but their individual characteristics, perceivable in their faces, were responsible for certain variations. Though they would not have used the word, they were like "specialists." Anthony's slow, searching reflections while with each one resulted in discoveries. One held charity to be of prime importance, another the tiring of the body. A third was careful always to have a joyful gleam in his eyes; a fourth devoted himself to study. When he went to visit them, instead of saying to himself that he was going to see Marcellus, the ascetic, or Old John, our young Anthony would call them Patient, Abstinent, Learned, and so on. He visited men and virtues at the same time. This was an arbitrary simplification but one that helped his spiritual development.

Once back in his hut and absorbed in his vigils or his basket making, Anthony marshaled his thoughts, compared, and ruminated. Those athletes of Christ who lived near Koma had started sooner and were keeping a certain number of cubits ahead of him, but he would overtake them. He had given his land to the poor; also his money. But it happened that he had kept his health for himself. His blood was ardent, his bones strong; his stomach functioned well, and his muscles were powerfully elastic. All these attributes would be concentrated upon accomplishing the task! Young Ascetic would become more patient than Patient, would eat and drink less than Abstinent. Young Ascetic had a good memory which he always kept well oiled, and, if he paid eager attention to passages read aloud from the Holy Scriptures, he would eventually know more than Learned, who had to bury his nose in his papyri before he could quote anything.

"He was jealous of his contemporaries in but one way," wrote Athanasius, "he could not endure any of them to be better than he was in achieving perfection." Jealousy is always jealousy;

and these feverish excesses would gradually be overcome by Anthony's holiness, for they were partly due to his insufficient trust in God and an exaggerated fear of His justice. One of the most important themes in desert literature was to be a warning to the young against sensational performances. There was always a risk of replacing one evil with a worse: a difficulty about eating overcome and then followed by pride which was offensive to God.

Let us forgive Anthony this passion to be a good pupil on grounds of his youth and physical vigor. He would overcome it and acquit himself well, for there was someone watching over him, waiting for his first sign of weakness — a person who broke into all silences and for whom there was room everywhere, even on an ascetic's sleeping mat which was made for only one man to lie on.

We learn from Athanasius' book that in 270 A.D. asceticism was in a fair way to become a kind of profession, rare no doubt, and eccentric, but with regulations which the ascetics obeyed, and which the uninitiated surmised were in existence.

The origin of Christian asceticism has long been thought to be a subject for endless conjecture. It would not have been displeasing to discover some heathen lineage there, and a thousand comparisons have been made — ingenious, learned, intelligent, none of them surviving the scrutiny of common sense. Christian asceticism is a Christian movement, or, if we must have another word, a human movement. All has not been said of man when he is called "ζῷον πολιτικόν," "political being," for there are so many times when that being, though loving groups and discussions, must have silence and solitude and calls himself "ζῷον μοναστικόν," "monastic being." In all religions and in all climes, there have always been men who have wanted to withdraw from the rest of mankind, and, to attain their ideal, live isolated lives of sustained privation.

There is no need to consider the infiltration of Brahminic thought, or, when speaking of Anthony and his peers, to mention the Essenes described by the Jewish historian Josephus (they never proselytized), or the Therapeutae discussed by Philo, the Jewish philosopher at Alexandria, who were thoroughly saturated by Platonian thought. And, rather than suggest that the first ascetics should have followed the example of the recluses in the Serapeum at Memphis — who, up to a certain point, could be called monks, heathen monks, shut up in cells (we remember that Memphis was only sixty miles from Koma)—it would be far better to point out plainly that the religion of Egypt gradually emerged with some splendid precepts, and promised a future life of blessedness to no one but the righteous. Let those hear who would hear! It disposed men to meditation, to examination of conscience, and so to seclusion.

But after all, the ascetics of Middle Egypt in the third century were uprooted Egyptians. They despised the mixture of Greek and Egyptian religions, with a bit of stale Roman thought for added flavor, and an Imperial seal of approval in the style of the day, which all the heathens of their district were forced to swallow, just as they despised the absurd funerary monuments, senseless in shape and size, which edged the desert—vainglorious tombs, dedicated to decrepitude. Their spiritual bread was the Bible. From end to end, the Bible is filled with incidents, even whole books, concerning the acts, thoughts, and words of men who made of themselves the rubbish and sweepings of the world — wild and solitary men, hairy hermits eating roots and sleeping in old river beds, who were seventy times seven times more pleasing to Jahveh than the kings, princes, and potentates, and other favorite victims of Beelzebub. And if we turn from the Old Testament to the New, we find praise of the ascetic life running through the Gospels like a pure stream of melody.

Patient, Abstinent, Learned, and Young Ascetic were following a path marked out by Christians. And not the least interesting thing about them was the discovery that they detached themselves from their co-religionists rather than from the heathens, whose thinking, to their sense, did not stand up and was not worth examining. Even though the wheel of time had turned, Christianity could still pass for a revolutionary scoop-net; but deep in their hearts these men had discovered that it crushed originality and was becoming too middle-class and matter-of-fact; that it was adorning itself with Greek tinsel; that it was becoming infected with heathen ideas and turning political. And each one (the decisions were separate and, of course, no one would have given the signal) had chosen to withdraw from these currents, separating himself from the Christian-Heathens and the Heathen-Christians and retreating into solitude to cultivate his asceticism.

But the discoveries they made would one day become common property, and, in the end, their service to Christianity was to be far greater than that of the Emperor Constantine himself, with all his legions and all his cleverness.

In the first sentence of Thaïs, Anatole France speaks of the "desert peopled with anchorites." Let us throw the ball back to him and say that the ascetic's hut was peopled with enemies. Enemies — and one enemy: Satan. And all his followers.

To Anthony, the first weeks, the first months of his ascetic life seemed like a long honeymoon. Alcibiades himself, when only temporary privations were involved, was able to give points to some Spartans. . . . When Anthony was with his ascetics he experienced a spiritual joy whose intensity he had never before dared to guess at. What happiness it was to have these friends everywhere, these accomplices in the Holy Cause, these watchers for the coming of the Lord, these righteous men who brought down mercy upon the earth! What happiness to hear from them the golden words of the Gospels in the midst of so much timid hesitation — it made the heart feel like a slave freed from bondage.

Anthony had taken the plunge — a difficult one; he was thankful that Providence had allowed him to do it correctly and did not blame Providence for seeing to it that the villagers took an increasingly sympathetic interest in his efforts. They doubtless had not actually believed that he would hold out so long and several wondered for quite a while whether he would not take back his land from them. But their anxiety was needless. He had built his new hut himself, as any other poor man would do, and in it he crouched, without disturbing anyone. He wouldn't have taken a penny from anyone; and if there were none but he, on moonless nights, to slink around the houses, the dogs could have slept peacefully. Even the heathens praised him: an abstainer is always an abstainer, but Anthony's God had really overwhelmed him. His example made people think harder than did the endless philosophical discussions about aeons or the person of the Godhead.

Satan was a wise old fox. He concluded immediately that Anthony was of the martyr breed, and that, at a time when the phrase, "all that is new is beautiful," held good for him regarding his ascetic privations, it would have been unwise to launch a frontal attack. Better to let him dream awhile and harass him with nameless silent enemies. That was the way then to deal with him. He would be like a surrounded garrison which could never discover what threatened it and was finally exhausted by internal revolts.

Anthony had scarcely completed his apprenticeship in asceticism and had not yet worked out his plan for the new life, when a fog seemed to rise up around him in which he could hear many voices calling: "Anthony! Come back! Give up your absurd way of living and your foolish, stubborn behavior. Think of those three hundred *aroures* which your forebears so patiently acquired: those pastures, and those fields which you harvested so thoughtlessly for the unworthy poor. Don't you remember the sister your parents left in your care? We are your cousins, your cousins' children, your uncles, and your great-uncles — we want you back with us again. We'll embrace and you'll have back some of your land, Anthony. You're young and serious-minded; you'll be rich again. Come, Anthony, give up your foolishness! Think of that wonderful bread your mother baked for you on your birthdays, and that goose's leg you devoured while everybody laughed at you! Come back — you can fish the Nile and hunt in the marshes. In the name of Christ, come back. We'll let you stay and we'll honor you because of your probation in asceticism. Here's Anthony, we'll be saying, the wise and generous young man who did not confuse virtue with stubbornness."

Obviously, if he took seriously these voices which were becoming angrier, Anthony was going to have a terrible existence. One did not play games with hunger and thirst, or amuse oneself by not sleeping. That would be a madness like wanting to split stones with one's fingernails.

Anthony endured this attack without weakening. His fellow ascetics had told him of the Evil One's traps so that his underhand maneuverings did not frighten him overmuch. Young Ascetic would never have been anyone but Young Ascetic if he had not been obliged to struggle against such odds. They were struggles without glory, but indispensable, and they were cherished by the Lord. Give up prayer and privation, and set his feet upon the path back to his village? He could scorn such stupid advice by merely increasing his devotions and his fasting. If the Other insisted: "You don't want to go back, and it is because you are proud; you are ashamed, and you are afraid that the children in the streets will make fun of you," then he must not hunt for clever replies, but pray harder and eat less.

The adversary realized that he was beaten and altered his strategy. He used weapons against Anthony which, since the very dawn of the world, had won for him his most famous

victories, weapons which had prevailed over Samson and Da-
vid. A thousand voluptuous thoughts swooped down upon
poor Anthony, like locusts upon a field of maize, and the chaste
young man whose loves, if he had them, never got beyond
tender glances and innocent words, knew that he was frittering
away his life. A plague on his heart! on his friendships with
dirty, shriveled old men; on these talks about the water ration
and the archangel. Women for him — all of them! Because of
his body's strength and life's acquiescence. When one had the
same name as Cleopatra's lover, there was nothing to fear.

Anthony looked at himself with the disgust of a medical
student viewing his first cadaver. Scenes from his young days
came into his mind, conveniently distorted. He imagined himself a dissolute Roman soldier or a young brawler from Alexandria, and he enjoyed himself in imagination with everyone he
saw — nothing forbidden, nothing sacred for the healthy brutality of men. . . .

With a bishop's fine audacity, Athanasius writes: "He [Sa-
tan] attacked the young man, perplexing him day and night,
pestering him in such a way that those who saw him were
aware of the fight he was making." It was a long struggle and
a terrible one, but never for a moment did those voluptuous
thoughts get the better of him. Anthony disposed of them all
with the boiling oil of his fasting, the black pitch of his prayers,
the javelins of his meditations on death and damnation, and
the sudden sorties of his amazing faith in Christ. He was continually remaking his hut — which might have become a brothel
— into a haven of spiritual refreshment, light, peace, and pious
solitude. His was the patience of a soldier cleansing himself of
lice, of a peasant crushing potato beetles. He would either
obtain peaceful repose, or die in the attempt and go to his
heavenly reward — two alternatives which did not displease
him.

The Devil got nowhere with this erotic imagery. The
youngster whom he was trying to rouse resisted his temptations

78

as successfully as a hermit with sixty years of fasting and abstinence behind him would have done. He was made of flesh and blood, but he did not feel it to be in any way necessary for him to mutilate himself as Origen had done.

In his rage — before attacking on another front — the Devil bestowed, as it were, a favor: he showed himself in human form! For this occasion, he took to himself the face and form of a little black boy. He appeared and at once admitted his defeat. Anthony suspected trickery and pretended not to understand. Boldly and forthrightly, he asked the boy who he was, whereupon, in a mournful voice, the boy replied, "I am the spirit of fornication," and went on to speak of his past triumphs and his present defeat. Anthony laughed at him contemptuously and the little black boy took himself off.

Should we say no more of this incident? We can guess at the suspicions such a visit would arouse in some minds. Wasn't it simply another temptation? Did not Anthony, who had not submitted to feminine seduction, and, in order to escape it more quickly, had persuaded himself that women were dangerous beings, risk yielding to other carnal pleasures? He would not have been the first to do so, in that part of the world. But let us not press the point. Whether the black boy appeared to him adorned with the beauty of Corydon, or not, Anthony brushed the whole incident aside. He was pure, determined, and unswerving.

a refusal to permit a reduction, a rise or a fall in the tide of his meditation, but to feel it grow wider and deeper, spread more and more majestically in its flowing towards the great delta of God. Yet we must consider that outer covering, even though it may be for us merely an effort to get closer to essentials, in our turn, and also because Anthony and his fellow ascetics were to establish a kind of ascetic civilization.

Anthony ate once a day. His meal was composed of bread, salt, and pure water. Contrary to English hygiene, he took this meal after sundown, no doubt in order to learn how to control his hunger and thirst, and to avoid the craving he would have, if he ate in the mornings, to munch a crust of bread towards evening. Furthermore, he frequently skipped a meal altogether, either because he had given his ration to some poor man, or because he wanted to strengthen his resistance or punish himself for having felt the pangs of hunger — or simply because he had completely forgotten to eat. On such occasions the meal was postponed till the following evening, but only the bread and salt, for ascetics had the good sense to be lenient about water. But we can be sure that they agreed upon the minimum amount, and the psalm, "As the hart panteth after the water brooks, so panteth my soul after thee, O God," took the place of their drinking, nine times out of ten. To eat every other day would be no mean feat for an average man of our times, but Anthony did better than that: he sometimes ate but once in four days. We can guess that he did this during Lent, but the accomplishment was in no way diminished thereby.

The bread he ate was doubtless the kind eaten by the poor of his day: a flat loaf made of spelt flour. When fresh, it was considered agreeable enough, but the ascetics allowed it to get stale. A sensible man eating stale bread! But when very dry and tasteless it was more acceptable to God, and better for the health. Let others eat bread made for rich men! Clement of Alexandria was already inveighing against fancy baking: "Even bread, a simple and easily made food, is at the mercy of their daintiness; they extract the most nourishing part of the wheat and thus destroy its goodness." Since medicine and penance were agreed, there must have been a fair amount of bran in the bread eaten by ascetics.

Today, when balanced meals are insisted upon: calories, vitamins, carbohydrates, and all the rest of it, some people will think it amazing that Anthony, who ate neither fats nor green vegetables, could have kept all his teeth until his dying day, and without getting eczema and other skin diseases. Perhaps Athanasius, who was more involved with the human soul than the chemistry of food, thought he ought to assemble some striking details of Anthony's eating — bread, salt, no meat — without suspecting that the pith of a papyrus reed, the root of some wild plant, or a capsule of sesame put in bread to give flavor, might interest his readers. Later on, almost all monks kept a small quantity of oil in their cells. Some of them — oh triumph of modern ideas! — suffered terribly from skin diseases . . . We do not claim to have provided a satisfactory solution of this problem of the fats as an essential of diet.

"Sleep is as useless and silent as death," said Clement of Alexandria. Christian ascetics remembered with shame Christ's last night on the Mount of Olives when Peter and the two sons of Zebedee slept, and how strangely this distressed the Master. "Watch ye and pray, lest ye enter into temptation. The spirit truly is ready, but the flesh is weak." And the Master, in speaking these words to three of His disciples, was addressing all ascetics in general and each one in particular. "If thou wilt be perfect, watch thou with me. . . . Yes Master, here am I. . . ." Could there have been a holier occupation? Or a more marvelous companion anywhere? He was just the other side of the wall, praying to His Father. . . . And the ascetic prayed; now and then he sang a hymn softly to himself, or sang it at the top of his lungs. There could not be any sleeping.

Anthony's vigils were so long, wrote Athanasius, "that he often went for a whole night without sleeping. We must admire him because this happened not only once but often." We can easily agree with this; also with another statement: "He had a mat to sleep on, but usually he stretched out on the bare earth." This discipline of sleep was one in which Christ's athletes were to perform more astonishing feats than Anthony who, compared to some others, practiced of his own accord a fair amount of discretion. First listen to Palladius and his *Lausiac History*. What shall we say of Dorotheus the Theban, "never sleeping deliberately, but often closing his eyes while eating because of excessive exhaustion, the bread falling from his mouth in his drowsiness," or of Macarius of Alexandria who won a kind of mystical wager that he could stay awake for twenty days, confessing nevertheless, later on, that he nearly lost his reason? On the other hand, we read with delight, in the *Apophtegmata Antonii* that Anthony, while paying one of his long visits to Athanasius, who spoke with great piety, fell asleep. Athanasius shook him and recalled that the Holy Ghost had said: "They fell into a deep sleep and it profited them nothing." Anthony agreed that he was a miserable wretch.

Anthony denied himself all anointing with oil, and twice Athanasius stresses the fact that he never washed his feet. Fortunately, he encountered a certain number of brooks and irrigation ditches in his travels, and he did not allow his scorn of bodily cleanliness to keep him from wading through them. A woman went further than he did: we read in the *Lausiac History* that Saint Melania once saw her son wash his hands and feet in a basin of cold water because he had been walking all day in the hot sun. She rebuked him. "Consider this, and consider it well," said she. "I am sixty years old; neither my feet, nor my face, nor any part of me except the ends of my fingers, have touched water. . . . I have not slept on a bed. . . ."

Anthony's physical austerities were his weapons of defense; he possessed a particularly effective weapon of offense, which was prayer. When enemies threatened, he used it again and again.

*　　*　　*

Time Spent in a Tomb

The French are jokingly skeptical about ascetics, and about monks especially. Go without meat and wine? Just imagine! The moment you turn your back on one of them, he scuttles off to the kitchen! However, since Buchenwald, Auschwitz, and other such hellish places, man's cruelty has had to be re-assessed; also his powers of resistance. Viewed in the light of what happened in those camps, Anthony's physical feats and those of his fellow ascetics become much more believable.

But considering the penitential frenzies of the ascetics, even a good Christian might regard them as showing a lack of pro-portion, and speak, as one speaks of an excess of gourmandizing, of an excess of privation, of gorgings of abstinence, debauches of fasting. He may regard it as childishness to postpone a meal indefinitely, or put it off till the next day in order to control the flow of the gastric juices. Christ went into the desert to fast for forty days, but at the Last Supper He drank wine with His disciples, and the object of His first miracle was to provide wine for a country wedding. The ascetics did not wash their feet; they were dirty (we must be accurate), but how could they have thought that Christ wanted men to let their beards get out of hand and never care for their nails? Was He not careful to wash His disciples' feet himself—a symbolic act, of course, but not entirely symbolic. All the way through the Gospels, when the *Leitmotiv* of penance is heard, do we not also hear a modifying note of sympathetic understanding? Are we not continually aware of something like respect—an almost feminine feeling for clean garments? Those ascetics who sup-posedly imitated Christ desired to be more Christian than He was. They sinned in their excessive zeal.

Such a discussion as this involves too many problems. Never-theless, we love our hero and when he puts his asceticism on a warlike footing, we want no suspicion to touch him. We would not want the man who was preparing to drive the Devil back to his last trench and attack him on his own territory, to be criticized for the dust and dirt on his feet.

We must turn to historical facts, and, first of all, to the re-corded mystical semi-madness of those early centuries when some Christians felt that they had the right to expect the return of Christ at any hour, at any minute. How then could they aban-don themselves to luxurious living? The degeneration of the heathen world irritated the neophytes. Without suspecting it, they were frequently less occupied with being real Christians than being anti-heathens, if we may use the word, and these malcontents launched violent attacks against innocent pleas-ures because the heathens seemed to have too much faith in human nature and sought satisfaction of carnal passions too freely. We should say, for instance, that Clement of Alexan-dria was an understanding man and not one to exaggerate without good reason. But those dainty Alexandrians went be-yond the limit, and their luxurious excesses turned Clement into one of God's policemen: "Notice: men and women feel a desire to bathe for four reasons: one, the wish to cleanse them-selves; two, for the purpose of combating the heat; three, to preserve health; four, because they enjoy it. Henceforth, men are forbidden to bathe for reasons one, two, and four. Men may bathe only for reasons of health, and women, only for these and for their cleanliness. . . ." But, as we can tell from these last words, Clement was not, strictly speaking, an ascetic.

Though modern medicine prides itself on having renovated alimentary chemistry, it cannot help subscribing to the com-mon-sense doctrines laid down by the earliest human beings regarding the connection between food and the life of the spirit. The necessity to fast, in order to have the mind clear as much as to do honor to God, is recognized by everyone. The thought of Anthony taking bread from his mouth and keeping a careful watch over the water ration makes us smile, but our smiles are polite and good-natured. If the ideal for which such mad sacrifices were made was a great one, then there should be no criticism. We may think of Balzac weighing his food even in grams, fearing lest the euphoria of repletion might dissipate his restless creative impulses; drinking cup after cup of coffee to hold back sleep as Joshua held back the sun, and prevent his words from becoming weary and ceasing to flow from his brain. The ascetic's coffee was watchful praying; it was the hymn sounding from the innermost recesses of his memory and glowing with poetry.

The Christian ascetic went on a hunger strike in Christ's name, as did Gandhi or the Lord Mayor of Cork in the names of their humiliated countries. He went on a sleeping strike, a bodily comfort strike, in Christ's name. And often, in the silence of his nocturnal solitude, when, a willing substitute for Peter and the two sons of Zebedee, weary and asleep, he stood guard over Christ like a faithful dog who does not know what his master's thoughts are but is sure that they are supremely important—often, he caught a sudden glimpse of God and basked in His radiance, like a mountain bird with wings held still, against the warm upflowing air. Public opinion is indulgent to the inventor who sacrifices everything to his invention. How could there be a more wonderful invention for the ascetic than Christ? Henri Poincaré said that very rarely, but each time unmistakably, he had been spatially aware of the famous and greatly disputed fourth dimension. These occasions were at night and when silence seemed complete (which it never actually is). Learned men who have turned night into day will easily subscribe to the opposite of Saint Francis of Assisi's *Hymn to the Sun:* Saint Anthony of the Desert's *Reproach to the Sun*. Anthony's work is far less important, but lovers of clear thinking will find there a condensation of their annoyances: "O Sun, why dost thou disturb me with thy rays, as though arising but to deprive me of the true light?"

Anthony had won the trial heats. He had conquered hunger, thirst, sleep, and carnal desires. His ascetic training was functioning smoothly. The fire was smoldering beneath the ashes, and a watchful Satan drew nearer now and then; but pious thinking gave the alarm. Excessive praying came to the rescue, and watchful peace was soon restored.

Anthony considered the visit of the black boy. The wretched whimpering devil had told him nothing worth listening to: "I have conquered many men (ascetics, perhaps, among them), but you have conquered me!" Anthony realized that he was only one of Christ's athletes, a nondescript little ascetic whose insignificant feats could never bring the Devil to his knees. He had given up being rich because it bored him, resisted carnal desires when many others had done likewise—and he was not yet out of the woods. The Devil was still trying to ensnare him, and those peevish felicitations concealed and symbolized a threat.

It was some years since Anthony had heard Christ's voice in that of the reader at Koma. His days of instruction had passed; he was winged for flight now. When he told his fellow ascetics of the unexpected visit of the black boy and asked them to say whether or not they thought he was sent by the Devil, they replied evasively; but they ended with sincere admiration. "Our brother is already a great athlete. How beautiful are the feet of him who walks in the light of the Lord!" Anthony returned their compliments, but he was troubled because he seemed to hear an echo of the black boy's words in theirs. . . . Henceforth, if an adolescent from some nearby village felt God's call to embark upon an ascetic career, Anthony would be sure to get a probationer. Little Novice would kneel before Young Ascetic, as before the dirtiest of the old ones, and ask for the special privilege of learning from him how to serve Christ. He would ask this of Young Ascetic, still an athlete with everything to learn.

Many years later, one of Anthony's disciples came back to him to find out what he should do to make himself acceptable to God. The old man thought for a while; then he enunciated three precepts. We pass over the first two and give the third:

Time Spent in a Tomb

"Wherever you find yourself, do not go forth from that place too quickly. Try to be patient and learn to stay in one place." Anthony was speaking to a monk, and many monks neglected solitude. They moved about too much. Certain of them, called vagabond monks, did nothing but wander from town to town. Nevertheless, this precept had a general value. To know how to remain in one place was one of the convenient ways of practicing the essential virtue of perseverance. In one word, *egredere*, meaning "to go away," has been condensed the break with the world which asceticism implies; but another word, *sta*, meaning "do not move," could serve as the emblem for the second stage. First: go away; second: stay.

Anthony's formula was more complicated: ". . . do not go forth from that place too quickly." He did not advise against departures, but he wanted them to be legitimate and carefully considered. For him, the stages of his ascetic life had been clearly marked, each one coinciding with a change of abode, but we can be sure that every time he moved, spatially or spiritually, he refrained from advancing without careful thought. If he suspected for a moment that he would not be acting in accordance with the will of God, he would give up the idea immediately.

The paragraph in which Anthony's departure is related begins with a "So therefore . . ." which is intended to convince the reader that his decision was perfectly natural. Perhaps the monks for whom Athanasius was writing possessed the ability to understand at once the imperative reasons for a saint's journeys here and there, but since we lack that power, we must inquire into them a little further.

Anthony's departure occurred after a long period of advancement in asceticism. Our first thought is that, while toughening himself with privations and increasing his meditations and prayers, he was considering the idea of setting forth one day to fight with the Devil, and reversing the Latin adage, of making his preparations for war in order to obtain such a combat. But a second thought should come to us at once: the normal place for the ascetic was always his hut, and in order to attain to perfection he had to smother his restless impulses and remain stubbornly in it.

Athanasius' conclusions are too far removed from the facts, and he is inclined to oversimplification. Events which occupy two or three of his pages, told with a minimum of detail, seem to us to be those of several weeks, several months at the most; actually they are the happenings of a number of full years of living. Soon, for instance, Anthony was to shut himself in a tomb on a certain night and endure the screaming of a menagerie of evil spirits—in the morning however, a celestial vision consoled him. Without warning, and with phlegmatic casualness, Athanasius declares: "He was soon to enter his thirty-fifth year," as though he were remarking that rain was needed for the crops. The reader is jolted by this, having scarcely realized the passage of time since the day when Anthony went into the church and heard the Gospel story of the rich young man. Lacking intermediate information, we can be fairly certain that he required about ten years of concentrated effort for his thorough grounding in asceticism, which amounts to the conclusion that when he left his hut he was about to be thirty.

When Anthony set forth to challenge the Devil, he was no longer a young man with a liking for solitude; he had had bitter experience and had grown a beard. The medals won in his early conflicts shone upon his breast for the angels to see.

But we must dig deeper still.

We believe that, while still in his hut, Anthony was the victim of a third kind of temptation, perhaps the most dangerous of them all: acedia. This word, from the language of asceticism, must be explained. It was used to denote a kind of moral anemia, a disgust with meditation, which could plunge the ascetic into a terrible physical weariness, particularly on hot afternoons when his stomach was empty and his eyelids drooping—a lurking mental drowsiness, not altogether unpleasing despite its distressing effects. The precious principles of faith tottered. Nothing mattered any longer. He was a withered leaf rendered lifeless by the sun. No belief in anything. No further desire to be an athlete. To sleep. . . . The old men who had passed through the storm belt of voluptuous thoughts without much difficulty spoke of acedia with real terror in their voices, and, in order to make certain that their young brothers were aware of its appalling dangers, they included it in the list of capital sins. They believed happiness to be an indispensable virtue: a melancholy, surly ascetic was a bad ascetic. . . . There are, in the *Apophtegmata Patrum*, several procedures outlined, by means of which the struggle against that slow and hateful disintegration was to be carried on; and it must not surprise us to find there the advice to give up ascetic life for a while so as to prevent a disgust for it from conquering. And perhaps this overwhelming discouragement and loss of faith in prayer could be overcome by drinking more water, eating more bread, and taking walks — neglecting incidentals in order to safeguard essentials.

Anthony spoke at length, in his maturity and old age, of his personal experiences with acedia. But where could he have acquired them if not in his little hut? With the knowledge of him that we possess, our persistent hero would not have fled; he would not have consumed more bread and water; and he would not have gone out walking. But all the same, he would have made some concessions. He would have meticulously considered the plan he had formulated for his combat with the Prince of Darkness on his own terrain, and, since he would one day be justified in opening the door and quitting the hut, he possessed his soul in patience. The hut and the straw mats regained their significance, and prayer its magic.

The whole world seemed to have been affected by a variety of acedia. Persecutions had ended; Christianity was making regular progress; the poor were still being converted. But of what use were those neophytes? Their sympathetic and touching adherence to the faith, seemingly sincere, was not in any way similar to the final result of a struggle, and it could not be regarded as genuine. They would have to be shown, these blind sheep, that religions were not to be changed like loincloths, and that from first to last, a Christian must continually instruct himself in the faith of Christ.

Year after year, Anthony had been arranging and classifying his reasons for "going to the Devil"—in the literal sense of the expression—and in company with Learned, Prudent, and Patient, he wished to be Anthony-Who-Fought-the-Devil. . . . Between himself and Christ there was always the hideous specter of Evil. The accursed beast had to be driven from his sight, and this would be a service rendered to the whole world. He would keep the Devil occupied. Who could tell? He might be able to deal the blackguard a blow that would put him out of the running for a good while. . . . All his scheming helped him to attain the perfecting of his desire to follow Christ's example: the Gospel according to Saint Matthew recorded that the Spirit led Him into the desert to be tempted.

Anthony came out of his hut carrying a little bundle. He fell upon his knees to say a prayer; then he walked away. That rugged Egyptian had a plan in the back of his mind. Today we would be hard put to it, even those of us who believe in the Devil, to say how he could best be found, and most of those who make a show of knowing everything are satisfied to sit still and summon him by means of trickery and magic. Anthony, if we may put it this way, was more fortunate than our contemporaries. A man of his temperament did not act without lengthy searches among the texts stored in his memory, and, as he went forth into the desert, he was at peace with himself and with God. Several passages from the Holy Writ which he was still brooding on served as his safe-conduct and his compass.

Time Spent in a Tomb

In his world, just beginning to emerge from superstition, the Evil Presence seemed to him to be very near. Anthony was no Manichaean; he did not regard the Creation as the work of two equally powerful antagonists: God, the Good and the Light; Satan, the Evil and the Darkness. For God was the sovereign Master. He had created everything. Beneath Him were the angels, and among them the great disorganized army of the fallen ones, moving restlessly between earth and sky. Saint Paul was a part of Anthony's daily bread: "Put on the whole armour of God, that ye may be able to stand against the wiles of the devil. For we wrestle not against flesh and blood, but against principalities, against powers, against the rulers of the darkness of this world, against spiritual wickedness in high places." Though he could not actually perceive all this tumult, the eyes of his faith came to his rescue. The evil spirits passing above and around him were many times more numerous than the particles of dust raised by his feet as he walked.

Wherever he was, and even in his hut in the valley, he felt a singular gathering together and a swarming, as it were, of winged spirits. Nowhere was there freedom from the emissaries of evil. Nevertheless, for Anthony, favored places existed, and his slow steps towards the northwest would take him to them.

He was not a child imbued with the world's innocence as he made his way towards those regions, his eyes resting upon an acacia tree, a field of beans, on the hills, the slopes, the tombs along the ridge. He was not there for the enjoyment of the changing light or the harmonious coloring of the landscape. He was rather one of God's laborers, a lesser apostle, a disciple of the second class wearing working clothes, on his way to the yards. The famous athletes of Christ, laboring in Rome, Alexandria, Antioch, and in all their dependent Christian groups, strove successfully to bring their fellow men to God; but too important a zeal for souls must not be allowed to obscure another indispensable labor: that of reconciling the physical world with God. Man would not discover Paradise until all the earth became a garden and the young lambs no longer feared the young wolves. Creation was weeping and waiting. "For we know," wrote Saint Paul, "that the whole creation groaneth...." There was sadness in the rocks, the water, and the dust.

Each one to his calling in the great work. Let preachers and apologists persuade and martyrs bear witness. Anthony, the peasant, was going to cleanse the desert, a place favored by evil powers—a land that had strayed from the flock of fertile fields.

But Anthony did not dare yet to go into the great desert. He understood his task but doubted his powers. His procedure was roundabout. Upon the little hills separating the green Nile valley from Faiyum, it was impossible to imagine oneself anywhere but in the desert. The desert was not a vague conception of the mind; it had stamped all things with its scorching die. It began where the kingdom of the waters yielded to the kingdom of drought, and the transition from peaceful to tyrannical rule was accomplished in a few cubits. In the valley, men went about their daily occupations. The water moved from large canal to secondary canal, and from that one to another, and from that other it was carried by hoisting machines to the upland fields, where it nourished the earth and caused the crops to grow. A few steps farther and a man found himself in another country.

Many tombs were spread along the parched plateau dominating those desolate slopes, from which huge birds of prey occasionally swooped down over the lowlands. The tombs were like the human dwellings of the region, cleverly placed because on each slope there was a quarry; the materials had thus been close at hand. And here there was no danger of the floodwaters reaching the corpses of the dead. Whole villages of tombs spread out endlessly in the direction of Memphis. The pyramid at Mêdûn, where the corpse of some Egyptian king had lain for three thousand years, rose up above them upon its huge, rugged foundations. What madness to build an artificial mountain over the remains of a man! Let the droppings of eagles foul it as it deserved! Around its base, other tombs clustered fittingly, the large ones of the rich measuring as much as sixty feet square, the small ones of the poor perhaps only six or eight. More or less in ruins, most of them; more or less sunk into the sand—their entrances violated by the Bedouins or brigands and left stupidly gaping; their sham doors broken or destroyed. Blocks of stone were lying here and there. Hieroglyphs and strange figures were depicted upon the flat surfaces of this rubble; also the fauna of this absurd mythology: gods with the heads of dogs, goats, or jackals; ibises or lionesses, feet one in front of the other, in frightened postures or standing foolishly at attention, their single eye always avoiding the spectator.

It was the kingdom of the dead and the kingdom of evil spirits. Anthony had gone there particularly for the tombs. He could feel blowing over him, more violently than the sandstorms, the winds of evil power bearing spirits that were more numerous than all the mummies hidden in the tombs and all the powdered skeletons heaped in the ditches for common burial. The earth had absorbed generations of human beings as it absorbed the rain, and above the fairgrounds of the centuries hovered the fallen angels. Anthony, our Christian ascetic, found himself on a battlefield of the first magnitude—the Gospels speak explicitly of the unclean spirits that inhabit tombs.

Perhaps he looked down into the valley for a moment, with an aching heart. But in the next moment his courage returned. The valley where not an inch of earth seemed wasted, the green and yellow valley stretching to the north and south like the trunk of a palm tree from which tufts grew artlessly, its rocks resembling buffaloes or men, the valley with its villages, its gardens, its crowing cocks, its bluish smoke, and its scattered churches (how peaceful they were!)—all that was by no means an earthly paradise, but already its reconciliation with God was evident. Neither in the Libyan desert with its clustering tombs nor in the Arabian desert behind the ridges, did it seem possible that a righteous man's blood had flowed to redeem the world.

Nothing had changed since the day of Divine vengeance. There was confusion and sterility; and to view the surrounding landscape was to recoginze one's duty at once.

With the curious indifference of a vagabond in a disused blockhouse, Anthony went into one of the tombs. He had a wide choice, but we may be sure that he did not elect to live in one of colossal proportions. Even there, something modest, about the size of his hut, would suffice. Besides, the outer extent of the monument had nothing to do with the size of the chamber hollowed out in its interior. Many of the most important tombs were little more than piles of well-graduated and cemented stones with a tiny room inside.

Anthony closed the door, but we may guess that there were several holes in the walls, eroded during the centuries, to let in a little light and some fresh air. Hieroglyphs and hieratic profiles grinned from the shadowy walls; a strange-looking man was pictured there, sitting in a huge chair with a whip in his hand, watching a desert dog with man's body weighing fagots. Several feet underground, at the end of a sloping passage with a blocked-up entrance, lay some wretched ancestor who must have sought protection against the dangers that would threaten during his time beyond the grave by paying someone to paint those figures. No need to worry, old fellow! The Christians have begun to clean up the world.

Anthony sat down exhausted; then he fell to his knees and prayed, sang a hymn, and broke bread. His weariness was so great that his eyes closed, but he did not sleep. He knew that boredom was keeping watch over him. And outside, the tender night flowed down upon a dissatisfied world.

Strange, incredible night! Anthony, settled in the tomb, did not feel that he was committing a sacrilege. (One of his disciples, sleeping by chance in a tomb, found a mummy's head on the floor, and calmly used it for a pillow.) He was at peace, at least he strove to be so, and to pray. He had come there to go into combat with the evil powers, without knowing when and in what shape they would rise against him. He was rather in the position of the new student in a great school, but apprehensive and curious about the hazing; of the detective waiting for the killer to return to the scene of his crime; of the Cid Campeador for whom love made courage ten times greater.

Asmodeus—Beelzebub! Come out of the darkness! Come out, evil spirits, nameless and numberless, that I may fight with you! I feel you swarming around me. Declare yourselves!

Night lay heavily upon the cemetery, upon all the cemeteries with their millions of corpses, or what was left of them; and still Satan did not allow his hordes to manifest themselves. But they were there, nevertheless! At any moment their flight this way and that in the darkness would be heard like the whining of mosquitoes. Time went by, slowly, darkly, heavily. Anthony kept himself from sleeping, but he had come a long way. His limbs were weary and his whole body ached. His eyes closed again and again and he sang a hymn to keep them open, finding that he could doze while he was singing. What a shameful thing! He was doing what the two sons of Zebedee had done! He heard a faint noise outside. Was it a bat's wings brushing against the wall? Was it an accidental noise? Perhaps only ... Anthony rubbed his eyes, fighting hard to stay awake.

It wasn't on *that* night but on *a* night—after months or years, we cannot know when—that, according to Athanasius, the tomb became the theater of the strange battles which have given Anthony's existence its unique fame. He had been seeking for a struggle, and he got it.

One night, then, Athanasius reports, a troop of demons entered the tomb. They beat Anthony black and blue and left him for dead. His pain was of a sort that made him certain it could not have been caused by human beings, and he lay on the floor of the tomb in a coma, unable to call out. Dawn came, then sunrise, and he had not stirred. The morning wore on....

Some time before leaving his hut, he had arranged with a
friend to come to the tomb at long intervals, bringing the bread
he had to have, and then taking his finished mats back to the
village. This friend had decided to visit him that very day.
Leading an ass with the bread on its back, he climbed the hillside and came to the tomb. He found Anthony motionless,
covered with wounds, lying on the floor among his poor belongings; and he believed him to be dead or dying. So he took
him in his arms and placed him upon the ass's back. The descent
was accomplished somehow, and towards evening they arrived
in the village.

Anthony, still unconscious, was carried inside the "church"
by his friend; the others soon came running, loud in their lamen-
tations, their "I told you so's," and their exhortations to prayer.
No doubt his sister was there, and the other Christian virgins
with her, also his cousins and their cousins, who had formerly
shared his goods, a few idlers, and the fine flower of the pious
villagers. A funerary vigil began. But those present were not
athletes of Christ; they had been at work all day, and they soon
feel asleep. All except Anthony's friend, who was upset by his
personal grief or by finding that he had become a man of the
hour, along with the ascetic.

Anthony came out of his coma. It did not take him long to
realize what had happened, and, with peasant astuteness, he
refrained from waking the snorers around him. After many
nights of lonely conflict in the tomb, the warmth and the odor
of those human bodies and the harsh sound of their breathing
were pleasant to him, but he could not linger there any longer.
He had a rendezvous with the powers of evil. Now or never
he must go back to the tomb. His determination was like that
of an aviator who has crashed and wants to get into another
plane at once, or a wounded matador whose one thought is to
leave the infirmary and finish off his bull.

He raised himself on his elbow and beckoned to his friend.
"Take me back to the tomb," he whispered. At first the friend

refused, but Anthony threatened to crawl outside by himself and the friend gave in.

Dogs began to bark as the ass moved through the dark narrow streets. When so many men in so many houses were asleep, surely it was an ascetic's duty to watch and pray for them like a sentinel crane standing in the marsh. In the presence of that unthinking and careless abandon of folk whose hands and feet were bound, as it were, by the need for rest, Anthony had no sentimental regrets at leaving, for he heard with such perfect clarity the well known voice telling him again: *"Egredere,* go away. . . ."

It was still night when they reached the plateau and walked among the tombs. Hyenas were laughing. Huge bats flew awkwardly overhead, clapping their eagle-like wings. Anthony's friend marveled that anyone could want to stay in such surroundings, but he kept these thoughts to himself. He decided to get away as soon as he could leave Anthony.

At last the door closed and Anthony was shut into his mortuary hut. His wounds prevented him from standing up, so he prayed lying on his mat, but the prayers were no less fervent and when he had finished, his challenge to the evil spirits was no less bold. "Here I am! Here is Anthony!" he shouted, and he proceeded to provoke his adversaries with arrogant phrases. "If thou be the son of God, come down from the cross," they said to Jesus. "Come nearer, if thou art the Devil," shouted Anthony to the Prince of Evil.

Blackmail was not a successful procedure with God, and the Devil had his pride. This accursed ascetic! Beat him and he asks for more. No, the trap must be avoided; he will not flinch at a second attack. We must change tactics. He is weak now and can be driven mad.

That very night, the Devil and his hordes broke loose. "They made such an uproar," says Athanasius, "that the tomb trembled." Suddenly it was as if the walls had crumbled and all the beasts of the desert and the mountains had rushed at him:

99

wolves, lions, bears, serpents, asps, scorpions, leopards—and bulls as well. The trampling and the noise were terrifying. The bulls bellowed, the lions roared, the serpents hissed; and there were sounds like teeth gnashing, horns knocking together, and jaws biting. An invisible circle of protection closely surrounded the weary athlete, but outside it a tempest was raging. Creation's most hideous and frightening figures offered insults to him who expected to reconcile all creation with God and bring it to His fold—a madman enraged at his doctor, flinging himself against his bars and foaming at the mouth. The desert had no use for those mystical physicians! The desert wanted to be left lying in its vomit and filth. Let that little presumptuous man make himself scarce and take his bundle down into the valley without a backward glance, or we will drive him out of his mind.

Anthony was not scratched, either by fang or claw, but he suffered atrocious pains and could not help groaning. But he kept up his courage. He guessed that the howling masquerade was a machination of the evil one, and he laughed at his enemies, with their leopards' or lions' bodies, who were plunging at him furiously but had to stop when quite near. They were like watchdogs leaping from their kennels and unable to get one tenth of a cubit farther than the length of their chains. He infuriated them with his mock politeness, urged them and advised them: "Why don't you attack me? If you cannot reach me, why disturb yourselves uselessly?" They leapt forward again and again, exasperated, but always powerless to harm him.

Then the tomb seemed to open, and a beam of dazzling light fell upon him. He was alone now—nothing evil in the tomb with him. No trace of the nocturnal uproar. Anthony understood that the Lord was with him and he breathed easily once more. He felt that he had made an important advance in the hierarchy and that, having survived such an attack, he was in a way one of God's lieutenants. Speaking with the familiarity of a veteran of Marengo or Austerlitz, he permitted himself to ask, "Where

wert Thou? Why didst Thou not appear sooner to bring my
struggles to an end?" Now that they were alone together, surely
some explanations could be made! And the General in command answered simply: "I was there, Anthony; I was waiting
to see thy struggles. I saw them, and I will always be there to
help thee and to make thy fame known to everyone." The athlete had not asked for as much as that. The words were like a
strength-giving ointment for his weary, sweating body. . . . He
rose from his mat and prayed.

It is a far cry from the account Athanasius has given us to
the paintings of Hieronymus Bosch. Set beside them it seems
moderate, middle-class, almost paltry. Athanasius' menagerie
of devils seems like a country fair compared with Barnum's
great circus. It is less a matter of numbers than one of aggressive
gruesomeness. The beasts produced by Athanasius, quite a respectable group, which included lions and serpents, acted perfectly naturally. If devils had not inhabited their bodies, they
would not have been in any way abnormal.

Bosch threw the created world off balance; he scoffed at
unity, individuality, and the human hierarchy; he manufactured
an unreal universe out of bits and pieces, truly monstrous and
likely to give an experienced ascetic gooseflesh. Serpents that
hissed and bulls that bellowed, however numerous and whatever their noisy commotion, were as nothing compared to those
bacchanals involving a whole region and all nature's kingdoms
— villages destroyed by fire; fish wearing cardinals' hats and
herded about by monkeys; imps excreting eggs; evil monks
with heron's heads, celebrating mass with their sides laid open
and their putrefied entrails showing; birds resembling fish; prostitutes who looked like sows—a huge palpitating hodgepodge
of the world. . . .

Bosch proceeded to present a medley of all the temptations
whose results Athanasius only wanted to know about super-

ficially. Nevertheless, the frightening universe he described was his own — the universe of Hieronymous Bosch — and it is ours too, in an epoch crammed with stimulants and exaggerated desires to live dangerously, and with inventions that have got out of control. But we cannot see how it could ever have been Anthony's. The skies of Anthony's mind were never leaden. He was a man of grave solemnity, no doubt, but his essential spirit was a happy one.

Athanasius' narrative arouses a certain skepticism even in the mind of an uncritical reader. He prudently does not declare that the animals had bodies: "Spectres of lions, of bears," and, so on, he writes, then, "Ghosts of wild beasts". . . . Anthony did not at any time touch one of them. He believed that he saw and heard them. At a moment indicated, when they were about to devour him, they stopped. Was it because a Divine power had encircled him?

Until the incursion of the diabolical menagerie broke loose, there is no real problem to solve. Anthony was back in the tomb again. Physically, he was in very bad shape. He had been left for dead, the night before, by his assailants, carried down to his village by his friend, and treated as dead when he got there. On regaining conciousness, he wanted to return to the tomb with no thought for his poor body. Twenty-four hours after having been put out of the running, he was back at his post, shouting: "Here I am," into the darkness.

For thousands of years Anthony's ancestors had worshiped animals; they had associated their gods with beasts, often casually giving them the faces of jackals or lions. They mummified regiments of cats and ibises. Since the mouth speaks from the fullness of the heart, they decorated their monuments with hieroglyphs abounding in pictures of birds and beasts. They . . . but why talk of the past? Pagan Egypt still maintains crocodiles and sacred bulls with extraordinary ceremonial. A man in Alexandria was recently mobbed for maltreating a dog. For

Anthony, the desert fauna was identical with the fauna of mythology. The bulls of Apis—their privileges directly threatened by Christianity—came to the aid, as it were, of their desert colleagues. The assault which Anthony saw plunging at him, all that riffraff of the animal kingdom which rushed into the tomb, expressed the sudden clear consciousness both of a physical terror caused by the desert—a thousand times conquered and thrown back but preparing to attack again—and of a grim determination to defeat heathenism: a preposterous collection of animal stories, odds and ends of lions' tails and jackals' jaws.

Such a possibility in no way suppresses the Devil's actions; it merely renders them less noisy and more deceitful. We can, of course, follow the example of the Curé d'Ars and reject all critical investigation. The devils that rained blows upon Anthony and then disguised themselves as animals in order to frighten him were real devils: we either believe in the Devil, a being whom we admit possesses considerable superhuman ability, or we do not believe in him—and that is heresy.

This is not our attitude, but it has the merit of frankness. In order to understand Anthony's struggles—though, to our sense, this is not essential—we must begin by asking ourselves whether or not we believe in the Devil, and do we regard him as an actual being or as an ancient literary myth?

But belief in him does not oblige us, with sound theology, to blame him for everything. He is not an imbecile, and in any case his powers are limited. The Church today is inclined to object to demonic manifestations that are too obvious. It has been said that the Devil would have far less power if his existence were denied a little less often. And we cannot help realizing the enormous advantage he possesses through being able to inspire distrust and to act secretly: a fallen angel, he is still a spirit and does not use tangible methods.

The desert athletes had an annoying way of finding the Devil everywhere. They were like the monk who sent his disciple to fetch water. The disciple returned quickly and empty-handed, because he saw a dead asp at the bottom of the well. "Don't you understand? That was the Devil. Go back to the well; the water is harmless." Nevertheless these ascetics were beginning to be less credulous. One matter on which they meditated was how to tell good spirits from bad; more and more they reduced the number of the Devil's minions. Except in the case of a few, among whom we must not number Anthony, the essential dogma was never cast aside: God and Satan were not the Good and the Evil, endowed with equal powers. God was the supreme Master, and Satan, whom He had one day created as the Spirit of Light, had sinned and was now fallen, and his realm was far below God's.

When Anthony told his friend Athanasius that he had been beaten by demons and that he had recognized them as such by the strength of their blows, perhaps, after all, he suspected that they were not demons in human form but prowling brigands. It mattered little to him what they were: the Devil had suddenly put it into the heads of those heathens to blame him, had whispered to them that a hermit was plotting their downfall.

Doubtless Anthony did not believe that the lions, the leopards, and the bulls were beasts of flesh and bone ("Spectres of lions . . . Ghosts of wild beasts . . .") and his own understatements to Athanasius were responsible for these loose expressions. He was a poor interpreter of the things that happened to him. A fever possessed him, and, since he had an iron constitution and no experience of sickness, it seemed to him that the Devil must have been the stage manager of the troupe of wild beasts which had rushed into the tomb. Did his delirium pass off the next day? Did the disturbance in his fevered brain last several days?

To attribute to an attack of fever what Anthony attributed to the Devil does not amount to a denial that the forces of evil were at work. It is true that Anthony challenged the Devil. His ambition to "reconcile" the desert was unpleasing to the one who thought himself master of it. Regarded merely as chance happenings: the attack by night prowlers; the friend carrying a comatose Anthony down to the village and a frantic Anthony up to the tomb again; the attack of fever; a man talking at the top of his voice, seeing animals rushing at him, and then being restored to calmness—all these events have a reassuring quality. Anthony proved himself to be far above the average, both as a man and as an ascetic. He was a mystical force. Illiterate, he knew what his mission was and he was sure that he could accomplish it. Thenceforth he wore the mark of his election upon his broad brow. He too was severe and uncompromising, like Peter on whom God founded His Church, and like Paul who went unwearied from town to town, carrying the torch of Christianity.

Chapter VI

THE ABANDONED FORT

ANTHONY took his degree in perseverence. No evil power had been able to throw him out of his tomb shaking with fear; he had defeated mythology, fever, and death. When he entered the tomb he loved God; he was to leave it loving God still more, if that were possible. For he had discovered that his hopes were to be satisfied; his time spent in the tomb was only a stage in his progress. The same small voice he had heard in his hut whispered again to him that he should depart.

In a few lines, Athanasius sends Anthony down into the valley and then up again into the mountains, but actually things went much more slowly. Anthony was thirty-five, and he trusted in God. Though he wasted no time, it was not like the day when he had quickly unfastened the straps that held the burden of his riches upon his shoulders; he acted in the good slow way of antiquity.

He would go down into his village if only to arrange about his food supply. And perhaps to kiss his sister? Let us say that he would ask for news of her anyway. He was to reach the threshold of old age before getting rid once for all of his masculine uncouthness.

It was agreed that his friends would replenish his supply of bread every six months. ("The Thebans made loaves of bread that would keep for a year," wrote Athanasius learnedly. For an equivalent of today we can think of what is called army biscuit.) Anthony intended to go quite far away and he could not ask for more frequent replenishments. Since this was in line with his desire to be disturbed as little as possible and to do penance as much as possible, the arrangement would suit everyone.

But his friends had to know exactly where to bring the fresh bread. It seemed that Anthony was vague about this and was going to leave the matter to Providence; when he had reached the cemetery he had not known which tomb he would live in; and this time he would cross the river, climb "the mountain" (thus the steep opposite bank was called), and then look about him. The friends bringing his bread could do likewise. It would be much easier to find an ascetic than a grain of wheat in a field.

Though Anthony's plan to cross the river and climb "the mountain" was vague, it needs to be discussed. The change of direction for this mystical adventure, this *Drang nach Osten* after a slow walk towards the west, cannot have been mere chance. Was not the Libyan desert more desolate than the Arabian, whose valleys were often green with vegetation and whose carpets of Jericho roses were praised by the Christians? But the discussion is not one of geography. Almost no one visited those places. It is enough to say that the two deserts were alike, one to the west and one to the east.

To walk towards the east was to find oneself where the Jews wandered during the Exodus, in the desert where Christ was tempted, on Mount Sinai where Moses stood, hidden from his people behind a cloud, face to face with the Eternal Father to receive the Tables of the Law. A desert interested Anthony, far less because of its great spaces, the dryness that ate into his skin, a mirage trembling on the horizon like a goblet on an unsteady table, than because of its atmosphere of abandonment and ruin. The desert's geological perfection did not impress him till later. First he needed to feel that men had been there once, but evil spirits that had to be destroyed were swarming among the ruins. A place where men had lived for centuries and which they had then abandoned because of a war or some catastrophe, provided just the sort of surroundings for the Devil's followers. In very early years, human beings had been plentiful in the Arabian desert; they had searched it almost everywhere, vainly, for a place to settle down. When the Nile valley became thickly populated, there had been schemes for opening up the desert by means of countless roads leading to the quarries, the mines, and the Red Sea ports from which the land of incense might be reached; but these projects could never be carried out. All that remained of such schemes were a few trails and, here and there, dilapidated shrines where ancient desert couriers were supposed to have regained strength and courage by reading (if they could read) that a company of soldiers or a caravan had passed that way, sent by a powerful king, and that they had prayed to the gods in the proper manner.

Anthony must have been fully aware of all this, but we cannot be sure. We do not know whether or not he had been given advice, particularly by his first instructor in asceticism, the "old man," whom he now visited, perhaps for several days. While with him, Anthony did a curious thing which seems to us to be entirely out of character; he asked his former instructor to go with him into the desert. It was as if he feared complete isolation; as if, having come through an ordeal in the tomb, he was loath to encounter another like it.

But we should not judge Anthony so quickly. He did not hesitate in the slightest after his host's refusal to accompany him. He set forth at once to climb the mountain. If he had wanted a companion so badly, why couldn't he have looked up Learned, Patient, or Abstinent; and if they had refused, what about the other young ascetics of the neighborhood? There were plenty of adventurous ones among them, and he could have found ten as easily as one.

Actually, we should congratulate Anthony on possessing a

very human feeling. He had a warm regard for the man who had guided his first steps, his spiritual "father and mother" in whose presence he had realized his many shortcomings. He had in no way developed a fear of the solitary life while in his tomb; on the contrary, he felt that his time there had been a triumph. Very soon he hoped to experience far greater joys, and it was natural that he should want, as one pays a debt, to share this marvelous banquet with the person who had generously given him formulas for happiness, with this calm old man, fixed and tied to his asceticism, this mirror of holiness offered by God to Egypt.

His reverential affection for his former professor and the young ardor of his thirty-five years had clouded his perception. When Anthony had first embraced asceticism, the old man was already an old man. More than fifteen years had gone by, and he was more than ninety years old. Even if asceticism conserved the strength of its adherents, we can be sure that he had less resistance to cold, privation, and fatigue than in his young days. He no longer felt equal to the role of desert evangelist. The day for "joining the Fathers" was drawing near and he must get ready to turn in his account. He had lived his life. So, politely, piously, he refused to go with Anthony.

Aside from being old and unaccustomed to moving about, perhaps his refusal was an indication of the flourishing condition of Christianity. When the game was practically won, why embark upon new offensives? It was 285 A. D. Diocletian had just taken over the leadership of the Empire in which "the Christian peace" reigned. He was a dynamic man without prejudice, and was not interested in persecuting a sect whose adherents were now too numerous, and to be found in all levels of the social hierarchy. Such people should be left unmolested. Were they not loyal to Caesar? There were at least ten more urgent tasks for the Master of the World to undertake than to cast their leaders to the beasts of the arena, or to burn their churches. The Empire was nearing the end of its third century and obviously approaching decrepitude. For perhaps a century now, it had been gradually but inevitably declining. It was turning into a great flabby thing which no longer responded to orders. Poverty was increasing. And the barbarians, like worms in the rotting hull of a ship, gathered at its frontiers and invaded it everywhere. Defense measures were imperative. Although he had no doubts of his own strength, Caesar called in Maximian, a "brilliant second" and one who shared almost all his prerogatives.

The Egyptian ascetics were not aware of the anxieties of their Emperor Number One. Christianity was spreading—that was all they noticed. The "old man" thanked God for the prevailing tranquility, and, in the hut where he crouched with stiffening legs, he imagined Diocletian to be a Christian. The scribes of *The Acts of the Martyrs* of the Coptic Church wrote similarly: "After nine months the king of whom we have spoken died. Diocletian reigned in his place. At the beginning of his reign, when he was Cosmocrat of the Realm, and a Christian, for he had not yet abandoned the God of Heaven . . ."[1] These words of the scribes undoubtedly reflected the general opinion of the populace in the early years of Diocletian's reign. This was the beginning of Christ's earthly triumph.

Whatever the old man's arguments, his reply disappointed Anthony; but this did not delay his departure. Bending under the weight of his sack of loaves (seventy or eighty pounds), he set forth briskly into the desert.

Anthony crossed the Nile. He knew how to swim, as did everyone in those days, ascetics included. But the river was the river, wide and with a strong current, and not a canal. He could not enter the water wearing his clothes and carrying his bread. His clothes could be wrapped around his head, but what could he do with the bread?

[1] Martyrdom of Saint John and Saint Simeon.

Fortunately, there was continuous traffic on the Nile. Economic difficulties were interfering more and more with navigation on the river, but many boats were still to be seen, with their white sails and their boatmen. There was plenty of acacia and papyrus of which small boats could be built; the flowing of the Nile and the wind on the Nile cost less than the tiniest chip of a drachma. It was a marvelous moving carpet. On it were placed wheat, oil, Faiyum wines, goat skins, melons, cucumbers, Augustan and Tiberian marble, red porphyry and porphyry flecked with white—and it was all hurried along on the river toward the Delta, or, less frequently and more slowly, towards the interior.

From one bank to the other there was a certain amount of ferrying. From the eastern bank were taken the corpses of the dead; in funerary barques they were carried to the western bank whence the mountain cemeteries could be reached. Here the heathen religion had decreed that the blessed should rest.

Anthony crossed the river on the first boat that came along, perhaps one that belonged to a regular ferryman. He paid for his crossing with blessings and pious quotations, and it is possible that, in the days when Christianity was gaining ground, he was already known among the river people as the famous young man who had given his property to the poor as easily as he might have taken off his loincloth. His legend had begun, like the first smoke from a fire not yet caught but soon to flame up. A young man named Anthony; a good young man, as hard as iron, who had fought with the Devil.

After crossing several small canals, Anthony looked about him. Above rose the steep ocher-colored slopes, turning to purple at their summits. From their bases to the edge of the river, the strip of arable land was no wider than a quarter or a half a mile, and it seemed still narrower in the wavering light. Birds rose up continually from the earth and the air smelled

like honey, for there were whole fields of flowers waving in
the soft breeze, pressing close together like waterplants in a
fast-running brook. This narrow strip along the river's edge,
despite the asps and scorpions which could do their work at any
moment from beneath rocks and roots, seemed like a small paradise. The palm trees were clacking, little frogs jumping, and
scarabs crawling. The landscape resembled the setting for a
Biblical allegory—a righteous man at peace with the beasts of
the fields, walking in the sight of Jahveh, and with laughter
upon his lips.

The difference between that little happy region, that fertile
and many-colored strip, and the ridge that rose up abruptly to
cut into the blue sky, was shocking to the eye. A sacrificial knife
had sliced down, inexorably dividing the earth into two inimical parts: the fertile soil and the barren rocks. Beyond that
wall, where the eye could barely pick out the shapes of gray
bushes as it vainly searched for the nests of birds of prey in the
invisible hollows, nothing could be seen, but a world of chaotic
sterility could be imagined—a compact world, completely re-
signed to its evil fate, and even more sluggish than the gorged
vulture which sailed silently above the ridge.

When Anthony had climbed the mountain, his ascetic mind
was intrigued by the sight of a building that he could scarcely
distinguish from the cliffs into whose faded lilac color it blended.
There would be the place for him, if, as seemed from a distance,
it were empty. A difficult winding path led up to it. An abandoned dwelling was the ideal abode for an ascetic, and his
friends could easily find him—several peasants had seen him go
towards it.

The fort must have been one of the small ones built by the
Romans after the barbarian invasions. Overlooking the Nile,
they had been used as barracks and lookout stations; then, when
the trouble was over, or troops were needed in the north, the
occupants had moved out on short notice. The little fort had
apparently been built at a stragetic point where the Nile valley

was intersected by a small one with no river, cut into the mountain. From it a part of the alluvial plain could be surveyed, and a watch could be kept on the desert salients whence danger might threaten. Since its occupants were liable to siege, the permanent presence of water was imperative, and, if we interpret Athanasius carefully, there was a spring close at hand which meant that Anthony's proposed dwelling was not on the ridge but slightly below it.

Though we cannot fix its position with exactitude and must beware of traditional certainties, the fort was undoubtedly situated but a few hours' walk from Aphroditopolis, or, if we like, Venus Town. Aphroditopolis, to the north on the same bank, was not such a dangerous spot or a particularly dissolute one, despite its cult of the white cow—an incarnation of Hathor, herself equal to Venus. It was certainly much less so than Alexandria, the Montmartre of the epoch. The matter is of small importance, but the coincidence is an amusing one. It undoubtedly made its impression upon Anthony when he entered his chaste retreat.

The fort was large compared to the tomb, and, when Anthony discovered the spring, must have affected him as a villa with every modern convenience would affect a homeless vagrant. How marvelous to have running water! Actually, the fort was a poor affair; the stones in the walls were uneven, piled carelessly, and awkwardly pointed with mortar. Perhaps it was square, with the main part enclosing a court, but more likely just a tower, round or square, and about twenty feet high.

With no human being in occupation, reptiles had taken over and were living there comfortably, breeding, hatching their eggs, digesting their food, keeping warm in winter and cool in summer. Their neutral coloring enabled them to blend themselves with the stonework and do their evil work more easily when they had to. But they did not harm Anthony (and actually the largest ones, despite their somewhat frightening appearance, were rather nice beasts; an ascetic should have been particularly understanding of them, with his ardent righteousness and his filthy exterior. But he had to be continually watchful for the Devil. . . .) The reptiles took themselves off at once, and, as soon as they had disappeared, Anthony blocked up the entrance.

If by chance anyone should think of a Beaux Arts student retiring into a studio and starting his work for the Prix de Rome, he would be very wide of the mark. Anthony was to stay in his fort for twenty consecutive years, breaking all records for his era in confined asceticism.

It was an amazing story—still more amazing when we remember that Anthony had challenged the demon world in his new abode. Shut in with these evil spirits, rushed at by their hordes, he waged an exhausting but enthusiastic war on them, day and night, for twenty consecutive years.

Upon cliffs overlooking the sea, upon rocky peaks, men who enjoy experiencing strong emotions build themselves solid dwellings from which they may watch the tempests roaring along the coast and hear them battering and howling in their unfettered violence. . . . Thus it was with that Egyptian fort. The seven hurricanes of Hell swept over Anthony; the armies of the Devil hurled themselves against those walls. Up to that time it had been a place of victory for them. Here men had set up an outpost, but they had abandoned it to be ignobly worn away and inhabited by reptiles. No small success had been scored there against that infamous race of humans, chosen by God to replace the spirits of light. It had nearly been vanquished by the Devil on the day of the Fall, but it had remained inexplicably dear to the heart of God who had sacrificed His Son Jesus, the "new Adam," in its behalf. There would never be an armistice in the war between evil spirits and men. This accursed one who had dared to climb the mountains, re-establish human occupation of the fort, drive out the reptiles, sing hymns of glorification and psalms of gratitude in the very faces of those whom God's anger had destroyed, and pursue patiently and faultlessly in the desert the kind of asceticism that would hasten the coming of the Lord—that accursed one would pay dearly for all his challenges.

The fury of the evil spirits exalted Anthony. There was no solitude to bore him, no feeling that he was accomplishing nothing, no trace of acedia. He was never alone, never idle never in doubt as to the value of his work. For him, his desert mountain was the center of the world. This illiterate man went far back against the current of history, beyond fallen kingdoms and ruined capitals, beyond the petrified forests of Mokattan and the plesiosauri, beyond the great dried-up river beds of the Libyan desert. When his enemies began their uproar, causing the walls to tremble and the ground to shake around him, above and below him, pitching and rolling and groaning like a ship on the point of foundering, he felt supremely happy and he jeered at their pitiful parody of Divine Vengeance and their imitation Chaos.

"Get out of our desert! What are you doing here?" shouted the demons, whereupon Anthony intoned a psalm and they quaked with fear. Athanasius does not say that they struck him, and they seemed to have found themselves less effective than they had expected. When Anthony had had himself carried up to his tomb after they had beaten him, the game was won without his suspecting it. Despite the violence of their hate for him, they could do nothing now but continue their noise and their groaning.

To Anthony's contemporaries goes the credit of being the first to find extraordinary his reputed struggles with the Devil. "His intimates went to see him," says Athanasius, without indicating whether or not they were the ones who had promised to bring him his bread. They halted before the pile of stones blocking the door. They called and Anthony answered them.

He thanked them for coming but refused absolutely to let them into the fort. They must go away. But they would not go, and they voiced their disappointment. They had brought food and wanted to share it with him. So they sat down, ate, and took their ease. When evening came and the unyielding Anthony realized that they could not reach the village or even cross the Nile before nightfall, he relented. Ascetics were usually unlike other men and very difficult in the matter of their solitude, so that it was frequently necessary to lay siege to them in their lairs as though they were animals, before catching so much as a glimpse of their noses. An ascetic might even refuse to admit another ascetic. Certain ones had been known to let pious visitors cool their heels for three days and three nights running. But Anthony would never have been so obstinate as that. There was nothing of the misanthrope in him and he would never have let anyone risk catching cold on his account.

Suddenly the friends stood up. The mountain seemed to tremble. Within the fort there were terrible noises as of soldiers attacking: shouts, jeering, "Off with you; get out!"—and blows striking the walls, sounds of men leaping and falling back. . . . The friends fled, leaving their belongings behind them; but in a few moments their curiosity brought them to a halt and they stood behind some rocks, considering what to do. The uproar had not ended. "Get out! We do not want you here. Off with you!" It was a terrifying experience. What had become of Anthony? They had certainly heard his voice.

When it appeared that nothing disagreeable was going to happen to them, the friends took advantage of a lull in the uproar and went back to the fort. The night prowlers must have got in through the upper windows. Anthony must be rescued, alive or dead. They inspected the fort carefully and found no ladders. Through cracks in the walls they could see inside, but no one was there. They crossed themselves. It was not prowlers, but evil spirits who were inside the fort attacking their friend.

"Anthony! Anthony!"

Then they heard a calm voice making fun of their fears for him: of course the noise was that of evil spirits, and what then? No reason to be afraid of them. They could not harm those who did not fear them. He was used to them. He could move about among them without risk of any sort. To say that they were making his life impossible was stupid. It was his being there that enraged them. Let his friends cross themselves and go quietly about their business; let them go back to the village and give the people there, the ascetics and especially the "old man," good news of Anthony and his nursery of demons.

The friends did not want to leave. Their curiosity far exceeded their fear. At nightfall they were still there. Anthony's calmness and courage were strangely refreshing. The demons groaned and howled; they flung themselves about and beat against the walls; and, while jackals screamed and night birds cried one to another under the narcissus-colored stars, the voice of the ascetic, a voice more serene than a peasant's voice in the village street at noonday, could be clearly heard:

> In Judah God is known:
> His name is great in Israel.
> In Salem also is His tabernacle,
> And His dwelling place in Zion.
> There brake He the arrows of the bow,
> And the sword and the battle.

And the desert, blasted by the anger of God, listened thoughtfully to Anthony, the reconciler.

When the friends were in the village again, they told of the wonder they had witnessed. Anthony was performing on the mountain exploits greater than those of any hunter before him, greater than those of the ancient Pharaohs who had hunted lions and tigers with hundreds of men. At a place a few hours this side of Aphroditopolis, Christ's athlete had established himself in a small fort, offering little protection, and there, day and night, he defeated demons in legions of full strength. The mountain was like a great trumpet sounding the glory of God. It was possible to imagine huge invisible tracts listening in silence. "Get out—get out!" the demons cried. Get out? No. Anthony searched his memory for a moment; then, without a single mistake, he intoned psalms one after the other at the top of his voice, and his enemies could be heard grinding their teeth in helpless rage.

> The hill of God is as the hill of Bashan,
> An high hill as the hill of Bashan.
> Why leap ye, ye high hills?
> This is the hill which God desireth to dwell in.

With only the evidence of Athanasius, we cannot state that crowds of people ever rushed to the mountaintop to witness Anthony's game with the forty thousand demons. The place would not have accommodated multitudes. On those dangerous ledges topping the steep, rocky slopes, there was hardly space, we may suppose, for more than a limited "audience." Also it was necessary to spend the night in the open air, enduring the sharp cold of the morning which would strike painfully between the shoulder blades; then would come the stifling heat of the day beating down on the head and blinding the eyes. The pleasure of overcoming obstacles, and, if one were a Christian, of killing two birds with one stone—mountain climbing and a pious pilgrimage—would hardly exist for the populace. Peasants were used to living from day to day, wavering continually between poverty and destitution; for them, climbing a mountain would be a back-breaking task, and not pleasant exercise for the muscles.

Almost no one but religious enthusiasts came to Anthony's retreat: the fine flower of asceticism and their friends, priests, persons of high degree in search of God, humble novices seeking perfection. It would be a mistake to visualize an incessant and varied stream of Egyptians arriving to see the ascetic thrash the Devil. The place kept its mysterious quality and the little fort was never interesting to sightseers. Except during the final years, we can take it that there were long stretches when Anthony received no visits, and when the sun and an occasional eagle sailed over a solitary mountain. The friends who brought bread for him every six months (the loaves were doubtless pulled up with rope by an invisible Anthony, according to the custom of today in Coptic convents) frequently found themselves alone when they performed this task.

Considerable idle curiosity was shown, but this was disparaged by veneration for the ascetic. His holiness and his intoning of psalms had made the demons harmless; they had lost their power to frighten. But had one the right to go up there and listen at cracks like a Peeping Tom at the door of someone's bedroom? Was the mysterious manifestation to be regarded as a spectacle? The walls of the fort concealed what was happening within, and Anthony's struggles involved much more silence than speech; but it would not be right to sit there. Even if one said nothing, might not that silence taint his isolation? Was it not a greater impudence to watch a man's meditations than to look at him when he was naked? Holy people deserved to be in high places, and let others keep away from them.

Despite their admiration and their certainty that God was in control of events on the mountains, many people experienced a very human reaction. As the years passed without Anthony's permitting himself the smallest deviation from his strict regime, they could not help fearing that his body would be less resistant to sickness, and they were afraid that he might be taken ill when there was no one there whom he could call upon for help. They did not doubt for a moment that he was engaged upon God's business, but he must not be allowed to die. He surely deserved to live until the day of Christianity's triumph, and that day could not be very far off. They went up to the fort unobtrusively and were filled with anxiety if they got no reply when they called "Anthony! Anthony!" And, like a hunter who ob-

jected to interruption while watching for his prey, he would
answer in a low voice that he was there. Would they please
go away.

Yet even if a few mystics and some overly curious persons
were the only people who ever went up to Anthony's retreat, the
fame of his penance on the mountain and his strivings to liberate
the earth from its demonic swindlers was considerable. Unmistakably and mysteriously, a change was taking place in Egypt,
in the whole Roman world, and even beyond the Empire's
frontiers. Anthony's fort haunted the thoughts of millions of
men who had never seen it but were moved by the idea of such
self-consecration. Christians took a greater pride than ever in
their faith, and many heathens who had hesitated to be converted felt their resistance melting away. This madman on his
mountain had obviously received assistance from Heaven. It
must then be true that Christ was God.

In a sense, Anthony the poor man, Anthony who did not
make up his eyes, Anthony who took bread from his mouth, became Egypt's national hero in the days of her increasing poverty. His appeal was much stronger with the people than that of
the heathen priests with their newly shaved heads, the white
linen and panther skins required by their calling—solemn fops
who never forgot to fill their stomachs. Soothsayers, keepers
of the celestial wardrobes, markers of victims for sacrifice, pilots
of the sacred barges, embalmers, musicians—all these were in one
way or another, profiteers. They received less than formerly,
but it was plenty to live on. The revenue department did not
neglect them; and their lack of concern about the difficulties of
their fellow men was insulting.

Anthony could play the role of the father of the people more
fittingly than Diocletian, who spoke Greek to his subjects and
almost never said anything to them but "Pay!" A dynamic man,
perhaps, but his methods were not popular. The money pump

was in full action, and the revenue officers pushed the taxpayers hard. Good times or hard times, Nile floods or no, it became strangely difficult, if not impossible, to pay taxes and dues of produce. The plight of the peasantry, already precarious, became much worse. The machine showed signs of wear; it did not run smoothly. Diocletian, though a man of energy, turned over the western part of the Empire to Galerius, his son-in-law, and to Constantius Chlorus (the Pale); and this must have meant that things were in a bad state.

For Diocletian had believed, at the outset, that the Empire was too large for one man to rule, and had brought in Maximian to help him in 286. Now, in 292, he made another important change: he cut the Empire in half, putting the west in the hands of Galerius and Constantius Chlorus, and keeping the east under his own and Maximian's control. From this military, financial, and political rearrangement, he expected great things. It would bring direction and execution closer and make it possible for the Emperors to show themselves more easily, to make personal appearances before cheering crowds carefully kept in order by the police, before all the diverse peoples brought together by Roman power and perseverance. But he was soon to be disappointed. Poverty and discontent increased alarmingly, and particularly in Egypt.

As the people's distress grew, the cult of magic became more and more frequent. "What will happen to me tomorrow? What about my wife? And my children?" Many Egyptians sought the answers to these simple questions in sorcery and magic. Anthony had held off the menagerie which burst into his tomb, but he had not been completely victorious. In the heathen religion there were many little animal divinities which enjoyed an unprecedented prestige. A large section of the Egyptian peasantry affectionately worshiped cats, ichneumons, crocodiles, scarabs, sharp-nosed fish, hippopotami. All of them were simple healthy animals that lived out-of-doors and asked only to be allowed to eat and multiply. They did not annoy humans (act-

ually, the contrary was sometimes true). They were nice beasts.
Ubu was the official chief, but in many hovels and cabins the
cat or one of its fellow creatures was adored.

The gods had perhaps given the signal for Egypt's disloyalty
to the Roman Emperors when the Colossus of Memnon at
Thebes, the stone of which, for some strange reason, gave forth
a melodious lament at dawn, became silent after the repairs made
to it by Septimus Severus at the beginning of the third century.
The silence of the god was tantamount to a reprimand.

The Emperor Decius (249-251) still had his statue in an
Egyptian temple—at Isna, between Thebes and Aswan—repre-
senting him as making a sacrifice to the goat-headed divinity
Khnemu of the Cataracts—and his name was carved in hiero-
glyphics on a cartouche; but after him, no Caesar ever claimed
the doubtful privilege of playing protector of the Egyptian
religion or of Egypt itself. And that fact represented far more
than a decaying of the hieroglyphic system. When Imperial
negligence forgot to respect the usual procedures and hinted
that Egypt was a Roman possession like all the rest, then the
Egyptian people, for its part, ceased to love its Emperor.

We learn from a papyrus that two people, armed with clubs,
entered the hovel of a peasant who still owed the Imperial gran-
ary a tenth of his dues in grain; the guilty man was not there,
so the righters of wrongs stole a cloak and treated his mother so
roughly that she was obliged to take to her bed. Almost everywhere the revenue administration employed spies to pounce on
the slightest cheating, and to recommend the names of rich citizens to the administration for its benevolence in entrusting to
them (that was the official phrase; it should have been "inflicting
upon them") the responsibility of collecting certain taxes.
These offices were called "liturgies"—a fine name which was
the only good thing about them. In many of the villages the atmosphere was unbearable. Among the letters of that time that
have come down to us, there are some, which were exchanged
by intimate friends, that remind us of the inter-zone postcards

during the German occupation of France, because of their necessarily vague phrases understood only by the writers.

Revolts broke out and were put down with much bloodshed, but the violence of these quellings accomplished nothing; and the Empire, as regards its defenses against the barbarians, showed signs of weakness. In order to control the incursions of the Blemmyes, a savage tribe who lived for fighting and were then pillaging Upper Egypt, Diocletian adopted maquis-like methods because he was reluctant to use a great expeditionary force. In Upper Egypt he installed, at high cost, a certain number of Nubians whom he ordered to control the Blemmyes. Then he bribed the Blemmyes to leave the Nubians alone—a piece of trickery that was easily seen through but had to be paid for by the taxpayers.

Caracalla, a hypocrite of the first water, had considerably increased the number of Egyptians who could claim Roman citizenship—a dubious concession. Proud Alexandria, the new Athens and the second city in the world, shuddered under the yoke. The sale of her luxury articles: cosmetic spoons, ivory-framed mirrors, and glassware, all the profitable traffic of her merchants and traders, was on the decline. But, in addition to material losses, the city was suffering in the matter of her prestige. Alexandria, which had not been afraid to lampoon Caracalla (unable to take a joke, he had replied with massacres), and whom coins represented facing Hadrian, both of them standing, could not see why she should now be treated as subservient to Rome. She knew that she could far outshine her rival in the things of the mind. Caustic, impressionable, quarrelsome, enthusiastic and then discouraged, Alexandria was brooding bitterly at having been made subservient to the Emperor Aurelian (270-275), at having kicked over the traces, and at losing the Bruchion, her most beautiful section. Some of those who lived there had backed the wrong horse and the Bruchion was barbarously destroyed. And yet again, Alexandria's hot blood brought trouble. An officer of the Roman garrison defied Diocletian, and everyone—gangsters, merchants, sailors, philosophers—took sides with him; he was named Emperor. He was Julius Domitianus—Achilles to the women and the populace. Diocletian arrived on the scene; the city refused to surrender and underwent a terrible siege lasting eight months. When there was an uprising because, among other reasons, food was lacking, it became impossible to repulse the besieging forces. The city was taken by storm and pillaged (295).

Diocletian was not overly pleased with his victory. He saw no reason why the offenders should die; and since famine threatened to carry off several hundreds of thousands of men, women, and children, when Alexandria fell, he gave up all thoughts of vengeance and busied himself with the feeding of the conquered. Then he did an unprecedented thing which shed light upon Egypt's plight: he reduced her grain dues and kept in the imperial granaries a part of that which was ordinarily sent across the sea. He rationed Rome in order to save Egypt from starving to death.

Diocletian reorganized the country, which had lost its pre-eminence in all this unfortunate business; the Latin language and Roman law filtered in. Egypt was now, in the practical and political sense, little more than an unimportant province.

However, Diocletian had his own opinion of Egypt. He was extremely anxious to attach to himself the most religious people in the world he ruled, even when he was in process of destroying the political independence of the separate states in the empire. He believed the cult of Imperialism to be of considerable importance. He wanted his subjects to make sacrifices. Could not a Caesar, worshiped in the religious sense, command his people's loyalty more easily than an out-and-out autocrat? That madman, Caligula, who made a consul of his horse, had been deified—why not Diocletian?

The Christians thought otherwise. Their one and only God would yield to no one, even an Emperor, the smallest shred of his sovereignty. They would have nothing to do with deifying

Caesar. Diocletian was in a rage. He was unaware of feeling any hostility towards Christianity in principle, and there were many Christians among his high functionaries. But he did not understand why a cheap and sure way of attaching his empire to him should be withheld.

What could the solitary man on the mountain know of the world's doings? Athanasius tells us that he was completely absorbed in his struggle, embedded, as it were, in the place where he had established himself, away from everyone; and we have no grounds for supposing that he ever had conversations of any length with his friends through the chinks in his walls. Besides, those Copts did not regard the fall of Alexandria as a national tragedy. Alexandria, to them, remained a Greek city whose importance was entirely due to the fact that it was the head-quarters of the patriarchate. . . . But it is hard to imagine the passing of twenty years without Anthony's asking for news, or even receiving it unasked-for, now and then.

Towards the end of his time in the little fort, the number of his visitors increased in a rhythmical crescendo. Sometimes there were those who did not go down the mountain again. These wanted to be ascetics, or more perfect ascetics; and they were sure that they would be better off under Anthony's guidance than anywhere else. Some found caves, but most of them put up tents. The group did not form a monastery, as we understand it, since there was no enclosure. Each man lived separately, and it was more like a gathering of solitudes. Clearly, there was some sort of neighborly intercourse; for those athletes of Christ sang their hymns together. Frequently more than one of them went to Anthony's wall for advice and consultation.

Sixteen, seventeen, eighteen years. During the twentieth, the cup seemed to be full to overflowing. No one had ever heard of an ascetic remaining in solitude under such conditions for so long! Anthony's friends were full of anxiety and apprehension.

They were afraid that he had reached the limit of his physical strength and they feared for their own future without him. During that last dark period which was taking on tragic proportions, they must have needed so terribly to see Anthony, to have him walk before their eyes, to see that amazing man sit down, stretch out his arms. To tell the truth, all Egypt must have felt the same need. Was there not talk of persecutions? Now or never was the moment for the conqueror of the powers of Evil to come to the rescue of his Christian brothers.

Chapter VII

FATHER OF MONKS

As ONE breaks the mold of a statue when it is believed to be completed, so Anthony's friends broke down his door after twenty years. Anthony came out and they were breathless with astonishment at the sight of him. Though convinced of the value of asceticism and of the wonder of the Holy Ghost's gifts, they expected to see a kind of specter appear on the threshold of the fort, an emaciated rag of a man whose eyes alone might retain their brilliance.

The man they now saw showed no trace of physical decline. Twenty years of desperate combat in an outpost of Christianity, without a single day's repose, had passed without leaving its mark upon Christ's soldier. As he was when he had shut himself away from the world, so he now appeared, but with an added look of supreme wisdom upon his features. He seemed, says Athanasius, "to have learned the secrets of the Temple of the Lord and to be endowed with the breath of divinity." He was the living statue of perfect asceticism. He had neither put on flesh nor lost it, and his appearance was sturdy and confident. His smile was not that of a man rejoicing at his escape from danger; and there was, in his expression, no trace of the bitterness or unhappiness of a man who remembered his past trials too often. He was not surprised that they had broken in his door, or that a throng of friends and people he did not know had gathered on the mountain. He moved among them with unassumed simplicity, answering questions politely and even asking some himself. His words came quickly to his lips, his tongue and his memory functioning perfectly. It was hard to believe that he had ever given up the habit of talking with his fellow men.

The throng showed its admiration. As a whole, it was impressed favorably by the ascetic, the champion of piety who had broken all records; but we are not obliged to idealize those Egyptians, and it is easy to imagine that there were, besides the priests who had come for purely religious reasons, a few skeptics, and some jealous Thomases who could believe only after they had seen. They saw and they believed. Martyrs were not the only witnesses for Christ, said Origen truthfully, and ascetics were also witnesses. Marcellus was thrown by his executioners into boiling pitch and he did not utter a groan, but his courage was no greater an omen than Anthony's calmness and restraint after his twenty years of complete seclusion. There was no need for tongues of fire to blaze above his head, for jewels to fall from his mouth, or for a radiance to come from his tunic. Twenty years had fled like shadows—fled as though they had never existed. The mountain exhaled the fragrance of Eternity. Christ was there, with Elias and Moses standing by His side.

It will be said that fasting keeps away physical decline. But Athanasius' account, which is fuller than other texts, is of considerable importance in this connection. The serenity of Anthony's mood, his quiet strength, and his holy youthfulness as he left his prison, qualities which were to be evident in his bearing day after day henceforward, prove conclusively that we need not regard him as a neurotic, as affected with hallucinations, or as a paranoiac. He had no imbecile grin on his face, no wild look in his eyes, no excessive hilarity or rubbing of the hands, no locomotor ataxia, no stammering, blushing, or quick, feverish activity followed by sudden depression.

His was a holiness mingled with good health, a robust, methodical power in which was mingled perhaps the slight heaviness
of a Bossuet or a Thomas Aquinas. The impulsive acts of his
youth, bordering on fanaticism, his lack of critical sense,
his fear of being unable to make decisions, were no more. *"Je
suis une force qui va,"* declared Hernani. But Anthony's
power was static. He ran almost no risk of suffering a mental
smash-up. A man of his sort, firmly established as to his trust
in God, was very unlikely ever to lose his reason.

We cannot therefore regard Anthony's visions as the rav-
ings of a starving man or the maunderings of a dreamer. The
man who was taken by his friends out of his embattled fortress
did not look starved, and he did not have the appearance of
a fantasy-ridden Don Quixote. Those who saw him believed
him, even though he talked of unremitting, unverifiable battles with the powers of evil.

In the early years of his mountain solitude, Anthony must
at least have been aware of the temptation offered by madness, but he put it from him. His good health and his well-
balanced mentality do not tell us the whole story. While strug-
gling with his demonic co-tenants, he must frequently have
felt a desire—partly subconscious but acutely present in his
weary flesh—to topple over into the irrational, to abandon himself forever to the confused images flashing through his mind:
to stop praying, to close his eyes, to stretch out on the ground,
to step down into madness—to lose his reason for good and
all, to see the Devil everywhere. . . .

Chroniclers of desert history did not try to conceal the fact
that hermits went mad after excessive privation. They let it
be understood that madness was one of the serious dangers
threatening the existence of an anchorite. Wouldn't it have
been better to call it one of the chief temptations that beset
a monk? The ethics of despair must have seemed very attrac-

tive to the man who struggled continually to reconcile his high principles with his wretched way of living. To crack up suddenly, to play havoc with intelligence the way debauchery did with the body, to feel oneself engulfed in a thick fog, to believe oneself no longer a responsible person. . . .

During acedia and all the loss of sleep from which ascetics suffered, madness lurked in the consciousness; in the case of Anthony, who seemed never to have a moment's inactivity in all his twenty years inside the fort, it must have declared itself in the midst of his struggles. But Anthony overrode it and kept his sanity.

He was not yet, however, altogether out of danger. If ever he thought he was, at that moment he was abundantly exposed. From all sides the temptation to show his pride assailed him. He had just accomplished a chef d'oeuvre of asceticism: twenty years without seeing a face or showing his own; twenty years of fasting and fighting the evil powers. Then, suddenly, he found himself plunged into public life, called Master by a multitude of people of all ages who sought to give him and receive from him the kiss of peace, to touch him as though he were a second Jesus Christ, to cut off a piece of his tunic without his knowing it, to learn ascetic principles from him, to question him on two meanings of a saying of Saint Paul, to bring him a sick man to console or cure. . . . The stones were hacked away. The entrance was open now. He crossed the threshold—and then, triumph! Every voice proclaimed him Saint. Voices near him said: "Happy the breasts that gave thee milk; happy the man that begat thee; happy the house where thy first cry was heard". . . . "Master, here is my son. Wilt thou consent to touch him, for he has erysipelas?" . . . . "What, Master, is to thee the greatest of all virtues?" . . . . "Share this loaf with me, Master, though I am unworthy." . . . . "Master, hear me." . . . "Master, look at me." . . . "Master!

Master!" Signals were given in the valley, and people kept arriving. A joyful throng recognized in Anthony their leader and their guide.

Some ascetics whose accomplishments had been far less important than those of Anthony of Koma, and whose fame was as nothing compared with his, had, according to Palladius, wallowed in pride. Such was Hero, who went for three months without eating, "contenting himself by communion with the mysteries and with edible weeds if he could find them." He bored every one so terribly with his talk of his exploits that the "fathers" put him in irons. Such was Albanius who, during a journey of forty miles when his companions ate twice and drank three times, refused food and drink altogether and recited passages from the Holy Writ by heart; when he was back in his cell he broke down and rushed off to Alexandria to celebrate. Such also was that Ptolemy who thought himself a famous athlete of Christ because he lived in a place supposed to be uninhabitable, eighteen miles from the nearest well. In December and January, when dew was abundant, he collected it from the rocks with a sponge and put it in Cilician jars, thereby insuring a supply for the whole year. He lived thus for fifteen years; then he discovered that he could not manage with his dew any longer. So he abandoned it for the juice of the grape and sank into vice.

Anthony was in the high tradition of the greatest mystics; he knew nothing of pride. His sense of the near presence of God was too intense for that; he submitted everything to his Master. The Christian forces, his contemporaries, could use him for propaganda all they liked, exhibit him and take his holiness for granted; but he would keep his simple humility till the end.

Immediately, we see him in action. Anthony, the hermit, became Anthony, the healer, the worker of miracles.

"Through him, the Lord cured several persons of their bodily ills; and he cast out demons from others," declares Athanasius, and the examples he gives at the end of his book, though connected with another period, explain this sentence . . . the healing of a man who had torn his tongue with his teeth; the healing, without seeing her, of a young girl with paralysis affecting her eyes ("her tears, the mucus and fluid that flowed from her nose and ears upon the earth were at once changed into worms"); the healing without seeing her of a young girl who had been weakened by the excessive severity of her existence and was suffering pain in her stomach.

Medical authorities have always invoked the law against those who call themselves and whom people call "healers"; they regard them as charlatans. . . . We must give Anthony credit for never calling himself a healer. Nine times out of ten people had to circumvent his hesitation, which was in no way caused by fear that his prayers might not be heard. Granted or not, God would still be the only true God. But he considered it unfitting for a hermit to put himself forward. Healing the sick was, generally speaking, too spectacular and people talked of it, attributing the merit for it—the ingrates!—to a man. Even during His active public life, Christ hesitated when people wanted Him to heal the sick—all the more reason for an ascetic to avoid such activities.

Anthony told everyone that he had no medical ability. Homeopathy, acupuncture, magnetic passes: he boasted no knowledge of these or similar practices. He could have given, without risk of error, advice regarding hygiene, though, with his dirty feet and his many privations, the idea of doing so never entered his head. Prayers, more prayers, always prayers—such was his only prescription. His role is not to be compared to that of the captain of a small ship or commander of a desert garrison, relying on a medical dictionary, on textbook medicine, and a field infirmary. He deliberately took his stand upon religious terrain. Trust in God — that was his instrument case and his quinine. Hence his attitude after his interventions. "Always," says Athanasius, "he gave thanks to the Lord." *Not my will but Thine.* "If his prayer was granted, he did not boast; if it was not granted, he did not complain." God had nothing in common with an idol of wood, stone, or metal, to which one addressed cajoleries, and which one turned to the wall if these were not successful. Man knew nothing of God's ways and was required on all occasions to praise Him.

An ecclesiastical medical commission examining with critical eye the miracles of pious personages whose "cause" the Vatican is examining would refuse to take into consideration cures reported in such terms as Athanasius used. He gave no thought to scientific precision. Clinical symptoms of illnesses, proofs of healing, all that remained extremely vague. Although we may remain uncertain as to these miracles, however, it would not be good sense to deny that they took place. In sound theology, the power to heal was equal to that of conquering the Devil and his minions. The shameful sickness with which Satan afflicted the world had two synonymous names: death and sin. The ascetic who triumphed over vice was conquered by Christ, Who then entered into him and Who, when He was willing, soothed all human suffering. "For whether is easier, to say, Thy sins be forgiven thee; or to say, Arise, and walk? But that ye may know that the Son of Man hath power on earth to forgive sins (then saith He to the sick of the palsy), Arise, take up thy bed, and go unto thine house."

In half the cases, at least (the proportion seems greater, if we scrutinize Athanasius), the sickness healed by Anthony was that of possession, bodies inhabited by evil spirits. Athanasius differentiates between the possessed and the madman: "Through him the Lord purified many of the possessed and healed those whose minds were affected."

Anthony's Egypt, like the Palestine of Christ's time, seems to have harbored a relatively large number of those "energumens" (an etymologically exact term) of whom, apparently,

the world, despite its reputation for being no better than formerly, contains fewer and fewer. Periodically, people have regarded the leaders of their enemies as creatures of the Devil:
Hitler, who succeeded in making himself the ideal henchman
of Satan, took his place in the long line. But individual opinions
cannot be taken into account.

The Church did not wait for progress in neurology, psychoanalysis, and psychiatry to check the zeal of those who
drew attention to cases of possession. "Before the priest under-
takes exorcism, he must carefully inquire into the life of the
possessed, his circumstances, his reputation, his health, and
other matters; and he must talk with a few wise, prudent, and
well-advised friends of the possessed, because the too credulous are frequently mistaken. It often happens that lunatics,
sufferers from melancholia, and the bewitched, deceive the
exorcist, saying that they are possessed and tormented by the
Devil; these persons have greater need of a doctor's prescription than of an exorcist's ministrations." This is contained in
the *Actes du Synode National de Reims* of 1583. The Roman
Ritual entreated the exorcist to be, above all else, suspicious:
In primis ne facile credat aliquem a daemonio obsessum esse.
And the specific symptoms of possession which he enumerated
(the use or knowledge of an unknown language; the knowledge of distant or secret events, the presence of extraordinary
physical strength), and which he offered as simple guarantees, justifying his claim, had to undergo a careful sifting.
The Church firmly discarded many symptoms of possession
which the average Catholic man would have considered un-
mistakable. The "itch to do evil, to wallow in it," for example,
was encountered in diseases like epilepsy. "This sickness,"
wrote de Tonquédec, "produces the most uncharacteristic
words and acts in those afflicted with it: coarse blasphemies,
rebellion against God, insulting behavior to priests and other
religious persons, mad brutality, defilements even before witnesses, sacrilege with sadistic refinements. . . . I discovered

young girls spitting out the Host after receiving it, or keeping it to profane it shamefully; also those who dirtied their crucifixes, trampled on their rosaries, etc. . . ." A whole black literature has sprung up around supposed cases of possession.

Modern theologians blame the clergy of the Middle Ages for not having acted with more enlightened critical sense in matters of sorcery, and for having too easily believed in stories of possession. Trials, several hundred years old, have been re-examined; most often there was no reason to suspect the honesty of the judges, but in too many cases it was found that the dossier was composed of rumors and anonymous accusations.

Do we ever find Anthony trying to discover whether or not the people, brought to him or described to him, were authentically possessed? Everything seemed to happen as though the matter were as clear to him as to the great mass of Christians of his day, who called a cat a cat and called mentally unbalanced people possessed (especially those claiming to be inhabited by the Devil). Did not Christ tell His disciples to "heal the sick, cleanse the lepers, raise the dead, *cast out devils*"? And did He not exemplify his precepts? In the list of miracles described in the Gospels, those of casting out devils figure largely; these Jesus regarded as authentic proofs of His power and He liked to perform them.

We can take exception to the Gospel passages, using the care that Jesus used when He conducted a kind of inquiry and adopting His differentiation between the various types of demons. Exorcism, in Christ's mind as in the daily life of Palestine, was nevertheless a procedure—perhaps not commonplace but at least natural and usual—deprived of the furtive and rather hesitant solemnity with which it is surrounded today, somewhat like a machine which may or may not be running properly. There was nothing surprising in that. Christ, and, following Him, the Apostles, the Saints, the Church Fathers, had turned the world upside down in their cleansing of it. We can take it that the devils learned a lesson and withdrew and became less easily seen. In Anthony's lifetime, Egypt was just coming out of the shell she had worn throughout many centuries of paganism; she was occupied by the powers of evil as though they had conquered her: air, water, earth, and the regions beneath the earth belonged to them—also many human beings, tied hand and foot, in whom they had made their dwelling. A reconciliation with God had to be made for the rocks, the fish, the plant roots and the buffaloes, the sand and the sunlight, and particularly for all those possessed beings whom the devils ill-treated at their pleasure.

At fifty-five, Anthony had a proud bearing, but his eyes blinked as he gazed at that throng. To each one in turn, he could have given advice, but they all seemed to want to question him at once and hear him give them a general program. But he did not draw himself up to his full height under the clear sky in that rocky embrasure and deliver one of those impressive orations which politicians knew how to improvise, and which, after his twenty years' retreat, they would willingly have listened to. After an hour's conversation and quiet enthusiasm, he stood there speechless before that gathering of poor and pious men. They represented the task he had accomplished, and now, with a look of gravity upon his face, he wondered what to do next. Christ's disciples had said: "It is late, Master, and these people have had nothing to eat. . . ."

It was going to be necessary to increase the number of ascetics, but there were too many people in the crowd before him, and too many sick ones for him to visualize a group of pure ascetics. Solitary retreat was his ideal and one that was almost impossible to realize. Christ's great athlete would always be the Lord's free lance, detailed to the outposts of the world, but the ordinary good athletes would not go far from their fellows. Strange villages were to be established in suitable places —villages which would contain nothing but lonely huts, scattered cells which would be strongholds of Christianity in the empty stretches of the universe.

Athanasius shows us Anthony going at his task with full energy, crossing the canals, climbing and descending the mountain, preaching to groups and exhorting individuals, returning quickly to keep up his backlog of silence and prayer, only to set forth again on visits to those who needed his help: he was the father of the new monks.

Athanasius' desires to praise led him to turn all his flood-lights upon his hero, but there is no doubt that Anthony's activities benefited from very precious cooperation. We do not think of him as an organizer. He supplied the ascetics with a model, and, up to a certain point, with a program. Once the movement was launched, he kept on as their model and was always ready to rouse them, criticize them, and encourage them; but he had his seconds: a team of practical religious who could transmit his orders, explain his metaphors and his precepts for daily use.

In his fashion, Anthony was also a man of action, and his life is to us a chef d'oeuvre of strong, pure lines. He thought, made his decisions, and then executed them. He knew exactly how far his strength would take him and he set a limit not to be exceeded. He never launched his mystical attacks nor got himself involved with desert retreats or the evil powers without carefully arranging for his supply of bread and water. . . . Nevertheless his power was in meditation. He could draw near to God far more easily than he could talk to men. When his pupils needed help in carrying out their programs—his commands were often too general—his faithful adjutants took charge of the detail.

Though Anthony's authentic inspiration is more or less clearly indicated in the various *Regulae Antonii*, they need not concern us here. They were assembled subsequently: "He persuaded many people to live solitary lives, and thus it was that monasteries were built upon the mountains and monks sought seclusion in the desert," wrote Athanasius. A curious sentence from which it definitely appears that Anthony was in a sense an adviser to, rather than a creator of monasteries. As soon as he had left his fort, a certain number of ascetics established themselves there, forming a company of which he acquired and kept the honorary directorship. It was not a monastery in the sense we give the word today, an absurd sense—for monastery means literally the dwelling of a single being and one which scarcely, if at all, distinguishes it from a convent: a holy barracks, a building that housed a community of religious. The contemporary term was "laura," indicating the intermediate stage between hermit life and monastic life: the point where Anthony's thinking was concentrated. The monks' cells were not actually next to each other, or grouped around one cloister and within one enclosure; they were scattered over the terrain. The collection thus formed was not perceptible to the eye, for great care was taken that no monk could see the cell of another. And some of the cells were simply caves.

It required a long period of wearing down before such groups could function smoothly; their organization produced endless problems to solve and obstacles to overcome. It had been impossible to foresee everything. Perhaps a hierarchy should have been established among the monks. What day should be chosen for collective training in asceticism, and what should the training be? Could a married man, taken with asceticism, install his wife near him, in a separate cell, if she too wished to live a solitary life? Would it be a good idea to have a monk who could bake bread in the group? Could the monks address one another if they met at the well? Should there be a common cash box? And so on.

Sooner or later these semi-hermit organizations, established upon a bastard system, were to come to grief. Either an ascetic wanted to be, literally, a monk, living alone and not associating at all with any other monk, or else a group of them believed in the value and necessity of being together and lived thus, within a vast, lonely enclosure. Before long, the monasteries that claimed to be Anthony's inventions would resemble those founded by Pachomius in Upper Egypt about 320.

What with first enthusiasm and the good will of the brothers who found the great Anthony's occasional presence invigorating, the serious faults of the system were not very noticeable. When the Master came, they thought, everything would be put in order. He would say a few words and the difficulties would disappear. Meantime the new groups of monks which began to form at that time in Lower Egypt, and which kept in more or less direct touch with Anthony, did not observe the original formula at all. It was as if, instinctively, the monastic movement had learned the lesson of experience and, even before Pachomius had begun to change his discipline, became aware of the need for a more rigid system. The monks built houses for collective use, in addition to their individual cells. Convents began to rise up along the eastern edge of the Nile, on the mountain where Anthony had conquered the Devil; then to the west of the river, upon the other mountain; then in the province of Faiyum; then near the oases close to Faiyum.

Between two approximate dates, 305 and 310, and between Anthony's fifty-fifth and sixtieth year, he managed to visit and take encouragement to all his spiritual children. And this effort was due not to a need to be on the move after his twenty long years in the fort, but to a feeling that his work required it of him. Though he cherished the numberless athletes whose vocation had been precipitated by his ardent piety, he had no illusions about many of them. He guessed, in fact he knew, that a considerable number of "opportunist monks" had slipped in to the ranks of the holy phalanx. The heroic days of asceticism had passed. Anthony and a few others had smoothed out the rough road to perfection, made less bitter the bread of solitude. Monkhood no longer seemed to involve terrible privations; instead, it carried with it a certain social standing. Many saw a way of escaping the poverty that was bearing down upon Egypt. They did not burn with love for Christ nor was it their conviction that they—Ammonius the near-sighted or Stephen the currier — were being personally addressed in the Gospels by Christ, always their living contemporary, holy, immaculate, and young. It was their quick and crafty conclusion that the monk's garb protected them against the revenue officers, bad crops, and the hazard of marriage. A roof over their head, bread to eat, peaceful surroundings— all these benefits would be theirs.

It could not be held against these poor wretched men that they treated asceticism as a profession and a way out of their troubles. They had to be taken as they were and then made into better monks. This was the reason for all Anthony's comings and goings. Later on, no doubt, he would find himself regarding certain ones with skepticism, as is borne out by a delightful story in Palladius' *Lausiac History*, told to him by a priest. Anthony was shuttling back and forth between his hermitage on the Red Sea and the great monastery of Pispir (near the famous fort) where he gave interviews. But not to everyone! It was his custom to send for Macarius and question him: "Brother Macarius, have our brothers been coming here?" Then Anthony told him; "If you see some that are more careless than the rest, you can be sure they are Egyptians. But the more meditative and sensible ones can be put down as 'Hierosolymans' (natives of Jerusalem). . . ." When Macarius said one day, "Here are some Egyptians," Saint Anthony replied, "Cook them some lentils;" and he prayed for them and sent them off. But when Macarius said, "Here are some Hierosolymans," Anthony sat up all night talking to them about salvation.

His compassionate sympathy for his compatriots—with its touch of contempt—must have come to Anthony after many disappointing experiences accumulated during the years between 305 and 310. He could have easily tested them, body and soul, but, after all, he had conquered his own and he believed himself to be no better than the next man. So he did nothing of the sort. He was overwhelmed by his longing for solitude, and his desire to lose himself in his silent and immediate drawing near to God, as he hurried here and there to pay visits to the monks. But he was able to rid himself of those tempting visions of peace and solitude, so that he could continue his visits with his customary eagerness.

The important speech to the monks which Athanasius attributes to Anthony—quite a substantial piece of oratorical bravura—would never have been delivered. We cannot imagine Anthony talking for any such length of time, with care for elegance of phrase and closely knit reasoning, and with an air of listening to his own words and enjoying his own earnestness. Public orations were not for him, and he would have been a most unsuitable occupant of the Notre Dame pulpit—also a wretched conversationalist for a Paris salon. His triumphs were achieved in small, spiritual gatherings, mystical conversations interrupted by the reading of psalms and long silences, where no more than a dozen ardent monks were present—preferably monks fifty years old or more. It was in such an atmosphere that his thoughts took shape most easily. Or in talks with one man who sought instruction and repentance for his sins. . . . He uttered phrases heavy with meaning, even hesitant, but full of sense: grave witticisms, robust imagery, and, occasionally, a quoted passage of soaring beauty.

Though Anthony never made that great oration with which his biographer credits him, his talks with the monks contained a close approximation of its principal theme: *the ascetic is defined as the enemy of the evil powers.* In his disciples' presence he took the role of the Devil's conqueror. They must have questioned him endlessly about his battles, and our soldier undoubtedly regaled them with many tales of his campaigns. Now that the noise of battle had faded into the past and the insistent voice of passion no longer troubled that austere heart, perceptions could be achieved in the calm light of serenity. The demons had not really been formidable; a determination to defeat them was all you needed. "But weren't you frightened when they took the shapes of animals?" "No." "And when the walls shook as though the earth were trembling?" "No, and if you had been in my place, you would not have been afraid."

A new race of men appeared. They lived on both sides of the Nile, in the mountains which had, till then, been deserted, and their pious clamor filled the air. They wore wretched woolen garments; they did not paint blue shadows round their eyes; they lived in tiny cells; they did severe penance. But there was joy in their hearts. They were sweeping the threshold of the world clean of empty terrors. Be happy, oh Egypt, and dance in the valley. The end of thy misery is drawing near. Men are living, unmolested, in the desert, and upon them may be raised up the proud dwelling place of thy joy.

Athanasius writes in admiration of the spectacle, and he adds that others admired also. The sight of those mountains brings at once to our minds the Bible verses:

> How goodly are thy tents, O Jacob,
> And thy tabernacles, O Israel!
> As the valleys are they spread forth,
> As the gardens by the river's side,
> As the trees of lign aloes which the Lord hath planted,
> And as cedar trees beside the waters.

Chapter VIII

ALEXANDRIA

WHILE Anthony's "monasteries" evoked the picture of aloe trees in the clear Egyptian morning, planted by Jahveh's hand, and called up visions of the Father of all monks, walking from one tree to the next, his feet black with dust but his head haloed with legend, sounding the mort of Satan from the mountain tops with his wool-clad brothers, the Roman Empire had come, more and more, to resemble a worm-eaten galley.

Diocletian had not succeeded in his effort to simplify the governing of the world, in 292, by parceling out the authority among four Emperors: two Augustuses and two Ceasars. He had merely underlined the fact that the Empire was a huge mosaic. The East and the West were cracking apart. Pax Romana, in many of the provinces, seemed to have been replaced by a kind of masked terror.

Diocletian, the dynamic Emperor who had an exalted idea of his task and of the Imperial purple, did not understand any better than any other despot in world history why his carefully considered policy was not successful and why, outside the palace in which men and slaves bowed and scraped before him, there was a resistance, like that of the elements, to the execution of his official program. So he began to hunt for those responsible.

It was likely that he would find them, sooner or later, among those who did not participate—even in a token sense—in the cult of emperor worship: namely, the Christians. For a long time, however, friends restrained him. Furthermore, Diocletian was not a bloodthirsty brute; he was intelligent and he weighed both sides of the question. Christianity had gained considerable ground and it was estimated that, in certain sections of the country, the proportion was one Christian out of every three Egyptians. The new religion had a strong wind behind it. Conversions were increasing. Though there were two out of every three Egyptians who had not abjured their gods, perhaps one of these was getting ready to do so. The Prefect's reports indicated that there was a strange man called Anthony in the neighborhood of Memphis, who had an enormous influence on the people, and that many now lived as outlaws in desert outposts, pretending to be ascetics.

But from the dawn of the world, there had never been a religion which lasted more than a few hundred years without changing drastically, unless it consisted only of the establishment of a sect that did not proselytize. What right had Catholicism to refuse to lend its Christ to the heathens, to open its churches to the heathen divinities? Were not all the gods on friendly terms? In its way, Christianity was as deeply torn by dissension as the Empire itself.

Policemen and philosophers claimed that one out of every two Christians was a heretic. Christianity was improving in quantity rather than in quality. Those who rallied to the flag were frequently lukewarm, slack, changeable, lazy men whom a good healthy persecution would start along the straight road.

The East was still the great manufactory of carpets, perfumery, and doctrines; the Christian religion was not the last of them. Would not the snobbism which was then favoring Christianity be involved tomorrow with Manicheanism, whose elements were, after all, acceptable to people of common sense and which returned to some ancient legends? That conflict between the Good and the Evil, between Ormuzd and Ahriman, was a familiar one, similar to many others which had been satisfying to the intelligence.

Diocletian was propelled by a sentimental logic when he

persecuted Christianity. So many Emperors had previously done it that there was an almost primeval reason for the action; also, an Imperial solidarity was brought into play in his particular case. It was strange that, at the very moment of the Empire's decline, Christianity should be increasing so vigorously—a religion thriving on poverty, growing upon rubble, filth, and vermin. Yes, but if a persecution were started, it had to be carried through to success.

The scribe of *The Martyrdom of Saint Apa-Ari* dealt with the event thus: "In the reign of Diocletian and Maximian, an impious thing was done. . . . The blasphemous Emperor Diocletian created seventy gods—thirty-five males and thirty-five females. . . ." The scribe of *The Panegyric of Saint Peter of Alexandria, the Pure, the Archbishop, the Martyr,* declared: "Peace still existed and the Christians had some freedom [to follow their religion]. The Devil, being unable to endure this, began a terrible persecution with Diocletian, the impious Emperor, as intermediary. He caused great bloodshed in Africa, in Mauretania, in Egypt, and in Asia. . . ." And the scribe of *The Martyrdom of Saint Eusebius* fixed the precise date of the edict against the Christians for the disobedience of Basilius (one of Diocletian's high officers and the father of Eusebius—himself a victorious general) who refused to sacrifice to the heathen gods: "Then the Emperor Diocletian, burning with the furious rage of the Devil, his father. . . ." On the other hand, the scribe of *The Martyrdom of Saints John and Simeon* took it for a certainty that Diocletian was an adherent of Christianity at the beginning of his reign.

Up to a point, the actual events were of less importance than the degree of contemporary awareness of them and their correct interpretation. *The Acts of the Martyrs* of the Coptic Church help the historian to measure the depth of Egyptian ignorance—that of the populace and the monks—regarding events of the very first importance which should on no account have been allowed to remain unknown. The scribe knew that Saint Eusebius' executioner "took him by the hair, pulled it forward, and, dealing him a savage blow with his sword, cut off his saintly head," but he proved himself incapable of describing the legal proceedings with even the slightest clarity. Thus the people had nothing to depend on except verbal accounts and a few inadequate papyri. The topography of Egypt makes it likely that news traveled slowly, but easily and surely, from one end of the country to the other. Perhaps it was enough for the news to be started down the Nile valley. The north wind filled the river boats' sails; the flat roads along the banks wearied neither pedestrians nor asses. Many of the clergy went "underground" before the police arrived, and the communication system could easily convey their letters of exhortation and comfort to all the churches.

But, owing to the country's poverty, there was a pervading bewilderment. Rumors were both disregarded and believed. The people waited. Persecutions—perhaps in the north, in the turmoil of Alexandria. Or in the south, in the Upper Thebaid. Many were killed there. But the persecutions did not become real until they reached the village. So many stories were going about!

The monks had so large a grapevine in Lower Egypt and were so closely united with the clergy that they got news more quickly than the rest of the population. It is astonishing to read in Athanasius, immediately following his description of the monasteries and the reinforcements for Anthony's ascetic campaign: "Then Maximinus' persecutions of the Church began. . . ." This phrase contradicts the known events between 303 and 310, and gives the impression that Anthony and his monks had been shouting their psalms for several years without suspecting for a moment that their brothers were being put to death in Alexandria and the Upper Thebaid.

There was actually nothing they did not know, but they awaited developments. In the early years there were no Holy Wars, so it never became necessary to call the Christians to arms or to march on Alexandria. "Did you ever hear of one of us Christians starting an uprising?" said a bishop to the tribunal. Anthony believed the Christians' role was to persevere in ascetic training. But Imperial decrees threatened them too. *The Acts of the Martyrs* of the Coptic Church mentions an anchorite who was tried by the Governor, as well as a monk called Paphnutius who brought several adolescents with him to the tribunal. When the Governor saw him he groaned: "By Hercules, these Christians are a torment to me, especially that little monk Paphnutius. . . ." Nevertheless, Paphnutius went to meet his destiny, while Anthony and his monks waited day after day. . . .

Solemn egocentricity and indifference to the sufferings of others did not explain this mystical unconcern. It was due to the feeling that martyrdom was the most desirable ending to the life of a Christian athlete, and that the grim persecution was a prelude to the coming of the Kingdom of God. When human beings were peacefully and continually won over to the doctrine of Christianity, that triumph also heralded the return of Christ. Persecutions which interfered with the administrative machine of Christianity did not delay the onward march of Christ. The blood that was shed in Alexandria or in Coptos was still blood of atonement, of Calvary. A veil would be lifted. . . . The martyrs went from earth to Heaven, where, like the Good Penitent, they firmly established themselves. The Church could lament their deaths, it could pray that those deaths might be less atrocious—yet what an enviable fate!

The relative tranquillity of the monasteries during the storm that shook Christian Egypt shows that asceticism was never regarded by Anthony as slow suicide, death by inches, or a polite way of killing oneself without transgressing the interdicts. Though he wearied his body by means of fearful privations, and though he truly, according to Athanasius, loved to repeat Paul's phrase: "For when I am weak, then am I strong," at least he tried not to destroy his body secretly and not to hasten his end. He was certainly expecting to die, saying to himself each morning that he would not last till evening, and in the evening that he would not see the dawn. But none of his acts or his prayers would bring his last breath nearer. Death was ignoble, recalling the momentary victory of the powers of evil. It was necessary to watch with Christ and one must die only in the usual manner—the death that lies in wait for each one of us.

Anthony did not wear a hair shirt or flagellate himself. His asceticism must never cause him to grumble and complain; there was no need for it to become spectacular or give him excessive pain in order to be the sister of martyrdom. Origen had said so and his doctrine on this point was authoritative. A discreet sister, yes, certainly—for human eyes. Compared to baptism with blood, an ascetic's concentrated thinking about Christ's presence, and his determination to bring the world back to righteousness, with all the daily effort involved, amounted to a kind of "witnessing" that had a lasting value. No need to pick and choose in the matter of fasting, or to be overwhelmed with jealousy of the brothers who were baptized with blood and who were cheered by the celestial phalanxes when they left the stadium—the important thing was for Christianity to win and for death to be beaten. The Christian athlete's heroism consisted first of all in running swiftly and obeying his captain's orders. Among those who died at Alexandria without abjuring their faith, how many were there who did not feel consoled and strengthened beforehand by the recital of the great performances of Christian ascetics? Had not Anthony shone on his mountain like a huge lighthouse casting its beams upon the gates of Heaven? And by the same token, while the slaughter of Christians continued in the north and south of Egypt, the souls of the new elect looked down upon the monks.

The persecutions did not lower the Christian flag to half-

mast or in any way take the joy out of the verses of the psalms.
Eternity was not affected by atmospheric changes.

The greatest saint sins seven times a day. Theoretically,
Anthony did not envy the martyrs. But actually, though he
disciplined himself endlessly on the subject, he coveted their
fate. Why they and not I? After more than forty years of
ascetic life, would not martyrdom be the natural end? He increased his privations, but the demons kept on whispering
that his struggle against sleeping and eating was paltry and
too fastidious, that it was the behavior of an old imbecile and
not worth nearly as much as a quick blow of the ax or a good
burning. He pondered the apostates, those who abjured their
God when tortured. Would he not be permitted to maneuver
himself into the place of a weakling? Since, in the Christian
apostolic brotherhood, the rich shared their goods with the
poor, could not a courageous man put himself at the disposal
of a coward? And was not the length of his vigils always set
forth in his ascetic program? He listened to the lament that was
rising up from the Egyptian earth. . . .

The persecutions did not open with a massacre. In March of
303, the nineteenth year of Diocletian's reign, and almost at
Easter—Christianity's most important festival day—two Imperial edicts were issued. The first one closed the churches
and houses of prayer, and it required that all religious objects
be turned over to the authorities; the second ordered the immediate imprisonment of the heads of all the Churches. But,
though a large number of the buildings with their Holy books
were burned, many of the priests escaped. They were not
afraid of death, which would have made martyrs of them, but
they had no wish to go out of their way to meet it.

The persecutions increased. The simple adherents were the
victims this time, and, according to classic procedure, they
were required to sacrifice to heathen divinities. Many gave in.

Towards those who resisted, the authorities vacillated between two procedures: some were executed, but the greater number were released. The judges had been ordered to be lenient and some comic scenes resulted. "I refuse to sacrifice," said the Christian. The governor stood up, shouting, "He has sacrificed," and the soldiers repeated, "He has sacrificed! He has sacrificed!" Then a group rushed on the dumbfounded Christian, beat him and dragged him away. No martyrs—that was the great objective.

Harsher treatment was thus postponed, but only temporarily. Diocletian, angry because many of his soldiers became converted to Christianity and then deserted for reasons of conscience, resorted to his *ultima ratio:* terror. The blood of Christians flowed in Phrygia, in Cappadocia, in Arabia, and in Phoenicia. And above all, in Egypt. The era upon which the Coptic calendar is based is called the Era of Diocletian or the Era of the Martyrs. In the Thebaid, on certain days the executioners killed their one hundred Christians. The historian Eusebius witnessed the killings and described their horror. The axes lost their keen edge from repeated use. The executioners relieved one another. Human ingenuity, coupled with cruelty, strove to prolong the torture and make it more agonizing. The women were hung head downwards by one foot till death came. The men were quartered, their arms and legs broken.

In 305, disheartened for one thing by this new failure—he would have much preferred to compromise with the Christians—Diocletian abdicated. Maximian followed his example. But the persecutions did not cease, at least in Egypt, which in 308 was subservient to three Augustuses: Galerius, his nephew Maximinus Daia, and Licinius.

A day came when the great Anthony decided to fly to the assistance of his brothers. We cannot be precise as to the reason for this new attitude. It was as if one of the heads of the Church had sent him a confidential message, instructing him to come out of his solitude. Anthony respected the bishops. He considered that the monks owed them military obedience.

If anyone took this step, Peter, the Patriarch of Alexandria, must have been the one to do it. He was a man of great thoughtfulness and courage. The authorities had arrested him and thrown him into prison, together with most of his entourage and several other bishops from Lower Egypt, thus plunging the Christian Church into confusion. In order to improve the situation, Peter may have thought of using the prestige of Anthony—Public Friend Number I—and, due to some fault in the system of surveillance over Peter, his message may have reached Anthony.

The Gandhi of the fourth century set out upon his journey. His decision was vigorous and determined, despite the several years he had taken to reach it: "Come, let us also fight if we are called, or at least watch those who are fighting." With several other monks he went down to the Nile, near Aphroditopolis, and the little group boarded the first river boat that would take them towards the sea. There, among the bags of grain and the dried vegetables, they meditated, chanted psalms, and discussed religious matters without stopping to enjoy the softly-flowing current or the changing beauty of the landscape—sudden glimpses of pink sandy shores covered with birds; bluish cliffs in the dawn light; distant villages seemingly piled on top of one another, like blocks of stone with trees growing amongst them; many-colored fields with men and animals moving about in them. At dusk, when navigation became dangerous, the boat was moored at the riverbank. The monks gave thanks to God and broke bread as though still upon their mountain, attending to their pious exercises. We can imagine them, very sleepy from being in the open air all day, lying down, even snoring—watched over by God and His starlit heavens, huddled close to protect each other from the cold river mists.

Dawn came again and found them in good spirits. The boat

moved out over the gold-fretted surface of the river. Fish jumped, and birds preened themselves on the shore, while Anthony pleaded with his companions to follow his ascetic precepts—they must suffer with Christ. Then his thoughts leapt ahead to Alexandria, and he thought deeply about the Patriarch. At last he spoke: "Peter is a great athlete." And the monks answered in unison: "Assuredly, Peter is a great athlete."

Sympathetically indifferent to the monks, the helmsman and his men gazed silently with their wide, blue-shadowed eyes at the shimmering waters. The north wind was already blowing against the current and it made small rippling noises.

They passed Memphis on the left, Babylon and its Roman citadel on the right, and they were filled with emotion at passing through the region that contained so many reminders of the Holy Family: the Virgin's well, the Virgin's sycamore tree. . . . Only yesterday *they* were seen here. What were three centuries, when one realized how old the Nile was? Nothing had changed. Nothing would change until the return of Christ.

They came to the Cow's Stomach—the traditional name for the forking of the river—and followed the western branch, with the desert close on the left and the fertile fields of the Delta stretching as far as the eye could see on the right. They were entering a new world, and their usual tranquillity would no doubt undergo a severe testing. They saw the vestiges of the Garden of Eden. Water, flowers, grass, corn in profusion; men and women in great numbers tilling the soil, cutting papyrus, herding buffaloes and geese, cleaning out irrigation ditches . . . . Ah, if only they had known how to avert the poverty of Egypt!

Farther on, both banks teemed with this abundance and the labor of the people. Boats passed them continually now, their sails bellying in the morning breeze. Helmsmen shouted to one another. Finally, at Schedia, they turned left into a canal with no winding—a street for boats. With scarcely any keel, they glided along steadily, propelled by oars and sails. They passed tiny boats loaded to the gunwales with melons and cucumbers;

lighters—mobile pens—of buffaloes that bellowed and locked horns with each other; little barges of salt that glistened in the sunlight. The great city was declaring itself from afar by the extent of its material needs. It was clear that the butchers of Alexandria would kill and sell the animals; that Alexandria's housewives would buy those cucumbers; that Alexandria's beggars would drink from the hollowed-out rinds of those melons. Anthony kept exhorting his companions: let no one weaken in the glamour of that astonishing city. Earthly wealth was nothing but a whited sepulcher . . . a cemetery, a skeleton, and all the rest of it.

There was something paroxysmal about the fertility of the soil. Vineyards delighted the eye by their similarity to an army in battle array. Vegetables and grain looked finer and healthier than elsewhere. Lake Mareotis, a little to the right, became joyously bluer. Men and caravans peopled its shores. Alexandria, Alexandria—the wonderful name floated in the golden air of the morning. Anthony tried to think of it only as the name of a city where Christians were suffering—where, for the glory of God, it was surely necessary to seek martyrdom. Like buffaloes from the Egyptian pastures, the monks proceeded towards the place where death awaited them.

In the "literature of the desert" there is the story of a monk who journeyed to Alexandria. On his return, his friends asked him, "Couldn't you tell us something about the city?" He replied, "I saw the Bishop but nothing else," and they lowered their eyes in silence.

Despite its ruins, Alexandria must have seemed like a collection of skyscrapers to the average Egyptian, but Christ's athletes were not of ordinary clay. It is likely, however, that, while refraining from craning their necks like provincials, they had a good look around them. They wanted to show that they were not afraid.

Finally, they came out into Lake Mareotis and glided past the southern part of the city; then they entered another canal which took them through the Rhakotis quarter with its noisy shipyards, drinking songs, and shouts of hawkers and teamsters. Then, at the edge of the Mediterranean, they entered the Kibotos (Casket), a little enclosed harbor within the Eunostos, the western port, and found themselves close to the Heptastadium, the famous sea wall that separated the eastern and western ports. The Island of Pharos lay beyond the Heptastadium, and was partly hidden by it, but its huge tower stood high above everything, like an enormous asp trying to strike at the sky. Old hulks, encrusted with mussels, were being repaired on the shores. The Kibotos, crowded with triremes, galleys, feluccas, tartans, resounded with oaths and songs; it was a kaleidoscope of colors, languages, races, and the rigging of boats. Women skinned fish and cats devoured pink entrails.

Apparently there were some Christians, in the crowd watching the ships, who knew of the imminent arrival of the monks and would give Anthony the kiss of peace. His name doubtless flew from mouth to mouth, rousing the curiosity of the idlers. Twenty years in a cell! Forty thousand men under him! He had thrashed the demons! They hurried forward to see what an ascetic and a worker of miracles looked like. They touched his clothes—perhaps that would bring them luck. These Egyptians from the interior smelled of the brush; they walked awkwardly with a rolling movement of the shoulders. They wore dirty woolen garments and were dirty themselves, for they never washed. Nevertheless, the Greeks liked them. The townsmen sensed in them a childish self-consciousness and a sense of humor, they told each other that their leader was famed for his powerful personality. Imagine that man, not knowing Greek, and, fresh from some village, mixing fearlessly with men selling secondhand goods and pottery, urchins, fishwives with high combs and jiggling earrings, scar-faced bullies, high-sandaled prostitutes. The laughter and jeering was stilled, and the Jewish street boys wondered if the hairy Christian might not be a prophet after all.

In scarcely any time at all, Anthony and his companions were mentally adopted as honorary citizens by the great majority in that big city whose curiosity and volatile moods were rather Parisian. What the monks had done moved the populace: Greeks, Jews, Syrians, and blacks. They had come from farther off than the Pyramids solely to help those they called brothers to die nobly. And in the gymnasiums, the taverns, the theaters, there was furious betting as to their fate. Would the police decide to give up their strange policy of indulgence and put them in prison? Or would they have the final word? Evidently the monks were looking for trouble, and this pleased the city's ruffians, despite their very different ideas on the question of the flesh. What would be the end of this strange conflict, in which death sentences were labeled martyrdoms and meant not defeats, but the most priceless triumphs?

The conflict was indeed strange, and it spoke eloquently of the confusion of those in power. They too realized that the blood of the martyrs became the seed of Christianity, which deprived them of the traditional trump card of violence. They had continually to tax their imagination and coolness to conceal their purpose and to give the impression that they would be pitiless and that the candidates for martyrdom must regret their obstinacy. But this was useless effort when it came to Anthony and his companions. Like strikers lying down to be trampled by policemen's horses or run over by locomotives, the monks offered themselves, baffling judges and the police, who were exasperated by this new kind of culprit. They were too gentle and too polite. "I am going to put you to death." "That is what I desire most. I kiss your hands."

At the very time when Christianity appeared to be at its darkest hour, Anthony and his group—in effect, with the consent of the police authorities—set themselves the task of destroying paganism. They went everywhere: into hairdressing shops, the houses of philosophers, gymnasiums, brothels. They visited courtesans of high degree, several of whom were flabbergasted by their audacity but suddenly became aware of the emptiness of fleshly pleasures. Accustomed to weariness, they slept anywhere: in public squares, on flights of steps, in boats hauled out of the water, in caravanserais with huts holding forty persons, in empty wagons.

Arrests and condemnations continued, but the authorities did not lay hands on the new arrivals; they pretended to scorn these up-country fellows who spoke no Greek. The monks acted as liaison officers between the prisoners and their families, between the faithful or the priests, hidden in the city or its suburbs, and their bishops whose trials were being prepared. Though they did not have direct access to the prisons, their many messages were somehow transmitted. Sympathetic guards were always to be found: an apostate, for example, tormented by remorse. Also, the prisoners were not all confined; the majority of them were put to work in the copper mines and underground quarries of the neighborhood, and, when they did not try to escape and the prefect ceased paying unannounced visits, guards closed their eyes if a monk accosted one of their charges. The poor souls never discussed even the most harmless sort of sabotage. Only the gentlest of pious talk: "Christ does not forsake his own . . . Thank Him for allowing thee to enter the school of suffering. . . ." Or perhaps they discussed details of parochial administration: someone's heresy, someone's plea for forgiveness, someone who would make an excellent priest. The guards saw no menace to the Empire in any of that. Because a monk offered bread to a prisoner and the prisoner shared it with his fellows, the guards did not believe Emperors would quake upon their thrones.

The little bands of monks took care not to neglect public questionings, during which they shared a twofold responsibility; some formed a nucleus of opposition in the crowd and managed to create a kind of Christian claque which cheered or booed at the right moments; the rest of them harassed the bench, and, by means of gestures and audible remarks, paying no attention to judge or soldiers, attracted the attention of the Christian under examination and encouraged him in his resistance.

The monks attended executions, anxious to see their brothers endure martyrdom bravely, to the bitter end; anxious too not to disturb the ceremonial that accompanied the entry of a Christian soul into Paradise. The spectacle of that suffering upset them deeply, but they strove to transmute their grief into joy. Then they removed the pitiful remains and saw to it that suitable burial was given them.

This went on till the authorities lost their tempers. Their leniency must not be regarded as weakness. The prefect issued a special decree, forbidding the monks to mingle with the crowds that besieged the tribunals, and, more sweepingly, ordering them not to stay in the city. Anthony gave thanks for this. Though martyrdom was his most cherished dream, he persuaded himself that, up to then, he had not attempted to bring it on. He could give up his cautious attitude now. "The others hid themselves," says Athanasius, seeming to hint that Anthony's companions had become frightened; but we prefer to believe that they were obeying their master's orders. He wanted to spare them the torture that he so urgently desired for himself. Then came a strange scene that would have been magnificent in a great silent film. Anthony had had his tunic washed. The following day he stood where the prefect and his guard would pass on their way to the tribunal. There was no trace of impudence in his steady gaze, but he was there, erect and clothed in shining white, standing a little apart from the crowd, which fell back in order to admire him more easily. He looked as if he were about to call out, "It is I, Anthony, the Father of Monks! If you are a man of your word, strike me!"

The prefect soon appeared in his open litter, and the escorting soldiers shouted at those who did not fall back quickly enough. Anthony stood now on the tips of his toes against a wall. His white tunic caught the prefect's attention, and their eyes met. The crowd held its breath in terror. Nothing happened. The prefect did not even have his litter halted so that he could force the insolent monk to stop gazing at the Emperor's representative. Perhaps his lips curled in a sneer, and that was all.

It is hard for us to decide whether or not this was a considered act on Anthony's part. His audacity could certainly have caught that self-important man off balance. But however this may have been, Anthony remained in Alexandria and the prefect kept himself free, apparently, to have him seized and put to death. Though the authorities disregarded Anthony's disobedience, they had carefully weighed the pros and cons. But, like so many magistrates in those first few centuries of Christianity, the prefect belonged to the spiritual family of Pilate. He was not a bloodthirsty man, but he wanted to be a good servant to the Emperor, not to confuse justice, and to keep his job. Being uncertain as to the rightness of persecution, he wavered. His orders were in no sense definite, and they did not cover the case of those monks who were not actually members of the clergy. They could have been arrested as ordinary Christians and urged to sacrifice to the gods to avoid the death penalty. More particularly, Anthony could have been seized for his disobedience of a definite order. But the number of martyrdoms had to be kept down and it would have been imprudent to lay hands upon those strange visitors who seemed to have the ear of the populace.

This gives a measure of the real power of Christianity at that time. Whenever the authorities got angry, they lost their equilibrium. Anthony stayed in Alexandria, right under their noses, comforting the Christians in prison, laying plans for conversions, and keeping the populace in a state of agitation.

Though there was indulgence in certain quarters, some of the most celebrated prisoners were executed. It was as if the prefect wanted to prove to himself that he was still a man. These executions came too late; they seemed to be the acts of authority in desperation—of spite, anger, and bad policy.

We are not familiar with the circumstances of the execution of the Patriarch, but we can take it that the police feared it might be the occasion for an uprising. It seems that they had reached some kind of agreement with Peter, who did not want the people to suffer or shed their blood for him. (In Carthage, where persecutions were also carried out, members of the clergy were accused later of having neglected the prisoners so as to avoid quarrels between Christians and pagans.) Peter was secretly taken from prison and led to the sanctuary of Saint Mark. There he was allowed to meditate for a few moments; then he was pulled away. In a lonely spot, in the presence of some of the faithful who had hastily assembled, he was beheaded.

A number of priests and bishops were executed at the same time, but Peter's death must have had the deepest effect on the Christian mentality. The Patriarch had enjoyed great popularity because of the purity of his life, the sureness of his understanding, and his generous heart. The son of a "protopresbyter," he had been dedicated to God at the age of seven. "Thanks to him," wrote Eusebius, "the poor received alms from the rich and became their equals, and the rich were in no way different from the poor." At once proclaimed a martyr, he was regarded as a great celestial protector of the Egyptian Church, and people awaited developments with more confidence than ever.

After that December of 311, the persecutions slowed down. The authorities became less severe, owing partly to boredom and partly to a fear of adopting an unwise policy. They maimed their victims, blinded them, hamstrung them, but they hesitated to kill them. Several priests came back to the city and celebrated mass semi-secretly. Scribes wrote accounts of the Patriarch's last moments.

According to strict ceremonial, Galerius recanted his mistakes and issued an edict of tolerance: *"The Emperor Caesar Galerius Valerius Maximianus, Invincible, August, Most High Sovereign Pontiff, Most High Germanicus, Most High Egyptian, Most High Thebaicus, Five Times Most High Sarmaticus, Twice Most High Persicus, Most High Armenicus, Most High Medicus, Most High Adiabenicus, Twenty Times in Tribunal Power, Nineteen Times Imperator, Eight Times Consul, Father of His Country, Proconsul . . ."* But Anthony had already left Alexandria. He felt out of place in that huge city which had been restored to peace, and he had heard the summons of the desert. If martyrdom did not require him, then let it be asceticism.

So he went back to asceticism.

Chapter IX

MORE MONK THAN EVER

THE game had been won, officially, by Christianity. In 312 Constantine defeated Maxentius just outside the walls of Rome; in 313 he issued the Edict of Milan, signed by himself and Licinius. Thus the reign of the false gods came to an end. Thus terminated the persecutions. Maximinus Daia gave in to his colleagues and hounded the Christians no longer.

Anthony did not undervalue the importance of this victory, and he did not overestimate it. The most splendid edicts ever issued could not change men's hearts in a day. Surely not Constantine's. *In hoc signo vinces* ... the *labarum* (banner) ... all this served him well on the day of battle, but then. . . . Though the Emperor owed his victory to God, he was in no hurry to seek baptism.

Yield to the prevailing optimism—relax his vigilance a little? Impossible! Would Christianity now possess the same virtues as during the persecutions? Wasn't there a risk of its weakening? The situation was too serious for the monks to take it calmly.

During the years immediately following, calmness was never general. After liquidating the too-ambitious Maximinus Daia, Licinius himself became too ambitious and started a conflict with his brother-in-law, Constantine. The conflict was both open and underhanded. Anti-Christian persecution broke out in many of his states. In 323, Constantine crushed Licinius' army but spared his brother-in-law. The latter was, nevertheless, put to death several months later, and unpleasant rumors went the rounds concerning Constantine's broken promise.

Putting oneself forward as the official champion of Christianity did not prevent one from sinning.

In Alexandria, Anthony had been closely aware of poverty and sin, the misery in the drab suburbs, the brawling, the exhausting labors of men, the neglected children, the disease, the dissolute houses. He knew how fickle was the mentality of those crowds, with what flippancy their laughter would burst forth over something not understood. He was aware of the confusion in souls never submitted to self-examination, of the superstitions, the passions, the tangle of virtues and vices. He himself—a man from lands south of the Cow's Stomach, with the country and the mountain in his blood—had experienced the giddy sense of isolation among thousands of men and their dwellings, and now and then he felt the dangerous longing to mingle in the life of an open-handed city like Alexandria, lying close to the sea waves in simple majesty. The great lighthouse on Pharos, the singing of sailors, the silence or the chattering of philosophers, the free and easy ways of the young women, the noise and color of the markets, the endless procession of faces and bright costumes—all of it could be wonderful on sultry evenings.

Such thoughts could not be allowed to turn him from the essential matter. Athanasius and the *Apothegms of the Fathers* speak of Anthony's anxieties in almost identical terms: "Fish die when taken out of the water, and it is thus with monks, who, lingering in the world away from their cells or spending time with the world's people, relax the intensity of solitude. We must therefore, like fish to the sea, return to our cells and keep our inner cares in mind. . . ." Solitude is the natural element of the monk.

* * *

When Anthony returned to his hut, he began by firmly taking himself in hand. Meekly obedient to the laws of hospitality, he had been obliged more than once to deviate from his regime of fasting. Moreover, his visits to prisons and his religious propaganda work had reduced to a minimum his opportunities for meditation. He had been a public personage, showing himself in the streets as such. He had defied pagan authority and had been treated as a Christian of superior rank, one whose arrest would have undoubtedly caused an uprising. The authorities had not dared to lay hands upon him, and, in refusing to martyr him, they had turned him into a man beyond the law, the moral leader, as it were, of the Egyptian Church.

He would have none of this title and every day he proved to himself, by fasting and various other austerities, that he was just an ordinary monk, a poor sinner like anyone else. He bothered less than ever with his clothing. No washing. Nothing comfortable to wear. No indulgences in eating. Once away from the Alexandrine parade, he took a cure of filth, silence, and scorn of food.

Unfortunately for Anthony, the world from which he expected to break away would have none of his wanting to escape. Those who had seen him at work in Alexandria followed him. They besieged him—the prophet, the performer of miracles, the saint. They besought him to cure this man's body and that man's soul. Poor Anthony had to be ruthless. Why couldn't they content themselves with prayer? He refused to open his door to them, and when they persisted he became stubborn and made them sleep outside. "Man, why do you nag me? I'm only another like you . . ." This to a soldier, writes Athanasius. And he replied similarly to many others. He did not admit for a moment that he could perform miracles, and it depressed him to contemplate the trickery practiced by so many others to the detriment of God's glory. God alone was all-powerful. God alone could perform miracles.

However, if we are to believe Athanasius, miracles were performed *through* Anthony. His visitors did not lose heart. New ones kept arriving continually and they knew how to take the welcome they got. They were not afraid to sleep under the stars. Anthony's presence sanctified everything—the earth near him was Christian earth.

Anthony's thinking was directly opposed to that of Moses—at least the Moses of Vigny. Though the latter suffered especially from a moral solitude, from the inability under which God had placed him to live on familiar terms with anyone whomsoever, his grievance was unqualified. All solitude seemed tedious to him. But to Anthony, all solitude was beneficial.

He did not put his desire for it above his duty to his brothers, but in his heart of hearts he longed to draw red herrings across the paths between him and the world.

And this time he decided that he could follow his inclination. Though not a man given to setting things down on the credit side of his balance sheet, he knew that there was an achievement which belonged there. And here he was, wanting at the same time to get away from it and to carry it through to perfection. "What shall it profit a man, if he shall gain the whole world, and lose his soul?" What good was it for the monastic movement to spread if it were to lose its original audacity and purity? A plague upon political Christianity. God—and again, God. God always!

One morning, apparently in the year 312, after the flooding, he went down and sat upon the river's bank. He had some loaves of bread with him, baked by the brothers. He looked for a boat, wanting to get away somewhere but not knowing in which direction.

He heard a voice from above, questioning him. "They will not let me live as a hermit," he explained. "They ask me to do things that are beyond my power." The voice spoke again, shrewdly and practically, and with no thought of tormenting him, saying that if he went to the Thebaid, or to Bucolia, which was a very wild part of the Delta, the people would bother him still more. "If you really want to be a hermit," the voice said finally, " go into the Arabian desert." Immediately won over to this idea, Anthony said only that he did not know the route. The voice told him of a Saracen caravan that was preparing to cross the desert in the direction of the Red Sea. So Anthony got up and went to find the Saracens. He begged the favor of letting him travel with them. "By a disposition of Providence," writes Athanasius, "they agreed heartily."

Though we may object strongly to the intervention of that celestial voice at just the right moment, it is no affair of ours. The account given by Athanasius, though idyllic, does not seem to us an unbelievable one. Agnostics will merely conclude that Anthony was talking to himself and that his ideas were suggested by seeing the caravan in process of forming. Our information is so scanty that we cannot argue about this. At this crucial point in Anthony's life, we should like to be able to follow every turn in his thinking. Climbing into the Thebaid, going to Bucolia, or setting forth into the heart of the Arabian desert are very different matters for the modern tourist, who wishes to know the details of his journey before departing. Considering the conditions of Anthony's time, Athanasius' account contains, we repeat, nothing unbelievable. In certain ways, Anthony, in his sixties, was able to hold himself completely and beautifully available. The fact that at eight o'clock one morning he thought of taking a boat for the Thebaid, and at ten decided to go into the Arabian desert, does not make a weather vane of him. He was very calm, very confident, and very humble.

The journey took three days, which was about right for the mileage. A camel's gait, unchanged through the years, is a little less than two and a half miles per hour, and the caravan stopped at night for sleeping and resting the animals. It was an invigorating journey. The atmosphere was dry and hot in daytime but very cool at night, with no flies or mosquitoes. Anthony had a weakness for camels; they knew how to conserve their strength. An ascetic would do well to copy them, rather than horses, which "ate all the time and immediately lost what they had eaten. . . ." The Saracens, their skins swarthy and eyes keen, moved with supple grace, and their scant speech, though not unsociable, was on a lofty poetic plane. Anthony prayed for his good companions during the starlit peace of the night, undisturbed by the invisible camels. The pagan world was reeling. The Milky Way, spreading over the sky, symbolized the invading Christian ideas that were being carried throughout the world by the four winds. The blood of Peter and the Alexandrine martyrs had flowed for these Saracens as well as for other men, and it had not flowed in vain.

From wadi to wadi and from stony ravine to bare plateau, the ground sloped upward. After the rust-colored foothills, which were the first to cut the horizon, the Kebril chain, running from north to south, rose up beyond. And beyond these, and much higher, the parallel chain of the southern Galalas, whose highest peak was Mount Qolzum. The caravan seemed to be heading for this peak, almost directly to the eastward. Anthony looked at it joyfully. Alexandria of the desert. Pharos on the sands. The peaks were etched against the sky with fantastic simplicity—tablets of stone, as it were, which told the tale of the longest and most meandering period in the earth's history.

The monotony of the journey, the weight of that stony, compact world, and that immense landscape out of which no man ever appeared, coming towards you with the new mystery of face, speech, and costume—these were sometimes enlivened by small things like the filmy grayish foliage of Jericho roses, pieces of petrified wood, little pools of silvery water among the rocks, low bushes, colocynth plants scattered over the sandy slope like jewels stitched on to a piece of material, fossil shells, even the sound of an underground stream. Anthony walked with a firm step. He was unfamiliar with his surroundings, and the names the Saracens gave to the irregularities in the desert's surface meant nothing to him. He had no precise ideas about where to settle. He merely wanted to choose a spot not too accessible, so that the endless visits would not begin all over again—though of course he realized full well that sooner or later his refuge would be discovered. And a nearby supply of water was imperative.

He probably left the caravan at the foot of Mount Qolzum. The Saracens' way led them around the mountain, but they doubtless mentioned to him a water supply that would serve his purpose, and he went alone to see it. Suddenly he knew the spot for the one God must have assigned to him in His original divine scheme. Athanasius' account is not picturesque, but it is moving: "He came to a very high mountain. At its foot flowed a limpid stream of fresh cold water. Farther on there was a clump of wild palm trees. As though by divine impulsion, he loved the place and recognized it as the one described by the voice beside the river. . . ." We perceive at once that Anthony experienced then a very simple, very human feeling. There was a smile on his face, at least for several seconds. We have proof that this blunt and constantly active man—this destroyer of Satan and the enemy of comfortable living—did at least once take pleasure in what he saw around him, as any traveler would who glimpsed a clear spring, with encircling trees, after days of sand and rock, Naturally it was still our pious Anthony who rejoiced, and for whom the trees and clear water evoked the sinless paradise that he wished with all his heart to recreate; but does not the feeling for beauty in everyone spring from a rediscovery of his lost paradise?

After the tomb and the abandoned fort, those trees and that spring formed a seemingly delightful landscape. The desolation, etymologically speaking, was complete. On all sides, the desert surrounded that sparse group of palm trees, which was merely a faint sketch of an oasis in this kingdom of burning sun and naked rocks. Far off, beyond the long slopes cut by twisting ravines, smoky blue water could be seen now and again. It was the Red Sea, whose waves were flaked, as it were, by the burning heat.

The very harshness of the panorama also moved Anthony; he was not seeking another Nile valley. A few trees in the rocky desert—that was the ideal place for him. And almost immediately he began to build a hut of large stones roofed with palm leaves. Then, perhaps the following day, he climbed the mountain in order to give thanks to God who had created him, to examine his surroundings, and to find a cave. When his hut was discovered and the monks came to bother him, he would need a more secluded place for his worshiping. What better way of effacing himself in prayer than to conceal and enclose himself in solid rock? A cool silence—darkness and solitude.

The cave which the present monks of the Monastery of Saint Anthony on the Red Sea indicate as that of their founder is more than twenty feet wide and ten feet high, and is reached by means of a forty-foot-long passage, about two feet wide and five feet high. There is no reason not to believe this to have been the secret refuge of the Father of all Monks, and our belief is surely buttressed by the magnificent panorama that meets the eye when one emerges from the passage. Mount Zion and the ramparts of Aigues-Mortes—praised by Barrès—are no more than replicas of Mount Qolzum, which gives a far more awe-inspiring impression. From it one sees, not the naive workmanship of human generations or the serene omnipotence of nature, but the divine craft of the Creator. The spirit of God and no other breathes there in that high place, as upon Sinai whose range spreads beyond the Red Sea; His creation bursts upon the eye in tormented unity. It was the finger of God which molded this lunar relief and which, with a single gesture, scooped out those deep cavities, scratched those rents in the rock, and started all the rounded crests marching in the same direction. Those cliffs and ridges, those swellings and crackings were reminders of the ageless conflict between Mind and Inorganic Matter. This was no crossroads where races met, no corridor where civilizations mingled. It was a sample of the earth in its most desperate form—stone, and again stone; a chaos controlled by divine thought, but where little creatures five or six feet tall, who were called men, continued to be as much out of place with their ploughs, their buffaloes, and their villages, as a caravan of camels on the surface of the sea.

There, Anthony was, if we may so express it, at his ease. It was just such great brutal stretches of earth that he hoped to reconcile with God. Under those burning skies, the rebellious spirits of light had been struck down, and Satan had tempted Christ—and a hermit should chant his hymns there.

That summit was one of the most poignantly significant in history. In that fourth century, when Christianity, in partnership with the Roman Empire, was officially playing a triumphant role, Anthony made it clear that his mission was not to live in the world and compromise with it, but to maintain a watchful and spiritual anxiety for its welfare. The finest churches and the most numerous gatherings of the faithful provided God's presence with a guard of honor which was scarcely necessary. Compared to a tomb, an old fort, or a cave, they were as nothing.

His message was mystical. Once in the passage leading to his cave, he forgot all about the majestic confusion of plateau and cliff under the scorching sun. As he drew near to his cave, a marvelous cleansing and lightening of his soul occurred, and when he knelt there the longed-for Presence was beside him. There, Anthony of Koma, Father of the Monks in Egypt and the world, saw God. There, in secret, some of the most portentous dialogues ever spoken took place between a man and his Master. There Anthony shed his peasant awkwardness and fully justified the severity of his asceticism. His eyes pierced the darkness with a keenness born of his faith, and he proved himself a mystic of extraordinary power, an outpost of human thinking for his time and for all time.

The demonic disturbances continued. Anthony had escaped into the desert, but, like the navigators of the Renaissance, he was working for his fellow men even if he seemed to be avoiding them. All humanity was involved in his meditations. The powers of evil could not respect his solitude without going back on their avowed threats. Satan was, if we dare to say it, more Anti-Man than Anti-Christ. He attacked Anthony, but it was now established that the hermit would not suffer from his onslaught. The temptations had lost their edge, the evil powers the strength of their convictions.

For several months Anthony was absolutely alone, in either his cave or his hut, in that occasionally gale-swept desert. Two or three caravans may have passed within eye-shot without his knowing it, or even caring. But the eyes of the Bedouins were as sharp as an eagle's; they saw the odd-looking hut, and perhaps the man, but they respected the hermit's solitude. The possibility of his being ill, or even dying, did not seem to them to justify an indiscretion on their part. However, when they reached the Nile valley and were asked by a monk whether they had seen any sign of Anthony, they told without hesitation of their discovery: a man living at the foot of Mount Qolzum, in the grove of palms. Actually there were no other such groves in those parts.

The brothers took advice and made their plans. Anthony would be running out of bread shortly, and therefore he would not object if they surprised him in his retreat. Several monks joined the first caravan to depart for the Red Sea, and thus, once again, a material bond was established between the Christian world and the hermit.

"Greeting, Anthony, athlete of the Lord!"

"Those who have discovered the way to my cell are the Lord's athletes. . . ."

The travelers and the hermit were united over pious repasts of bread and water, punctuated by the chanting of hymns. Then it was time for separate meditation, and at evening when they were together again the brothers voiced their demands.

"We are like bodies without heads when our Father Anthony is not with us. Our Father must not give up his visits. Who but he can advise us how to come back to the narrow path of right-eousness when we stray from it?"

"The father's knowledge is very small. Praying and reading the Holy Writ will teach my brothers much more than I can..."

The visitors did not insist further. It was enough that they had resumed contact with him. And when Anthony, anxious about his independence and embarrassed that he had had to have bread brought to him across the desert by monks of his own age, asked for a hoe, an axe, and some wheat for sowing, they were delighted. What an excellent excuse for another visit!

Later on, we find Anthony cultivating his garden. He had taken all the stones out of the little patch of earth, turned it over, watered it, and planted it. The following year, he ate his own bread and offered it to his visitors. Better still, he grew vegetables. Sympathetic towards visitors who undertook the exhausting journey to his hut, he wished to give them nourishment. Bread and water were not enough; he would add a large platter of lentils and beans. The desert had been conquered and he must profit by the victory, set up a little monastic inn in the former kingdom of Satan!

Sometimes there was a Walt Disney atmosphere about his daily existence. Desert foxes and gazelles trampled his sowings and his growing wheat when they came to drink at the spring in the early morning. Anthony watched and succeeded in catching one of them. Reproving it with Franciscan politeness, he asked, "Why do you do this? I have never harmed any of you. Be off!" And he was sure the beast would repeat his words to the others. According to Athanasius, they took it to heart and never disturbed his garden again.

Nevertheless we must not imagine that Anthony had retired, in the suburban sense of that word, and discovered the joys of gardening in his declining years, like some thrifty laborer. We are speaking, not of the Ile-de-France or of Touraine, but of the land near the Red Sea—the scorching, silent desert. And that return to Eden-like joy which Anthony strove to accomplish upon those few square feet was no more than a vague suggestion of it. Though the gazelles and foxes made their appearance upon the scene, it was still sullen and dourly threatening. Anthony did not overlook this, nor did he neglect the progress of monasticism in the Nile valley. He continued his unflinching asceticism with severe regularity; he wove his mats and baskets, ploughed, prayed, chanted, fasted, meditated. He had established himself in that desolate place for the express purpose of challenging his former enemies, the powers of evil, and they had begun to attack him. The gazelles and foxes had made a gentlemen's agreement with him, but that did not mean that Satan no longer knew how to mobilize the animals into the howling menagerie which had been launched against Anthony in the tomb and in the old fort. The monks who visited him—they had gradually succeeded in making an arrangement whereby they would bring him a monthly sack of produce: olives, vegetables, and oil—were amazed and terrified by these attacks. At night the desert would throw off its cloak of deadly silence and unloose its shouting, sword-rattling, howling armies. Appalling animals leapt from rock to rock in the moonlight and galloped among the crumbling boulders. A great noise of jeering burst from the mountainsides, reverberating and echoing contemptuously across the valleys. "Anthony! Anthony!" One voice roared; then thousands of other voices together: "Anthony! Anthony!" But he was deep in prayer. He saw nothing, heard nothing: neither the heat lightning on the horizon, nor the flickering stars, nor the sudden flashes thrown here and there on the black slopes, nor the trembling of the earth at the approach of that formidable army.

At that period, groups of monks established themselves at different times near his hut, not to watch over him (as they did later on), for he was full of vigor, but to receive instruction. And in 316 or 317 it would seem likely that there was an

early visit from Athanasius, still adolescent and entirely unknown, for purposes of initiation. Nothing is definitely known
of his stay with Anthony, and it is not certain that it ever occurred; but there are several good reasons for believing that
it did, and for taking several lines in the preface to the *Vita
Antonii* as a delicately veiled allusion to the happy occasion:
"I have therefore lost no time in writing to your piety *what I
know myself because I have often seen him; what I was able
to learn from him, having gone to him many times, and having
poured water on his hands.*" Throughout his active life, Athanasius maintained relationships with the monks, staying with
them on several occasions (sometimes of secret necessity). The
champion of the militant Church and defender of the divinity
of Christ had always the active support of the monastic army,
and it was as if, in protecting him, they felt that he was a man
trained by themselves and imbued with their own thinking. In
this relationship which united them to the Bishop of Alexandria there was something of the bond existing between master
and former pupil, and its origin seems to lie in this phrase:
"... *having gone to him many times, and having poured water
on his hands.*" Athanasius appears here as a postulant doing
homage to his superior.

Athanasius' dynamic intransigence in his battle with Arius
and the public authorities grew out of the abundance of his
energy. But, as the tender skies and woodlands of Tagaste are
present in the prose of Augustine, we are aware in Athanasius'
writings of his ascetic training and more particularly of his
stay with Anthony at the foot of Mount Qolzum. There was
no one like Anthony for inspiring disgust with slackness, and
nowhere could this be done more easily than in his desert retreat, when he pointed out that the oncoming of age, the blazing heat, and the surrounding desolation did not constitute
excuses for lessening the rigors of the ascetic schedule. Athanasius speaks of Mount Qolzum only in his *Vita Antonii*, and
there very briefly and without indicating that he had seen it

himself, but this does not prove that he never went there; it could mean that he preferred not to speak of a personal experience which was still upsetting to him. The formidable fighter may have been hiding a longing for the solitude he had once known.

Several years passed by. Anthony prayed to God, fought the Devil, and kept in touch with his brothers. He grew older in years and even more in holiness.

The monks kept begging him to visit them, and he gave in at last, telling his brothers one day that he would go back with them to the monastery. A camel went along to carry the loaves and the water, and they must have lost their way or drunk too deeply in the scorching heat, for the supply was soon exhausted. They searched everywhere, with feet bleeding because of worn sandals that had been burnt by the hot rocks; and in their starting eyes, reddened from the sand, the desert glimmered away into the distance. No spring could be found, no grass to suck and deceive their lips.

Their hearts beat violently. Once or twice the young monks became exhausted and collapsed on the ground. Anthony raised them up and got them started walking again, but the time came when they said they could go no farther, stretching out on the sand and closing their eyes in order to see no longer the mirage lakes coming towards them. Thus they awaited madness or death, and one of them began to rave in delirium.

While the camel moved off unconcernedly under the blinding sun and thousands of imaginary crickets chirped in the poor monks' ears, Anthony, suffering but trusting God stepped a little to one side and prayed. "God, give us water to drink!" To die in the desert was a fitting end for a hermit, but the young ones did not appear to understand and were panting pitifully. "God, give us water to drink!" And almost at his feet, a spring gushed forth.

When they heard this joyful sound of flowing water, the brothers ran towards Anthony, and when everyone had quenched his thirst the goatskin bottles were filled. But it was then discovered that the camel was nowhere to be seen. Here was fresh trouble. Was their escape from death an illusion? Half-heartedly they started to look for the beast and almost immediately found it hidden behind a boulder, kneeling as if waiting for them. Its leading rope had got wrapped around a stone.

It was a double miracle which has undoubtedly caused skeptics to smile. Perhaps the monks had embellished the tale of their adventures? But how to decide as to its occurrence? If the truth were that Anthony, courageous when his companions were not, had discovered a spring, could it not have been a miracle of faith?

They proceeded then without further difficulty, and on the fourth, perhaps the fifth day, they came to the "outer mountain" close to the Nile, which marked the end of the desert and upon which the monastery had been established close to the abandoned fort.

> How goodly are thy tents, O Jacob,
> Thy tabernacles, O Israel!

It was a triumphant welcome, partaking of the atmosphere of "the return of the prodigal son." The monks would have liked him to stay among them and they lavished attentions on him. Was it so necessary for him to be at Mount Qolzum when there were so many problems here? They consulted him about everything and brought him visitors every day, both lay and clerical, who wanted to talk to him about their troubled souls. The charmer of gazelles and foxes changed himself into a religious director; the man of silence became a great chooser of words; the hermit chained to his cell a traveler from monastery to monastery, an active master to whom accounts had to be rendered and who required enthusiasm and perseverance.

Meetings like pious vigils were held. Veterans and novices alike questioned him about his struggles with the Devil or discussed a problem in religion, asking him finally to solve it, as though they were whippers-in at a royal hunt, tiring the beast before driving it within reach of the King. Many of the sayings attributed to Anthony originated at those meetings. Most of them were extremely unpolished and could easily be regarded as too simple, but they possessed the magic of desert flowers—small, not bright-colored, and but faintly perfumed—which outlast all others. Such reflections, with their touch of blunt witticism and pungency, were those of a mind inured to silence and solitude; they were aimed at similar minds and contained themes for meditation rather than discussion.

Here is a characteristic incident. The monks were discussing a passage from the Bible which seemed to them obscure. Each one set forth and shrewdly defended his interpretation, except for one father who kept repeating that he did not understand it. The moment came for Anthony to arbitrate. He turned to the self-confessed incompetent. "You" he said, "are the one who has spoken most wisely." The infiniteness of Anthony's faith is contained in that naively forthright anecdote. "Let not the sun set upon your anger, neither upon your doubt nor your hesitation" was a precept that he loved to repeat to them. Another saying began with questions asked of God; Anthony was turning over in his mind the problem of evil. "Why are certain ones rich and others poor?" The reply came back, "Anthony, look to thyself." In its relation to Anthony's solitary life, this second saying might have resulted in one or several monastic discussions.

According to contemporary writing, it was only then that Anthony laid down rules for the monk's costume. Ascetics had been clothing themselves as they saw fit, but it is probable that, from the whimsical disorder of their poverty (patterned on that of contemporary destitution and of the Old Testament hermits), there was gradually evolved a special costume, under the most authoritative influence, and that the monks' garb followed it on general lines. There was a belt; a linen tunic—the colobium—with sleeves only to the elbow; a woolen scapulary with an oval cap of camel's hair, split down the middle, making the cowl; a small cloak, narrow and roughly woven, and the skin of a goat or a sheep.

Each part of this costume had its mystical significance in either its shape or its material, or even in the use to which it was put. About the whole there was a feeling of poverty and submission to a divine will. Linen was the material worn by the poor, as certain lines in *Athalie* indicate. The wearing of wool was anathema to the pagan priests, who said it was the 'result of a secretion'; Plutarch and Apuleius are positive on this matter. Their goatskins placed the monks in the line of Elias, Elisha, and John the Baptist. Monks were soldiers of Christ, valiant humble soldiers of the second class. They carried staffs and walked barefoot. For long journeys and when the weather was too hot, they wore sandals.

Monks came in through the side door in the history of costume; they resembled the poor of their time, with the insignificant difference that even in extreme heat they never undressed. And it was just as well if no one reminded Anthony playfully that clothes did not make the monk. He would have felt obliged in his humility to agree but would have been fully justified in answering: "No need to tell me that!"

Athanasius speaks briefly of a meeting between Anthony and his sister. "Anthony was delighted . . . to find his sister, an elderly virgin at the head of a group of other virgins." We could hardly read a drier account and would have liked, even if emotion was weakness, to hear of his showing a little. "When Anthony arrived at the various monasteries, all the monks . . . embraced him." Excellent. Those were people who seemed to be fond of one another, and we would have cheered if Anthony had fondly clasped his sister to his breast. But it is entirely possible that Athanasius, who was writing for monks, may have been afraid of giving too intimate a picture of his hero. The meeting of brother and sister was probably attended by more simple emotion than he wanted to disclose. We should imagine the pious women made a great fuss over him at their table and that he politely drank a glass of wine with them. For the Devil was not lurking in that goblet! Though the brother and sister did not have any intimate conversation or give themselves over to evoking their young days in the presence of strangers, their eyes must have met and overflowed with old memories: the sound of their mother's voice; the asp they had found in the fireplace; the wounded stork; the people crowded into the Lord's House; the slowly falling darkness at evening; the oily foam on the canals after the Nile's flooding.

Anthony in his seventies traveled the region round about Memphis, up and down the Nile, as through a country occupied in force by Christianity. Henceforth the monks had their recognized place among the different trades, and it was not only the exceptional people who wore the garments of monkhood. The average Egyptian had no prejudice against the religious state, and an incredible number, making a virtue of necessity, poured into the monasteries. At Oxyrhynchus, for instance, a city seventy-five miles south of Koma, Rufinus declares that, in 356, there were about ten thousand monks and twenty thousand nuns—figures that give us pause.

Shortly after 313, Pachomius, a young soldier demobilized from the Roman army, a native of Upper Egypt, whose heart had often warmed towards the Christians for their care of him and his comrades, weary and sweating under the weight of their packs, had himself baptized and became the pupil of an anchorite, taking up the ascetic life and meditating day and night. Such things happened during epochs richer than

ours in determined people. Pachomius' existence with Pala-
mon, his aged instructor, filled him with joy—a joy that he
dreamed of sharing with many others. When a celestial voice
addressed him—as it had Anthony—advising him to build a
monastery at Tabennesi, on the east bank of the Nile, a few
miles from Kena (thus about three hundred miles from Koma,
and fifty north of Luxor) he obeyed immediately.

Anthony was the father of monks and Pachomius the father
of monasteries, using this term in its modern sense. The religious
communities in Lower Egypt which claimed Anthony as their
founder, and which were now hailing their chief on his arrival
from the desert, were not closely unified, but represented, if we
may so express it, monasticism in scattered units. These ascetics,
except for communal worship which often occurred but once
a week, lived theoretically in separate cells, which could be far
apart. This situation reflected the desire of monks to go back in
time, to obtain a new deal, to be a new Adam placed like the
first one in the midst of creation but taking advice from none
but God.

Within himself and in speech to others, Pachomius recognized in that arrangement the ideal monasticism. Silence and
solitude—that was what kept the mind upon essentials. But one
had to take human weakness into account. Already the monasteries stemming from Anthony had undergone changes. The
monks lived separately but were frequently together. The
land they occupied had no actual limits; men and beasts had
free access to it and it was difficult to fix any boundaries at
all. However, there was an invisible but very real cohesion;
the little cells and their occupants were closely centered.

Pachomius went all the way with this evolution, which
gradually substituted monks, who compromised with the
gregarious instinct, for the hermits of the heroic epoch; and the
first monastery he founded, as well as those that followed,
were like little closed worlds. The cells were not scattered
but contained in one enclosure, in which there was also a

church and the usual buildings for refectory, kitchen, and so on. And this is, except for a few details, the plan still in effect.

As far as we can tell, and our information is scanty, Anthony does not appear to have had—as would be the natural conclusion—any direct effect upon Pachomius' vocation. It all happened as though the young soldier, then the young candidate for monasticism, was entirely unaware of the magic name of his senior. Despite his voyages up and down the Nile, the spiritual revelation that shook the lower Thebaid seems to have made no impression upon him. But we must realize that Pachomius had started from zero in matters religious. The first time his boat passed the cliffs upon which Anthony had shut himself in an old fort for twenty years, the story, if indeed it had been told him at all, probably did not interest him. He was a simple soldier then; people and things passed before him like a succession of more or less meaningless pictures.

Pachomius was not a disciple of Anthony, not even of the sort who criticize and then outstrip their masters. But it is certain that, indirectly, the eccentric of the desert had an effect on him. Many of those Christians whose easy philanthropy and affectionate ways had seduced the dissatisfied temporary warrior, knew of Anthony's activities and admired them and would have been less generous to the military if the famous hermit had not proclaimed in his every act the emptiness of this world's goods and the coming of the Kingdom of God.

Since we cannot be precise, we are in no position to deny that Anthony had a certain influence, perhaps indirect, upon Pachomius. But it was not one of those pronounced influences which affect a man all his life. Pachomius seems to have followed only his own ideas and those of God Himself, Who was just as exacting and just as near at hand for him as for Anthony—a God who spoke and made Himself known. Which is not to say that Pachomius' territory was barbarian and closed to Christianity. The upper Thebaid had had its martyrs; it had had and was still having its hermits, and on the whole, as in the days of the Pharaohs, it lived at peace with the rest of the country. There too, Christianity triumphed officially, and the name of the poor was legion. An instinctive need to be at odds with society and to have solitude and silence tormented the souls of many. The monastic crops were growing fast.

Pachomius would gather in the harvest according to scientific methods. It was no longer a crop of hermits scattered here and there like brothers who could not get on together. Only those who were exceptionally privileged for long service could live apart from the rest. One had to think of the poor devils, not thoroughly bad and not very good either, who had taken up monasticism as an escape, and, if left to themselves six days out of the week, would undoubtedly pray very little and stagnate in laziness.

Pachomius' scheme rapidly bore fruit, and, between his conversion and his death in 346, he was to establish in the upper Thebaid nine brotherhoods and two sisterhoods which lived by what was called his "rule" and included some which had several hundred members. A subtle bond began to form between Pachomius and Anthony, whose intermediate formula, combining anchoritism and the conventional group system, was still succeeding in Lower Egypt. The two never met, as was the case with Saint Francis and Saint Dominic, but each one had heard of the other and after a time a mystical comradeship was established, above and beyond space. Each one had messages sent to the other, congratulating him on his work. There was no trace of jealousy between them. Undoubtedly they knew that they were operating in different regions, but there would have been a certain vulgarity in stressing this point. We must remember our chronology; Anthony and Pachomius were not the heads of religious orders which had recruiting troubles. Monks poured into their brotherhoods; there was a surplus rather than an insufficiency of those with vocations. Anthony, because of his natural kindness and anxiety not to dodge his responsibilities, allowed himself to be called "Father" and authorized certain monasteries to adopt his name and his principles. He was no organizer and no arranger of statistics, and his ideal—if only he were free to follow him—was Elias, the hairy man with the leather belt around his loins.

The fact that the old Anthony and the middle-aged Pachomius understood one another was responsible for their special kind of comradeship. They knew that their labors complemented each other. When a delegation of Pachomian monks on their way to Alexandria interrupted their journey to pay respects to Anthony, he received them with charming courtesy and figuratively took off his hat to Pachomius in a little speech. It was as if the old technician were praising the inventor of a device to spare the new generation the difficulties encountered by the old: "When I began to live the life of a monk there was no *coenobium* where each one might concern himself with the salvation of his brothers, but each . . . lived the monastic life separately. Your Father has brought about a great benefit, with God's help."

Thus an exchange of good will. The Pachomian monks deferred to Anthony in their turn. Though Pachomius was a better organizer, Anthony kept his supremacy: the unquestioned merit of having founded monasticism. He it was who set everything going. "Σὺ μᾶλλον, Πάτερ, παντὸς τοῦ κόσμου τὸ φῶς τυγχάνεις," they replied to Anthony: "Father, you are, more than he, the light that illuminates the world." Far from intending a criticism of anchoritism, they seemed to admit its superiority. And they were not talking like Orientals, whose hearts belied their flowery speech, but as good disciples of Pachomius, who had sung the older man's praises to them, praises of the one he called not only "the completed model for all anchorites," but "one of the three wonders of the world."

Though the relative positions of Anthony and Pachomius were more or less equal, and though Pachomius' brotherhoods were responsible to their founder alone, and to episcopal and priestly authority through him, we may conclude that, in a definite and subtle way, Anthony was the sovereign lord of monks in Upper Egypt. They owed him no allegiance; he was not their "Father;" their rule of life did not come from him. But without him their brotherhoods would not have come into existence, and they knew it.

At about the same time, religious communities of a semi-hermit sort—large church and scattered cells—sprang up in Lower Egypt and in the Libyan desert towards which Anthony walked as a young ascetic. There, to the northwest of the Faiyum, a long day's march from the western branch of the Nile or the Delta country, lay the Wadi Natron, an elongated hollow dotted with little red lakes; and in and around this valley had long existed a kind of hermit center. Few hermits had hearts like Anthony's, and, though we may feel as he did, that the breath of the Holy Spirit was more noticeable upon Mount Qolzum and the chaotic solitudes it dominated, less determined souls who were not anxious to come to grips with an ill-tempered cosmos, found the valley an ideal spot. In winter the nights were cold but the days mild. In summer the dryness and the north breezes made the heat endurable. The lakes were invisibly connected with the Nile, rising in winter and their waters joining. To the south they were edged with low hillocks of sand and rock which the mirages repeated into the far blue distance. There was enough water and arable land to deserve the name of oasis; the desert was near enough and sufficiently wide in all directions, the water bitter enough, to insure a lack of comfort in that oasis. Caravans stopped there to get sodium carbonate, but the vast spaces were scarcely disturbed by such minor activity. The mystics were content to find in this local industry the occasion for a play on words; and the surrounding country was named a holy region where penance wiped out sins as sodium carbonate took spots out of cloth.

The monasteries of Nitria, founded by a friend of Anthony's young days, Ammon, called Ammon the Nitrian, and others to the northwest at Skete, founded by Macarius, called the Egyptian, the Great, the Cameldriver, or Macarius of Skete —none of these flourished till after Anthony had died and Macarius had permanently established himself in the neighborhood. (At the end of the fourth century, Palladius writes of five thousand monks on "the mountain" at Nitria, not including six hundred hermits in the nearby desert, at a place appropriately called "The Cells." But as far as we know, the purely hermit stage in that locality was a thing of the past, and groups of hermits existed who were monks save for name and garments. Thus, for example, is to be interpreted an odd encounter described in *The Life of Macarius the Great* which is undoubtedly founded on fact. After a four-day march the ascetic arrived at a wadi where he suspected the presence of monks. He suddenly came upon some men "whose flesh had turned black and was coarsened by the desert winds, and whose nails and hair had grown long." Believing the information he had received, he had no doubt that they were devils, but no, they were well-meaning and friendly monks who greeted him in the name of the Lord.

This encounter, occurring after Anthony's death in 356, shows how powerfully the monastic movement was affecting Egypt. Anthony had not created the movement himself, but had helped considerably in its development, and the initiative for the transformation from asceticism to monasticism had been his. In any case, from Ammon and Macarius, who were called Anthony's disciples, he held a very definite moral option on the future monasteries at Nitria and Skete. When Anthony went to Nitria, Ammon asked him where to put new cells, and the two men walked over the ground to find a location for them. Macarius stayed with Anthony at least twice, the first time in the role of chief probationer. He trained as a hermit and underwent several testings, but the demons annoyed him and he wanted to learn how to conquer them. At first Anthony gave him a rule to follow. He was assailed by the evil hordes and at the end of a year he returned to Anthony, who made him a monk.

Macarius was a noble-looking man, and people must have been glad that Anthony had such disciples, who provided eloquent proof of his own virtues. Pachomius, with his genius for organization, fixed once and for all—although small details varied with each order—the running of monasteries. There is no reason to condemn him for the evolution of his Tabennesian establishments which, in the fifth century under Schenoudi, were not peaceful refuges but were to be spoken of as barracks where iron discipline was in force. After all, the idyllic monasteries of Nitria and Skete had quickly enough fallen into decay. We must base our judgment of Anthony's and Pachomius' actions not upon the fruits they bore in Egypt, but upon their influence on all Christianity. The two Saints —obviously this was important—were very different in character. Pachomius' ideas, in many ways so liberal, were extremely rigid. He was always the administrator who saw things as they would affect the masses, risking annoyance to individuals. He gave the letter of the law a certain power over the mind without intending to. Anthony was the theorist and, to tell the truth, cared less for others than Pachomius. He longed to find them in God, prayed to in solitude, rather than to see the presence of Christ showing on their faces. A great and unbridled desire for holiness stirred him deeply. It was the others who had actual need to see him and they besought him to come down to them. Perhaps, all the same, he respected them more and understood better the unique mystery of their souls.

The Virtues of Saint Macarius, tenderly and familiarly poetic, contradicts several of the collections of sayings left us by the scribes of the Fathers. Saint Macarius is compared to Francis of Assisi; Francis of Sales should also be mentioned. The book is full of naive and ingenuous comparisons, and Macarius seems to us to possess the soul of a dreamer, dwelling between earth and sky, and keenly interested in both: "I know that when I was a child in my father's house I noticed that the old women and young girls chewed something—probably mastic —to keep their saliva sweet and take away the bad smell of their mouths, to keep their livers and their bowels in order. This substance gave sweetness to those who broke it and chewed it, but how much more the sweet sustenance of heavenly joy, the clear stream of salvation. . . ." Legend has it that this new Adam, like Anthony on Mount Qolzum, had recreated about him a circle of Eden-like innocence. One day an ermine entered his hut and took hold of the edge of his tunic; it was weeping because its three young had twisted necks. He cured them for her and she gave them her teats, which they began to suck ravenously. And, the story goes, Macarius watched in silent amazement, forgetting that he had just accomplished something far more difficult.

It would be best, perhaps, for us not to skip over the years in this way and lose sight of Anthony in his seventies, still hale and hearty, inspecting *his* monasteries and thus doing magnificent propaganda for asceticism quite unconsciously. "Hurry! Hurry! Here is Anthony who made the demons tremble; Anthony who defied the Governor of Egypt, Anthony of the desert, twenty years in a fort, several years in a tomb, seventy years old and an ascetic for fifty—all his teeth and not a wrinkle! Run! Run!" We must take into account, too, the pious gossip of the monks, the kisses of peace, the enthusiasm of the populace, the air of holiness that enveloped this astonishing person from his arrival to his departure. Nothing can take the place of a person's physical presence, so we who desire to know Anthony should imagine ourselves among the brothers who listened to his words or the villagers who watched him pass by, elbowing our way and standing on our toes. Then he would be there before us, very near, humble and glowing with inner light, his features dominated by the brightness of his eyes and his thick eyebrows, his cheeks pale and flat, his mouth wide and peaceful, his chest broad and solid. A pillar of wisdom. The world champion of asceticism, defeating all comers. A veteran of the severest campaigns.

No doubt of all that, but we have no landmarks; and the last years of Anthony's life seem, in the present state of historical knowledge, more obscure than the earlier ones. We have no reason to doubt the writers who declare that he reached extreme old age, keeping a proud bearing—ascetically speaking—to the end. However, it would seem that eternity laid hands upon him long before his death, and that, despite his unrelenting struggles with the Devil, which continued to the last, the bets were placed and nothing could alter the course of his life. But that can scarcely be true, and we shall try to show in our final chapter that Anthony avoided stationary perfection. Athlete of Christ he had lived, athlete of Christ he would die, active to the end and with no other thought than to die in the image of Christ. The almost complete absence, during his long life, of events that were not spiritual, the apparent regularity of his devotions, give us the feeling that, from the age of seventy onward, he had come into port. He had reached his spiritual summit, but he continued to influence others and, as it were, himself.

"This man, so celebrated and so little known, who owes his fame to impossible things and not to factual certainties," Amelineau calls him with resignation. Distorted or not, these words are fair. We know—for all our information points to it—that Anthony made a second journey to Alexandria. We also know the reason for it, but we cannot come within twenty years of its date. Some say it was between 326 and 335; others that it was in 355 or 356. These are guesses, of course. The only event in Anthony's last years which history might have captured is still unsettled in many details.

But let us be consoled. Sensational events have no place in his life. Anthony's was an interior drama, and his amazing career cannot be assessed in terms of showy adventures.

After Anthony had visited the brothers and showed himself to the impatient populace, he would set forth again across the desert. What joy it was to be back again! Ah, the air of those high places; the infinite despondency of that battered landscape; the pleasure of his fasting and his solitude! God must come to him, must return to those tortured cliffs which He held in bondage and which were waiting for His coming. Neither Sinai, nor Qolzum, nor the Red Sea had danced to the sound of the tambourine in the joy of early dawn. Nothing but the burning heat of the sun gripping the mountaintops. Night and day—day and night, Anthony waited for his God in that nightmarish country.

Preposterous and marvelous lookout man for Christianity in those Arabian solitudes, he interrupted his regular existence by making short visits to the outer monasteries. Once or twice a year, we imagine, he saw the brothers and held consultations. The monks acted as his secretaries and they handpicked the visitors so that he would not be overwhelmed. We can be sure, however, that he never refused to see anyone. And each time he returned and stood on the terrace near his cave, he experienced an almost childish exaltation at the sight of that harsh landscape, scarred and seamed, which gave him welcome and ground its teeth because God had still not come. There were seethings and angry noises because the Master was so close at hand and refused to appear. God was behind the wall, behind the clouds, beneath the blazing surface of the sea. . . . A panting landscape— reconciliation was at hand! Men would not have crucified the Son of God; Adam would not have sinned; everything would begin again and a new race of human beings—men, women, and children—would set their feet upon the paths of righteousness. The heat would no longer drip like loathsome wax down the living skin of the mountains; the palm trees would spring up, strange deer fill the meadows, fish sleep in schools close to the quiet shores.

Between two ecstasies, two battles with the demons, two visions of struggles awaiting the Church, Anthony, spading his garden, meditating in his hut, or praying fervently in his cave, perceived in a flash of lightning the new humanity for which the wild desert and he himself had been prepared. It already existed; it existed then. All those men clad in wool who had chosen silence and privation, those monks who had risen up and cleansed the Egyptian land of its absurd terrors: Macarius, Ammon, Pachomius, Isidorus, John, Paphnutius—thousands of them, tens of thousands. . . .

He could envisage the whole panorama, when necessary, without sacrificing his power of discrimination. The true monk was so rare! Many had wanted to live the ascetic life, and how many had made a success of it?

One day when a man knocked at his door and asked for help in becoming a monk, Anthony came out of his hut. He questioned his visitor. Sixty years old? The man's reason for coming seemed clear. "Go back and live in your village," said Anthony, "you cannot stay in the desert." Then he went back into his hut and closed the door. But the other was bluntly persistent; he had come because he had caught his wife in adultery. At this he had merely burst out laughing and decided to become a monk. So now he would be a monk! He waited outside the hut for three days and nights. "Even to attend to the calls of nature," says the *Lausiac History*, naively, Anthony did not come out of his hut. On the fourth day he emerged and roundly scolded his ill-behaved visitor, who let him finish and then repeated his demand. Anthony decided to question him more carefully; the man had had nothing to eat or drink and Anthony took him into his hut and set him to weaving palm leaves, despite his lack of experience. At evening he seized the work and pulled it apart, declaring it to be of no value. "Begin all over again," he ordered, and the man took the palm leaves and began to weave again.

Anthony was ashamed of his severity and suggested that his visitor, who had fasted for three days, should eat a piece of bread. "Whatever you say, Father." A good reply. But Anthony stiffened. He insisted on three psalms and twelve prayers before eating; then he consumed a loaf, and when his visitor, who ate more slowly, had finished, he offered him another. Salaams.

"I will eat only if you do."

"That is enough for me, because I am a monk," said Anthony.

"It is also enough for me, because I wish to become a monk." Another good reply, but the examination continued: twelve psalms and twelve prayers were decreed at once. The man followed him in these devotions. Then came a short nap, and, at midnight, Anthony woke up and chanted more psalms. The visitor matched his senior's forceful devotions with his own loud voice, going from one penance to another so satisfactorily that Anthony ended by saying: "If you can chant and pray like that every day, you can stay with me."

It was not an affectionate compliment (the visitor imagined, perhaps, that he had been put through an exceptional testing), but a monk, after all, had to toil hard over his devotions. In any case, the praise and the threat it concealed passed over him, and he said calmly and frankly: "If you should sometimes pray more than that, I don't know whether I can keep up with you; but what I have done already, I can easily do." Anthony thought for a little while and then gave his decision: "You have become a monk."

The new brother's name was Paul, but he was soon called Paul the Simple. He had to be distinguished from the other Pauls, of whom there were many among the monks, and the preceding account justifies the chosen adjective. He was a good and worthy monk who always remained wonderfully simple, and his devotion to Anthony was like that of a sheep dog to his master. The Father, pretending to be too busy himself, once brought him a man possessed by a demon. Let us quote the text: "Paul spoke to the possessed victim: 'Father Anthony said to come out of that man,' but the demon shouted, cursing loudly: 'I will not come out, old fool!' Paul struck the possessed man on the back, saying: 'Anthony said to come out!' The demon swore more violently, and at last Paul said: 'Come out, or I will tell Christ.' Again the demon blasphemed, shouting: 'I will not come out!' At midday Paul went out of the hut into the scorching heat—in Egypt it was like the burning fiery furnace of Babylon—and, standing against a boulder, he prayed: 'You see, Jesus Christ, that I can't come down, or eat, or drink, if you don't make the demon leave this man.' Then, before he had finished speaking, the demon cried out: 'O outrage, I am cast out! The simplicity of Paul did it.' "

The severity of the first examination to which Anthony submitted Paul the Simple shows what great care was taken by the Father of Monks. The words, "You have become a monk," would mean today "You have become a novice," and it remained for the brother to prove, by a year of solitude valiantly endured, that the Devil had no power over him. The passing years, those fleeting ones which normally bring death closer, did not prevent Anthony from believing in the iminence of the new Kingdom of God, and he did not feel that he could relax or rest from his devotional labors. Moses was not allowed to set his feet upon the land towards which, for so many years and in the face of so much hardship, he had led his people. Why should Anthony be luckier and see with his own eyes the approach of God upon a bank of clouds out of the heavens above him? He waited, full of hope; but his waiting was one of well-ordered zeal, that of a man whose task

Chapter X

ALEXANDRIA AGAIN

If a simple man could find Anthony's hut and besiege him for three days, it meant that there were many others who crossed the desert to Mount Qolzum. There were people who were sick, apprehensive, neurasthenic, who needed faith, others who merely wanted to discuss religion; curious people, snobs, rich men and foolish ones. Especially there were the zealous, the restless, the sincere who desired the reconciliation of their principles with their ways of living. Sometimes Anthony was alone for long periods. Then one day a caravan would bring a large party. People made their arrangements on the banks of the Nile. Monks and Bedouins had set up a return trip scheme: Pispir-Mount Qolzum and back again.

Anthony's vigorous reactions to the visit of Paul the Simple showed that if necessary he could stand his ground and shut his door. We do not know if his visitors realized that he had a cave up in the mountains. We would gladly believe that they did not and that more than once, when he spied an approaching caravan, he would hurry up to his mystical lair.

However that may have been, it appears that, willingly or not, he was in close touch with the world and that he was aware of everything important that happened outside the desert.

* * *

Thus there is nothing to prevent our believing the story about the coming of several supporters of Arius' heresy who wished to win Anthony over to their views. He was furious and sent them about their business. He had long known of the doings of the man who had given the hierarchy so much trouble. When the persecutions had been at their worst and Anthony had gone to Alexandria to give his moral support to the Christians there, he had already heard of Arius, a deacon in the great city, whose disturbances were so upsetting to Peter, the holy patriarch, in his dungeon, up to the very day before his death. It was anything but amusing to that cleric, at a time when the Church was in such straits, to have to endure a heretic whose ideas he so disliked. The heresy which at the time had thrown the Christians in Alexandria into confusion was that of Meletius, ex-Bishop of Lycopolis, and a difficult man. He had once again brought up the knotty question of the *lapsi* (apostates), whose return to the community of the faithful he recommended, but with severe rules for their deportment. Peter had fought this intransigence; he was a peaceful man and he did not think the Church should limit itself to a narrow circle of fanatics. Meletius did not give in and took an aggressive position. Peter pronounced his excommunication.

This measure, then Meletius' arrest by the pagan authorities, with several of his chief disciples, and their subsequent banishment, failed to stop the heresy from spreading. When Constantine became the master of the Empire, there was a kind of Meletian Church in Egypt which claimed to be the sole recipient of Christ's teachings, and calmly took credit for absolute purity.

Meanwhile Arius, ordained priest by the Bishop Achillas, had been making progress and had a very important parish. He knew how to push himself and his vivid, turbulent personality appealed strongly to the populace. And his opinions were easily accessible. They were not his own, for he was not creative; he got them from Lucian of Antioch. (Parenthetically, this skilled interpreter of the Scriptures in the third century abjured his errors shortly before his martyrdom.) He leaned towards the idea that Christ was not God. His slogan, which gained weight, was the famous formula, "Ἦν ὅτε οὐκ ἦν," "Then was a time when He did not exist," which contradicts the Gospel of Saint John: "In the beginning was the Word." This formula stripped Christ of one of the chief attributes of divinity and was pleasing to many who admired Christian morality and were ready to believe in one God only, but who balked at the Incarnation. Compared to Arius, the Trinitarians, those who believed in the Father and in the Son, and in the Holy Ghost who proceeded from the Father and from the Son—seemed like abstracters of quintessence. It was no good saying that to deny or simply to reduce the divinity of Christ amounted to the defeat of Christianity; such reasoning would scarcely affect the populace, who objected to using their brains.

The great majority of priests and bishops should have risen up against Arius, and, as a matter of fact, the clergy as a whole denounced the heresy. However, several bishops and a certain number of priests took up with the new doctrine. We can imagine that they were aware of its popular appeal, of the great opportunities it offered for the conversion, with a minimum of trouble, of heathens, perhaps Jews, and for the starting of discussions with the last gnostics and the Manicheans, and the building up of a great Church. Others, not interested in metaphysics and preoccupied with moral instruction, maintained a friendly reserve.

We do not wish to defame a person who was not commonplace, who had undeniable good qualities, and in whom the great restless city whence he came was epitomized. But in the circumstances, and considering the quarrels and intrigues of those who started theological controversies, Arius behaved with blamable craftiness. He got round Achillas, the calm and pious successor to Peter, the bishop. Alexander, Achillas' successor (he was perhaps the lucky rival of Arius), and particularly Athanasius, a deacon of Alexandria and a merciless opponent, were not men to be satisfied with making faces at Arius. When Arius began to put forth his doctrine publicly, the Egyptian bishops sat in council and, after being anathematized and excommunicated, he went to Palestine. But he kept on talking. He made up to Eusebius, Bishop of Nicomedia, a man of intrigue who had a certain power in the Christian world, and succeeded in involving him in his projects, thereby causing a furore. Eusebius of Cesarea, the religious historian, a bishop himself and an upright and sincere man, endorsed Arius, who then began to spread his doctrine by means of popular songs which traveled like wildfire, after the manner of modern tracts. The Emperor Constantine was appealed to, but he left matters in the hands of the religious authorities. He hoped for a reconciliation. The discussions seemed to him a little absurd—mere bishops' bickerings — and being a statesman he was concerned for the cohesion of the great empire, under the control of one man. In the realm of religion he undertook nothing showy. He was more dependent upon Christianity than he liked to be, and, considering the fact that he had never asked to be baptized, he had no right to call himself a Christian. "There was a time when He did not exist" ... "In the beginning was the Word." Those phrases did not mean very much to a man who was jealous of his power and full of trickery. And common sense leads us to believe that, in the tragic and tedious dispute which was prolonged much more by his vacillations than by Athanasius' real or imagined aggressiveness, political considerations swayed Constantine almost entirely. He too must have realized the powerful impact of Arianism on the heathen populace. This Christianity—without its most paradoxical and staggering mystery—which anyone could understand, must have seemed to him capable of one day uniting the Empire.

Nothing had been settled. The council at Alexandria expressed the opinion of the Egyptian Church only. The "verities of the faith" were still indefinite, and Arianism, to put things at their worst, amounted to heresy raised to the nth power. The Emperor convoked a council of all the Churches of the East and the West, called "oecumenical." The State undertook to pay all expenses: transportation, lodging, food. And thus, in 325, three hundred and eighteen bishops, almost all of them from the Orient, came together at the Empire's expense, at Nicaea, a city of Asia Minor.

It is not our purpose here to stress the accomplishments of a council which undertook nothing less than the task of establishing the chief articles of the Christian faith in brief but exact language. Let us say that the Church of Egypt shone there with a special brilliance. It owed its prestige to the tradition which gave the Patriarch of Alexandria a position immediately after the two Papal legates, and also to the persecutions of Diocletian and Maximinus, which were more violent in Egypt than elsewhere. Several mutilated Egyptian bishops in prison, like Paphnutius of the upper Thebaid, whose sightless eye was kissed by Constantine, and others without right arms or left legs, were objects of special veneration. They caused some Arian bishops, mutilated like themselves, to adopt their opinions in the name of what we might call solidarity. But more than that, it was the extent of its monastic movement that helped the Egyptian Church. The Western bishops spoke with emotion of the "flight into the desert" which had carried off so many noble people, and of Anthony, thrice blessed, who had destroyed Satan's legions.

Athanasius had come to Nicaea as a mere deacon; he belonged to Alexander's retinue, but he quickly made himself felt. Behind the scenes and in the council itself, he played an influential role. The Credo, sung at high mass and embodying, except for small details, the Nicene Creed exactly, owed much to him, even if its drafting was attributed to Osius. We might say that Anthony was present in a mystical sense with that former disciple who had tried aseticism and still longed for it, and the dryness of the lines of the Credo, its lack of color, its strict exactitude, suggest the cells of Skete and the Faiyum and their big, stale loaves that had to be dipped in water to make them edible. *"Factorem coeli et terrae, visibilium omnium et invisibilium . . ."* Although the word *invisibilium* recalls the teachings of the whole Church, we seem to see in it especially the hand of the monks — for those men who lived in silence and solitude, the existence of invisible spirits, cherished or hated, was essential dogma.

Arius counted eighteen adherents among the bishops of the council — a small number, but the decision was a long way from being made, and a certain number were still hesitating. Athanasius marshaled his forces, the victims of Egyptian persecutions seconding his efforts, and, when it came to voting for or against the wording of the "creed," only two bishops refused their signatures. The tussle was a lively one. Only in appearance did it resemble an academic contest. The discussion was confined to a question of adjectives: "ὅμοιος," **"similar,"** "ἀνόμοιος," "dissimilar"; "ὁμοιούσιος," "of similar nature," "ὁμοούσιος," "of the same nature," "consubstantial." They were discussing the essential point of Christianity, and the members of the council understood it as such. The term "ὁμοούσιος," "consubstantial," which triumphed, did not allow of any misunderstanding, but it had to be cleansed in advance of all suspicion of heresy.

The council adopted measures against the doctrine of Meletius, which, being excessively austere, could scarcely increase the number of its adherents but played havoc among the Egyptian priests. Twenty-nine bishops were in the group, undermining the Patriarch's authority in the eyes of the pagans. But since the heresy dealt with a point of discipline rather than of dogma, the measures taken were not severe.

However, the Meletians revolted. Alexander, Patriarch of Alexandria, having died on April 17, in 326, five months after his return from Nicaea, they launched a violent campaign to prevent the election of Athanasius. They — the ultra-Christians who insisted upon such guarantees and penances from the apostates — joined with the Arians. Parliamentary customs were not established yesterday! Despite this opposition of "right and left united," if we may be forgiven the anachronism, the dynamic Athanasius, who was known to have been the choice of the late bishop and who had just maintained so brilliantly at Nicaea the prestige of the Egyptian Church, was elected.

Arius did not give up because of this second serious setback; his machinations continued. Among the people of Alexandria he could count on a real following, and, besides the thankful pagans and the Jews (he had offered them a more accessible Christianity), there were the middle-of-the-roaders and the idle ones who were grateful to him for the exhilarating atmosphere of combat that proved Alexandria to be still alive and to contain the most active men on the Mediterranean seaboard. Of the same nature; of similar nature — six of one and half-dozen of the other; yes, yes, but all that was the very spice of life. What did it matter to them whether Christ was or was not consubstantial with the Father? What *was* important, they felt, was that people should take sides. All this shouting about subtleties was amusing enough and provided excuses for fine rumpuses, however small one's part in them might be. Nor was Athanasius — and let us not forget it — an insignificant man. And the verses in which Arius had couched his doctrine were sung to popular tunes, no more and no less than love ditties.

The Arians worked at influencing the Emperor from another angle. His sister Constantia was an Arian; she was dying. Eusebius of Nicomedia saw to it that she was briefed and could in turn brief her brother and get him to consider the whole problem. The voice of a dying woman would have a certain authority. Constantine was going through difficult times. The Roman populace had welcomed him coldly on his return from Nicaea. Seditious shouting had been heard, and he was criticized for being sulky at a pagan festival. Such misunderstanding was deeply offensive to him.

Constantine succeeded in making a botch of his private life and became a character out of Sophocles or Shakespeare — a man drawn into evil ways by fate. He had his eldest son executed, then his intimates, who had not stopped that execution, and finally his wife, whose end came in a Grand Guignolesque manner. If his father had been called Constantius the Pale, he himself deserved the name of Constantine the Red.

He fled from Rome, too full of unpleasant memories, and went to the Orient, drawn by its glamor and luxury. He wanted to found a Christian capital in a more central position than Rome, and where his power would be supreme. His choice fell upon Byzantium, which became Constantinople in 330 with magnificent festivity. The Imperial palace, as is always the case in the Orient, quickly became a nest of intrigue. The Arians kept hammering cheerfully at this grim sovereign with his gnawing secret troubles.

At Nicaea, Constantine had approved the bishop's decision. He would not have considered it good policy to break with the majority, but he had regretted, except insofar as this concerned himself, their lack of flexibility. From the moment that Arius proved to him that his followers were far more numerous than people said, everything was altered. Constantine remembered his sister. He listened with a certain submission to Eusebius of Nicomedia. What a mistake those Egyptians had made at the time of the Nicene Council in being so unyielding! He would show them. Their Emperor was their master.

Constantine recalled Arius from exile and joined with Eusebius in asking Athanasius to reinstate him in his former position. Athanasius refused. Alexandria became stormier than ever with the seething activities of Arius and his followers and of the Emperor's secret agents.

It was then, we believe, that Athanasius sent out an SOS,

pleading his years of asceticism, for the intercession of Anthony. The Father of Monks now more than eighty years old, probably in 334, set forth a second time for Alexandria.

We have said that there were possible dates for this journey: either some year between 326 and 335, or one somewhere near 355. If we showed that Anthony, at the age of a hundred and three or more, took up his staff, crossed the desert of Qolzum to the Nile, and boarded a boat for Alexandria in order to have a set-to with Arius, we should be emphasizing still more the Claudelian aspect of our hero. We should have an exact picture of the force of the supernatural in action. Once again and more authentically, Anthony would be the Titan of Monasticism, the Giant of the Desert.

Without actual proof, we should prefer not to envisage such a possibility. During his very last years, Anthony was still what might be called a handsome old man, but, says Athanasius, "there were two monks with him . . . practicing asceticism and waiting on him in his old age," and that implies a certain diminution of vitality. On the other hand, if he made this long journey and undertook the exhausting role of defender of the faith at the age of eighty-three, it would still amount to a proud feat and one which present-day politicians would be glad to be able to accomplish.

For us, this second journey to Alexandria occurred in 334 or 335. We may take as a basis for discussion the sentence from the *Verba Seniorum:* "Once when the blessed Anthony had been brought to the city by Saint Athanasius, Bishop of Alexandria, in order to defeat the heretics, Didymus, a very wise man who had lost the sight of his eyes, went to visit him. . . ." Then, if we agree with Canon Bardy, the modern biographer of Didymus, that the blind man was born in 313, we find that Anthony's journey could not have occurred after 335, when Constantine exiled

Athanasius, and not very much before that, since Didymus would have been too young to dare to knock at the door of Anthony's hosts and ask for him. Can this statement be used against us? In 335, Didymus would have been little more than twenty years old, and this seems to us to be conclusive.

We will add that the picture of Anthony rising out of the incident mentioned in the *Verba Seniorum*, gives us good reason to believe that the man visited by Didymus had not yet reached extreme old age. As a rule we greatly admire the blunt words attributed to Anthony, but frankly, the following give us pause. Didymus and Anthony talked for a while about the Holy Writ to their mutual satisfaction; then Anthony asked: "Are you not sorry to be without your sight?" Didymus was embarrassed and remained silent, but Anthony persisted, and after the fourth or fifth questioning Didymus admitted simply that it was a sorrow to him. Then Anthony continued: "It amazes me that a wise man should complain of the loss of something that is possessed by ants, flies, and mosquitoes, and that he should not rejoice at possessing what the saints and apostles have earned. It is far better to see with the spirit than with the flesh, and to have eyes that will not permit sin instead of those which with a single covetous glance can send a man to his death and damnation." No doubt. But this is like clumsily breaking down a door already opened, and an easy way of making preachments. . . .

And thus it seems to us that Anthony, at the very end of his life, would have been incapable of delivering such a direct and fanatical blow—Anthony whose doctrines delighted the Fathers, who included them in each of their collections—Anthony who believed discretion to be the essential virtue.

At eighty-three or eighty-four, Anthony set forth. There was no unusual incident during the first part of his journey; his way was the one he took when visiting the outer monasteries. He apparently had with him a large group of monks, especially chosen for their seriousness and their eloquence, who would go down the Nile with him.

It is easy to believe that the old man—with his well-known devotion to the Church, his obedience to the hierarchy, and the affection of contemplative master for active disciple which he felt for Athanasius—left his desert, his cave, and his garden at the first summons, just as he had once abandoned his fervent asceticism and the new monasteries to go to the aid of Peter the Patriarch.

We will not say that he went at great speed, but he did not drag his feet. He was country-bred, his knees were not stiff, and he made his two and a half miles an hour with the sun scorching down on the back of his neck; thus Father Anthony (in the country sense of the word father), a well-preserved old man with a will of his own.

For our beloved Father Anthony knew very well where he was going. The Church had summoned him, Athanasius had summoned him, and the heretics had to be fought; and to fight the heretics was, with asceticism, yet another substitute for martyrdom. Tertullian had said this, and if Anthony had not read Tertullian he had encountered men thoroughly familiar with the idea, which was also Paul's and was now adopted by Anthony.

Among the heretics, the Arians seemed to be the monks' worst enemies. We have stressed the fact that Anthony was not an intellectual, and the dispute over ῏Ην ὅτε οὐκ ἦν, "There was a time when He did not exist"; the pros and cons of the argument regarding the terms "consubstantial" and "of similar nature," had no doubt bored him in his young days as a land-owner and during the years of his ardent asceticism. He was still not an intellectual, and we have discovered, after his mild scolding of Didymus the Blind, that on occasion he could be clumsy, but there is no doubt that his meditations and his asceticism had greatly increased his shrewdness and his wisdom. He could judge men and ideas; he had become a psychologist and a logician, and he saw in Arius not only an undisciplined priest who had saddened Peter the Patriarch, but a man who wished to destroy Christianity.

He would not, however, have left his desert if he had not been summoned. He believed in discipline and he trusted in God who would protect His Church. And, once and for all, he was certain that monks belonged in the desert as surely as fish in the sea. But he had been called, and instead of confining himself to prayer he would take his place in the front line of battle. It would amount to shirking a duty if he were to remain in his hermitage.

The future of Christianity and the future of the monastic movement were bound together; a wrong done to Christ was a wrong done to the monks who called themselves His athletes or soldiers and set themselves joyfully the varied tasks which would show their love and devotion to a God who had become Incarnate. "Then was Jesus led up of the spirit into the wilderness to be tempted of the devil. And when he had fasted forty days and forty nights, he was afterward an hungered. And when the tempter came to him, he said, If thou be the Son of God, command that these stones be made bread." How many times had the monks, Anthony or any of the brothers, been so tempted? How many times had the Devil tried to extract a word from them against Christ, to make them deny that Christ was the Son of God, consubstantial with the Father? "We believe as you do," the good apostle might have whispered, "that God exists. The darkness of this night that surrounds your cell, pricked by stars that ride in the heavens like kingfishers above the shallow green water near the banks of the Nile; and to-morrow the yellow splendor of the sun that scatters handfuls of its heavy grains of heat upon the sands—what further proofs do we need? We deny nothing by rote—only by sensible reasoning. When we say that God could not become man, we know what we are saying. Think—you cannot believe otherwise. . . ." And the monks cried with their master: "Get thee behind me,

Satan!" Simple belief did not explain the ardent fire that burned within them, their need to fight and at the same time their passion for solitude, privation, and weariness. Satan arrived too late with his theology of a street orator. Christ came earlier and had marked the souls of his followers with a cross. When they saw it, they acknowledged their allegiance. These voluntary ascetics of the Arabian and Libyan deserts could not be expected to deny that Christ had always existed, like His eternal Father. . . . Nor could Anthony of Mount Qolzum be expected to make any such wretched denial.

The Meletians, who were more Christian than the Pope himself, had allied themselves with the Arian despisers of Christ against Athanasius—a mingling of fire and water which fully explains the disturbed atmosphere of Alexandria. As soon as Arius was recalled from exile, his Egyptian disciples started their propaganda. Athanasius was an arrivist! A favorite of the Bishop Alexander whom he had deceived! A little errand boy trying for advancement! "Of the same nature," "of similar nature," let decent people's ears not be assailed any longer by such ridiculous words!

"But the Emperor?"

"The Emperor? But he's on our side, along with Eusebius of Nicomedia—and all other intelligent men, as a matter of fact."

The Trinitarian hesitated here, somewhat shocked, and tried to recover his self-control.

"But Father Anthony! At least he is not on your side!"

"But, of course," lied the Arian shamelessly. "He is in the very front rank. Father Anthony is one of Arius' oldest friends."

"But I thought . . ."

"Lies! And those who speak the contrary are liars! Athanasius will say anything in order to be taken seriously."

"Oh well—if Father Anthony . . ." began the Trinitarian, moving away thoughtfully, while the Arian laughed at his discomfiture. What a splendid sight: Father Anthony, no longer in the prime of his youth, hurrying from the heart of the desert where he was quartered next to the Red Sea in order to close the mouths of those who were saying that he was on Arius' side.

That is, however, what happened. Anthony was approaching; he was about to enter the city. "There he is! There he is!" "Who is it?" the children wanted to know. "It's Father Anthony, who lives in the desert with lions and devils." "Bravo, Anthony! Bravo, Father of Monks! . . . oh, it's Anthony all right. Looks just the same as last time. Remember? In Diocletian's days he came quickly. To visit prisoners, to go to the tribunals, to . . . look—he's stopped! Someone has brought a boy with his legs paralyzed. Long live Anthony! Long live the Father of Monks!"

We can believe Athanasius when he says that Anthony achieved a great personal success. The Alexandrine populace hailed him all the more delightedly because it had almost succumbed to Arianism (tomorrow, perhaps, it *would* succumb), and the Arians were caught in their own trap.

"Arius is an impostor," repeated Anthony in the daily meetings he attended with Athanasius, who was just as obstinate as Arius and a born organizer, "And here is the man you must follow." He gave the kiss of peace to the Patriarch, while an interpreter translated his words and the crowd cheered joyfully.

"If there are any Arians here, let them stand up," shouted Athanasius; but the Arians did not move. What could they have said? It would have been an impossible discussion. Anthony stood up and Athanasius again introduced him: "He is eighty-three years old and has been a soldier of Christ for sixty-four of them. He has come here from the desert especially to tell you that Arius is an impostor!" What was there to say to those whose son, daughter, wife, husband, or aged mother Anthony had cured? That Arius too had performed miracles? But Arius had not performed miracles.

Aside from the large meetings, where enemies concealed

themselves, Anthony appeared at intimate conferences with only a few persons present: Christian priests who had not chosen between Athanasius and Arius, pagan priests and philosophers, high functionaries, people interested in asceticism—some clever and talkative, some already serious and faithful to Anthony's precepts. And in those circles he also triumphed; he had many opponents who were more intelligent and wiser than he, but he did not fall into their traps. They all played the secondary roles.

We must put but a limited faith in the details of Athanasius' accounts of the encounters between Anthony and the educated pagans. Here, as in the long speeches he has his hero make, Athanasius does not fail to put forward his own ideas and some purple patches of eloquence. But at the same time, we must not be too skeptical. Athanasius did not put into Anthony's mouth ideas that were alien to him. The two men understood one another perfectly. There was between them, as between veterans of the desert, the close fellowship of heat and privation, and Anthony subscribed in advance to the opinions of his disciple, whose pre-eminence both as a bishop and as a theologian he fully recognized. (This did not prevent Athanasius from venerating Anthony and always letting him occupy the first place. Of his own accord, Anthony could merely fight Arius and a doubtful wisdom which was not founded on faith in an incarnate God; and he could not, of his own accord, make use of subtle arguments. Athanasius supplied him with the details of his dialectic, and it is entirely plausible that, with Anthony's prestige added, excellent results were accomplished.

Between Didymus the Blind and Anthony, there was to be a close friendship. The young man, stirred by the holiness of his hero whom God had favored, and whom he must lose no time in getting to know, awakened the old one's admiration because of the knowledge he had in spite of his blindness, though he was almost as young as the adolescent named Anthony who had once distributed his earthly goods among the poor. But un-

happily we know no more than this. The personality of Didymus, despite the books of his which are available to us, remains
hidden. We can only guess that he was a young man of great
gentleness and sensitivity who, because of his blindness, was
charmed by the face of the world; who was not a poet but an
Egyptian who loved his country. In his works we have several
times discovered things which would not be significant in a
modern, but are striking in a religious writer of that period. For
instance, he hoped that God would provide a good harvest and
that the Nile would flood its banks properly—all of which
makes him sound like a man with his feet on the ground and one
who did not lose himself in abstract ideas. To think that Athanasius wrote a whole book about Anthony without mentioning
the color of his eyes or saying whether he was tall or short!

The talks which gave Anthony and Didymus so much pleasure and which, according to official texts, concerned religious
matters, drew together an old man and a young one, a hermit
and a blind man in love with reality. But perhaps also (and the
hypothesis is not absurd) they were two men who thought like
Egyptians. Their close fellowship went farther, perhaps, than
the anecdote in the *Verba Seniorum* would suggest, and our
interpretation of it remains doubtful. The writings of the
Church Fathers often have a certain coldness which can be disregarded. The tirade to which, according to Athanasuis, Anthony submitted Didymus could quite easily have been spoken
in tones of polite joking—in somewhat bad taste but gruffly
sympathetic. "Come, my friend, when Providence has pampered you to such an extent in the matter of brains, you surely
can't complain like a blind man wandering in the streets. Flies
have eyes and do not see. You have lost yours, yet you can
see. . . ."

And there was nothing there of the false good humor of an
official giving out decorations and wanting to bolster up the

morale of a man who had lost both legs: "You're lucky, my man; no more corns on your feet now!" Army humor or re-proof, Anthony's tirade was from one ascetic to another, at least to one who understood and respected asceticism. Since we do not, as a rule, live on mountaintops, we perhaps have no right to judge this. Anthony believed in what he said. The eyes of the body had permitted him to recognize the scene described to him by that celestial voice on the bank of the Nile, to be of assistance to the martyrs, to estimate the sincerity of Athanasius, or as now, to watch the effect of his words upon Didymus' face. He would be unable to say in advance what were the joys that blindness might take from him, but, besides knowing how to stifle pain, he had gone beyond certain limitations imposed upon ordinary human beings; and he depended less than anyone upon the light of day. We have already mentioned his outburst against the sun, blaming it for distracting the hermit and hiding the true light from him. His finest hours of asceticism were noc-turnal, due less to their silence—desert beasts were apt to be noisier at night—than to a weariness which subordinated the body to the mind. Then the flesh, and all doubts, were dormant; and the soul soared alone, like an unknown star, in a new sky. There was no acedia, but perfect happiness: a bodiless glowing serenity.

Thus, along with what we shall call the "simple" faith of the worker, and not to be confused with it, there came into existence in the fourth century in Egypt, the faith of the monk, the opposite of that of theologians. The "simple" faith has been accorded a favorable consideration which it scarcely deserves. It was a lazy, obstinate faith, full of superstition and fanaticism; it could almost be spoken of with indulgence, but not offered as an example. The faith of the monk was not founded upon reasoning either, but there were fundamental texts involved. It was not the falsely virile pretension of the wretched human being in the grip of daily existence and choosing to declare prematurely that he has solved all problems, but the superb ripening of a personal and constant friendship with God.

The faith of the monk was continually threatened with impoverishment and weakening; it made no provision for the workings of a critical sense; it assumed that there would be tension and discipline constantly. "I believe because I am a friend of God." "The Lord is living, and I am in His presence today." Thus Anthony spoke, as Elias had spoken, and if the monk did not maintain this high degree of exaltation he sank to paltry justifications. His faith needed bolstering on bad days by that of the theologian. The faith of nightly adoration and the divine friendship which the practice of asceticism deserves and obtains, needed to be supported by another faith—eloquent and nimble, rich and spirited. In a human way, the Anthony-Didymus combination was very moving; but, for the defense of religion, the Anthony-Athanasius team was the ideal one— the best pair that fourth-century Christianity could put forward: the champion of the desert with the champion of the crowded cities; the champion of solitude with the champion of propaganda. Credit the first with astonishing privations—the second with masses of sermons, pastorals, and pamphlets. Anthony will set you going, O philosopher, and if he does not convert you entirely, go to Athanasius. And you, longshoreman— you, currier, if Athanasius' speeches are too much for you, go to Anthony.

Anthony's success was considerable, both with the populace and with the rich and worldly. "Here am I, Anthony; I have all my wits about me, and I declare to you that Arius is a liar. He lies when he says that I am one of his supporters; and, speaking of supporting him, I had to put two madmen out of my cell a year ago. They were sent by him. And he lies when he declares that the Word has not always existed. People like him speak nothing but falsehoods. . . ."

The crowds gathered round to see, hear, and applaud the marvel of the desert, the Moses of Egypt. The Arian heresy, yesterday a fine field of growing grain, was little more now than a pile of straw kicked about by many feet.

We can imagine Anthony's departure to have been something of an apotheosis. It must have occurred in the early morning. A great multitude of children, beggars, soldiers, Christian widows, and virgins, was there. Before the astonished gaze of philosophers, pagan priests, and soldiers of all the countries of the world, passed the chanting, perspiring procession of Christian priests, bishops, and monks:

> O God, thou art my God; early will I seek thee:
> My soul thirsteth for thee,
> My flesh longeth for thee
> When I remember thee upon my bed,
> And meditate on thee in the night watches.
> Because thou hast been my help,
> Therefore in the shadow of thy wings will I rejoice. . . .

In the narrow cross streets, the asses and horses had to stop; the flies, stirred up by the confusion, buzzed loudly. There was a smell of humanity and spoiled fruit. "There! There! Look!" The two pillars of the Church of Egypt appeared, and the people's gaze went from one to the other, admiring and on the lookout for the smallest differences. Athanasius, orator and intellectual, with his searching eyes, bushy hair, and shaven chin, and hurried walk; Anthony, visionary and man of solitude, his face alight with supreme joy, his mouth wide and calm between mustache and beard. Both men had the shoulders of wrestlers, easily visible under their tunics, and as straight as the horizontal beam of the Cross. Both had smooth brows—there were no faults in their structure. And both of them—the Bishop in Greek, because it was his duty to set an example, and the monk in Coptic, because of his training and his desire to accompany his dreaming, sang fervently:

> Behold, how good and how pleasant it is
> For brethren to dwell together in unity!
> It is like the precious ointment upon the head
> That ran down upon the beard, even Aaron's beard . . .

This last psalm was repeated again and again; it was the national hymn of the monks and they chanted it on that day of separation as though there was in it an implied *au revoir*. The brothers who had lived together in Alexandria would meet in Heaven.

At the city gate, a woman cried out, beseeching Anthony to take pity on her young daughter who was possessed by a demon. The procession halted, and a long silence followed; it was as though they were back in Christ's time and in Jerusalem instead of Alexandria. Athanasius leaned close to his friend and whispered nervously: "Father Anthony, you cannot possibly avoid this." He knew what the Arians would make of a refusal—they would say that Athanasius did not love the people or that he was not sure of Anthony's power to heal. "As you wish," replied Anthony, and he walked unhesitatingly through the crowd. It never entered his mind, despite his modesty, that God could fail him. Too often had he refused to take advantage of Christ's friendship. God would not abandon him today. The little girl was laid on the ground before him and he cast out the demon at once.

Cheers and shouts of elation went up, and the women wept for joy. There were more psalms chanted; then a final:

> Behold, how good and how pleasant it is
> For brethren to dwell together in unity!
> It is like the precious ointment upon the head
> That ran down upon the beard, even Aaron's beard . . .

As this was chanted by the clergy and the monks, the crowd listened eagerly.

The sun rose higher into the heavens. Priests and monks gave Anthony the kiss of peace. Athanasius knelt before him, asking his blessing. People came as close as possible in order to photograph on their minds every detail of the scene: the champion of all ascetics calling down the grace of God upon the supreme head of the Egyptian Church.

A small delegation accompanied Anthony as he passed beneath the cool arches of the gate; then he set off alone, in the glaring sun, towards the nearby canal where the brothers and the boatmen were waiting for him.

"He went to the mountain as if to his house"; thus ends Athanasius' description of Anthony's departure. A man hurrying away. And Athanasius seems to be bordering on irony, perhaps without realizing it. "What on earth was I doing there?" Would not that have been the thought of the man who hurried away?—that new Elias, that second Moses who needed to rest his head somewhere in the desert? An old dog, according to the popular phrase, does not change his tricks at the age of eighty-four. Anthony had worked hard in the city: in the noise, the dust; among the men, beasts, wagons, ships—milling about among those so-called Christians who wore such fancy clothes and gorged themselves with food and wine. And the discussions, the meetings: Arius, Arius, Arius! To think that his mountain was waiting for him, so far away! And his cave! And in that cave, the peace from which sprang meditation as naturally as a hymn from a monk's lips.

Glad to arrive; glad to depart! But he was no yokel scuttling off as if escape were imperative; we can justifiably suppose that Father Anthony, in that year of 335, was acting from other motives than the deep and almost visceral need to go back to what had become his familiar surroundings.

In the light of events that were to follow, namely Athanasius' exile by Constantine and the vigorous recurrence of the Arian heresy, there is good reason, not to be skeptical as to Anthony's obviously considerable success with the Alexandrines, but to realize that he was in no way fooled by it. He felt that his and Athanasius' campaign had not been successful beyond a certain point. Its impact had been powerful and there had been a great *succès d'estime;* but the inner consciousness of all their listeners had not really been reached. Thus a region of doubt and indifference remained which they had been unable to touch. Someone had shouted; "Long live Anthony, the Father of Monks!" But Peter himself had denied Christ, and this man in the crowd who had not the staunchness of Peter would perhaps be shouting tomorrow with similar enthusiasm, "Long live Arius!" At the thought of such changefulness. Anthony's soul longed for the desert. He needed the hot dry taste of it in his mouth, heat lightning flashing across the mountaintops, and that dark cave where there unfolded continually before his eyes his friendship with Christ and the fury of the demons.

Even from Athanasius' pages, we discover that Anthony was troubled by the Arian heresy after he returned to Mount Qolzum. It was never for an instant that he was beset with regret, but he was eating his heart out because he knew that the heresy was still there, that it would flame up again. And while he remained on his precious mountain, looking at the flattened face of creation which bore the mark of God's hand, with the desert enfolding him, his thoughts took him back to far-off Alexandria and he had prophetic visions of dreadful things to come. "God's anger is about to fall upon the Church. . . ." he said one day to those about him. And if we accept Athanasius' text, Anthony predicted almost in every detail the lootings of churches and other profanations which the Arians were to carry out in 356.

Such revelations saddened his disciples, but he comforted them: clear skies would follow the storm. The Church of Christ would stand firm again. Exiles like Athanasius would return to their proud land. And yet for a moment Anthony let drop his complacent optimism: "The persecuted ones will come into their own, *and Godlessness will slink back into its hiding places.*" In other words, Godlessness would not be stamped out. Until the end of time, the Church's existence would be one of ebbing and flowing.

Unless we believe that Athanasius deliberately misrepresented his master, and we refuse to believe that, it appears that Anthony was not satisfied with the practical results of his journey to Alexandria. "Sometimes when the old man was sitting down to do his work, he would go into a kind of trance, sighing deeply at the visions that came to him. Then, turning to his companions, he would begin to tremble, get down on his knees, and remain there for a long time. . . ." This is the first time, since his youthful struggles against carnal temptation, that we hear of Anthony's robust body showing signs of unsteadiness. "He wept and said again: 'God's anger is about to fall upon the Church.' "

Anthony's departure from Alexandria was in no way similar to the gesture of a great actor or musician who wished to end his career while still in his prime. Besides experiencing the natural fish-out-of-water feeling of a monk in a large cosmopolitan city, he undoubtedly realized that the Church was not functioning smoothly and was afraid of getting himself involved in clerical intrigues. He had come with great willingness when Athanasius summoned him, and he had thrown the weight of his influence into the defense of their common religion. He respected the hierarchy and had quickly complied with the request for his presence in Alexandria. But let us read our Athanasius carefully; there is not much left. "There were certainly as many people who became Christians in that period of several days," he writes, "as in a whole ordinary year." Even if those "several days" meant, as is probable, several weeks, it was not very long. Does it not seem strange that no pressure was put upon Anthony to prolong his stay. We should have expected such lines as: "We besought him to remain longer with us and pursue further this harvest of souls. . . ." But nothing of the sort. Athanasius describes Anthony's enormous success and then, without any warning, simply begins a new paragraph with the words, "When he departed," as though it was to be taken for granted that Anthony's stay in Alexandria would be a short one.

By suggesting a possibility here, I risk giving the impression of quibbling, but the point is significant. When Anthony said, "As fish die if they stay on dry land, so do monks who stay outside their cells or spend time *with worldly people*," he could quite well have included Church people, people of the Egyptian Church, although he respected the Church. Between the Alexandrine theologians and the Father of Monks, there were many grounds for friendly understanding. Anthony was just as firm in his obedience to the Church as were the theologians in their respect for asceticism. Both he and they wanted to have done with mediocre learning. The theologians were glib talkers, while Anthony was ponderous and silent. Those hundred-percent Christians, with their terrible subtlety, frightened the old man who was born far from the Delta and who had become a true mountaineer and a citizen of the deep desert. Of course he was antagonistic to Arius, but he also knew, in his heart of hearts, that chatter and empty speechifying were not confined to the Arians alone.

A humble man among humble men, Anthony regarded himself as a countryman, a crude person, a monk. Rather than come to the point of believing that the theologians — those good soldiers of Christian philosophy—were in danger of involving themselves in quibbles and losing contact with the living God just for the sake of manipulating words, let the monk take himself off.

But the humble man was given to examining his conscience; it was not his habit to hide things from himself. Once back in his desert, he went over in his mind all that had occurred in Alexandria, and he realized his failure. He would gladly have taken the responsibility for everything; he would once again have regarded himself as a crude bear from the mountains, had he not had good sense as well, and the inner conviction that it would be far from true to believe that all of the Alexandrine battles of ideas served the cause of God. The Arian heresy, and all heresies, were wrong and must be fought against, but the fight should never be allowed to become envenomed. Like street brawlers who enjoyed brawling for its own sake, there were bad theologians who enjoyed disputes for the sake of disputing. Those were the ones God would strike down: "God's anger is about to fall upon the Church."

Extreme caution is required here. Every time the historian quotes a word attributed by Athanasius to his master, he must remember that Athanasius, in all good faith and in order to make Anthony's life seem more important, did a certain amount of "fixing." There is a good chance that a phrase may not be accurate to the letter. Since that is the case, and for precisely the same reasons, the historian whose task it is to interpret the *Vita Antonii,* that document of prime importance, has the privilege of singling out sentences and scrutinizing them carefully.

To all appearances, Anthony had won an easy victory in Alexandria. *Veni, vidi, vici.* He had come down from his mountain, mounted on a Coptic charger, and with one blow of his trusty lance had split open Arius' pentecostal monster. Then, amid the plaudits of the people, he had gone back to his desert.

We know from the facts, however, that although the monster must have been badly wounded, it was not put out of action. Anthony had no sooner left the city than Arius and his henchmen reversed the situation. Whether or not the Alexandrines took their side, they more or less weakly permitted the Arians to do as they wished. Can we seriously believe that Anthony, who was nobody's fool, whose insight was sharpened by meditation and the practice of asceticism, had foreseen nothing of this?

Anthony's faith in God, Athanasius' tactical obligation to act as though his master's success had been complete, and, finally, the great Christian friendship existing between the two men, could have made that last day a delightfully festive one. But there was a deep uneasiness in Anthony's mind. "He went to the mountains as if to his house." What hidden impulse caused Athanasius to use those words? Did not the phrase, despite its pleasant connotations, give the lie to the optimism of his pages? Anthony hurrying, hurrying with all the strength in his old legs, as if he wanted to end the Alexandrine interlude quickly and get back to serious things; as if he could not be completely reassured until he was back in the depths of his cave, with a desert between him and the great, noisy city. . . .

It is possible that Athanasius put in just a touch of levity here: Anthony, an old man, a little eccentric, unused to city streets, tempted to feel that, if he could have his desert and his cave again, the city might take back its Arian heresy. But that would not lessen the grave anxiety which Anthony carried in his heart, perhaps without knowing it—an anxiety which was to become still more grave in the future.

Arius died; the fact that his death took place in the public lavatory of a Constantinople market was regarded by his adversaries as a divine punishment, and as a symbol of the dissolution of Arianism. But they took too much for granted. Arius' ideas did not die with him. Far from it. In 359, after the curious Council of Rimini and in spite of Athanasius' tremendous activity, the entire Church seemed to turn Arian.

Meanwhile Anthony's soul had taken flight; but it had seen the catastrophe in many visions and had prophesied it. Those visions may have been pure gifts from God, but there had been no interior change, separating Anthony the visionary from Anthony the meditator. In these meditations he foretold the misfortunes with which his special enlightenment had familiarized him in detail before they occurred. His deliberate good sense brooded over the remote Alexandrine adventure and he learned lessons from it. Theologians discussed things too much; they used too many Greek phrases. Mystical knowledge must not be changed into matter for endless discussion. The clarity of words, the enlightenment of cities—all that was superficiality! Singing, cheering, smiles, and even some of the conversions—childish nonsense!

And while Athanasius, in the light of Anthony's visions, allowed his gaze and his pen to wander proudly over the immediate future—doubtless the years directly after 358—we can permit ourselves to look further ahead: "You will see . . . Godlessness will slip back into its hiding places. . . ." Godlessness was first of all the Arian heresy, but in a literal sense. More than that it was all heresy, all inadequate and distorted religion, all worship of empty words spoken against the Divinity of Christ. And yet that evil, which had ceased to be an immediate danger, was alive and near at hand.

In the fifth century, an archimandrite from Constantinople named Eutyches, claimed that, after the Incarnation, there was but one nature in Christ. The oecumenical council at Chalcedon condemned this doctrine, which was called Monophysitism, but most of the Egyptians had already adopted it and remained faithful to it.

In the sixth century, the Monophysites chose a patriarch and split off from the Church. Many small sects were to flourish, with very slight shades of difference and perhaps for this reason all the more hostile to each other. Their conflicts were bloody. And, as Arians and Meletians had joined to prevent Athanasius from being elected, so now there were some bewildering intrigues cooked up between the unsuspecting Christians and the Mussulman invaders. It was a matter of hood-winking other Christians over doctrinary details.

We cannot state that Anthony's prophecies covered so long a period and that he foresaw the triumph of Islam and the subordination of the Christian religion throughout the whole of Egypt, but, between Athanasius' lines, we get the impression that Anthony detected misfortune. He refused to be deluded, and, after declaring that clear skies would follow the storm, he offered further advice: "This is my only instruction: do not compromise with the Arians." Here Athanasius spoke for himself, from the thick of the conflict, and he used Anthony's prestige for purposes of propaganda; but he did not invent the gravity of his master's tone. At ninety-four, Anthony had seen terrible things happen. While he was converting the solitudes to Christianity and keeping the demons of Mount Qolzum at bay, he realized that there were other demons patiently and slyly harassing the cities. Christianity had withstood the persecutions and had then met up with heresy. Other sins and temptations were added to those of lust, greed, power, boredom; these others did not affect the monks, but they were dangerous to the intellectuals and the Greeks: the temptations of eloquence, of empty words, of systems built upon airy nothings—a religion of resounding futility. Christ was not apt to manifest Himself between the fifth and sixth points in the demonstration of some specious theory; but He would be present on the darkest of dark nights, after long years of asceticism and slow monotonous drawing near. "I am that I am," declared the God of the Bible, and not: "I am what I prove myself. . . ." Away with wordy battles! Away with circumlocutions! Go straight towards God!

And now we wonder—it will not invalidate the preceding conclusions—why Athanasius did not beseech Anthony to come to Constantinople and say to the Emperor: "Sire, you are being deceived!" And then confound Arius to his face. This would have been more effective than his visit to Alexandria, important though that had been. At least it would have provided a sequel to Alexandria. The Emperor had the key to the situation and he wrote to Anthony with respect and cordiality, which augured well for an interview.

Anthony and Constantine the Red exchanged several letters.

Alexandria Again

The Emperor took the initiative; he was not at all sure of his salvation and gave money to the churches to quiet his anxiety. He felt that friendly relations with Anthony would strengthen his case in the sight of God. So he asked Anthony for advice and this was somewhat bewildering to the man of the desert. What could he say to an earthly sovereign? However, Anthony replied, at first out of ordinary politeness; then he began to put propaganda for Athanasius' cause in his letters—and for the cause of all the weaklings, all the poor, so numerous in Egypt, and, alas, probably in all the countries that made up the empire.

Despite his great age, Anthony, the countryman, might have gone to Constantinople without getting too weary, by land through Palestine and Asia Minor, or, to make time, by sea. Several of the Nicaean bishops had also been no longer in their first youth. Duty always came first! According to an apothegm Constantius (one of the sons and successors to Constantine, with whom Anthony also exchanged letters) asked him several years later to come to Constantinople. Anthony hesitated. He asked the advice of one of his disciples, who answered in Eastern fashion: "If you go, you will be called Anthony; if you stay, it will be Father Anthony." We can easily challenge the accuracy of this anecdote; but if we accept it—and it sounds authentic[1]—it would be difficult to see why Athanasius, with the authority of Patriarch and former pupil, did not say the word that would have sent Anthony to Constantinople. The reasons for this silence are hard to find and the search is fascinating. Doubtless Athanasius deplored the encroachments of Imperial authority upon the domain of religion and would do nothing to increase them. He did not wish to seem to kowtow to the man wearing an Imperial crown who had not asked for baptism and took sides in religious controversies. No compro-

---

[1] Constantius, who reigned in Italy, was hostile to Arianism, while Constans, Lord of the East, favored it. Constantius, who had several times tried to change his brother's opinions, could easily have managed a meeting of the Big Three—himself, Constans, and Anthony—in Constantinople.

mising! No equivocal proposals! Athanasius was by no means
a man of peace first of all. Yet perhaps, in his affectionate admiration for Anthony, there was something of distrust. He was
afraid the man of the desert might not fulminate to his order.
Naturally Anthony was strongly opposed to the Arian heresy,
and what concerned Christ concerned the monks, and so on;
but we have too much the feeling that, in his holiness, he had
reached a place above and beyond polemics; and the sly characters of the Imperial Court would certainly feel the same.
They would get around Anthony with sentimentality and
would try to win him over to more flexible formulas. Must
the practice of asceticism, they would say, be encumbered
with such details as the terms, "ὁμοούσιος," "of the same nature," and "ὁμοιούσιος," "of similar nature"? What good was
a religion that rested completely upon a question of one letter
of the alphabet? Did the two commandments to which Christ
reduced the law and the prophets even touch upon the question? They implied, by a whole system of acts and consequences, that the theologians might split doctrinary hairs. But
wouldn't an open heart be enough, in the meantime, for all
those whom Anthony was defending: the conquered, the
slaves, those whom life had crushed, the homeless, the plague-
ridden, the outcast, and the millions of poor wretches who did
not have the power to think logically?

In the present state of history, it scarcely seems possible to
answer satisfactorily the question we have just asked. Some
will no doubt feel that it does not arise. But let them reflect
that we are at a crucial point in the evolution of Christianity,
and that the prevailing custom today is to deplore the loss of
the purity, authenticity, and tenderness of the faith that
flourished before Constantine's triumph and became somewhat faded afterwards. But this is anticipating, although the
effects of politics in Christianity were bad; the Church had paid

with a part of its independence for large material advantages which it had not sought.

In any case, Anthony had no stomach for such things, whose savor and freshness would have aroused his suspicion. Christianity still retained, for him, its explosive quality. If he had accepted the invitation of Constantius, if he had complied with orders from Athanasius and gone to confer with Constantine, and had been made to subscribe to less rigid formulas by his Arian Brain Trust, he would have hurried back to his desert. Hunter and fisher for the Absolute, he would have continued his great task: the reconciliation of the material universe, the Christian recovery of the earth's surface—the rocks, the sand, the caves, and the storms that swept above them. *Monachus in aeternum.* And he would have continued, as he did immediately after Alexandria, to explore the depths of solitude, poverty, and prayer—thus maintaining the pristine splendor of Christian dynamism with which so many bishops were soon to stupefy and lead to baptism Verlaine's "great white barbarians."

Saint Anthony of the Desert

We must not put this phrase in a context of any sort; it came after an interior conversation, that is, after a silence. It has not the sound of a clarion-like affirmation made in the presence of a questioner, but of a quiet and a happy response to what had seemed an enigma within oneself. Not a grandiose and stirring Eureka, not a shout, but a very personal confidence.

There is no reason to insist further. In itself, the statement is not clever; upon another's lips it would almost certainly have gone unnoticed—but it came from Anthony, from a man without pride who never spoke about himself, and who would not have mentioned this, if it had not involved a special discovery.

The Fathers, from whom we have the apothegm—a stern term which seems out of key with the statement—do not put a date upon it. We are not justified, objectively, in placing it in the final years of Anthony's life. It could have been spoken during the persecutions of Maximinus, before his first journey to Alexandria. Without definite knowledge, we should think it might, at the earliest, have been uttered during the first conversation Anthony had with the brothers who came to Mount Qolzum to surprise him. It possesses, in addition to a mild exclamatory value which gives it a pleasant pungency, a kind of statement-value which, for the biographer who carefully follows the steady development of his chief character, seems to fix the apothegm definitely after his establishment in the desert—that culminating point in Anthony's life. "I have considered my whole life," said Anthony, " and I find that I no longer fear God; I love Him." He who spoke those words understood, not only with his mind but with his whole being, that God did not require all good Christians to be baptized in blood, and that monks could bear witness equally with martyrs. He who spoke had meditated in a cave, on a mountaintop, and the logic of his inner acts had come to him in a blaze of understanding.

Spoken in his last years or not, the apothegm introduces them magnificently. A firm and considered repudiation of one of his former stages of belief was thus made. *Timor Dei initium sap-*

ientiae. But *initium* only! It was not a matter of condemning his early beliefs but of leaving them behind, of forgetting them in order to build a better order.

"I have considered my life, and I find that I no longer fear God; I love Him. How could I fear Him who has revealed Himself to me, who filled the desert with His Presence? How could I fear my Comrade, my one Friend, my Host, my Father?"

Penances followed, one after another. A repudiation of the fear of God did not mean that Anthony, the methodical, was repudiating the first and essential principle of asceticism: redouble one's watchfulness, in order not to let one's effort diminish. The evil spirits, those famous powers of the air, were ever-present. His love of God did not permit him to relax his discipline.

Nevertheless, Anthony's life was more serene now. Dating from a certain time which we cannot fix exactly—it was probably about 340—he had two monks living with him permanently. They were his confidants, his servants, and, if necessary, his secretaries and interpreters; they stood guard to keep his meditations inviolate. When the monks at Pispir had first talked of putting two monks at his disposal, Anthony had probably said to them: "I do not need anyone; I am still in good health. Do not worry about me, and do not get ready to bury me yet." It is likely that he had just had what we of today call "a warning," excessive fatigue, an attack of fever, a fear that he might be discovered stretched out on his mat, very sick indeed; and from such thoughts sprang the idea of not leaving him entirely alone. His ascetic feelings might have taken offense at a reminder of this "warning." They could have argued that the brothers would be his disciples rather than his attendants. Chosen from among the young and most gifted—that is to say the most pious—they might be replaced now and then, thus giving them practical experience in asceticism, as a master class; and

Anthony would report to their superiors on their conduct and progress in virtue.

Whether or not he was taken in by this, Anthony doubtless agreed to the arrangement. He remembered his own ardent beginning when no one had as yet dared to establish himself in the desert, and he was delighted to help those young ones. Though he had no doctrine of his own and was more than pleased to turn over to people like Athanasius the task of deciphering texts and elaborating dogma, he had an independent turn of mind, a liking for intellectual simplicity, and a distrust of big words which he could not have regretted inculcating in others also. It was not a bad idea to place a few good straightforward monks, for leveling purposes, among the Alexandrines, with their startling ability to put everything into formulas and systems. The other monasteries that claimed Anthony as their founder, and whose Fathers occasionally received visits from him, had already considered doing the same thing, and it would have given them a leg up, if their young monks could have gone regularly to Mount Qolzum:

> Behold how good and how pleasant it is
> For brethren to dwell together. . . .

An irreplaceable element, and one hard to define, went out of Anthony's life: a sort of broad, invigorating anxiety; the unfathomable sense of mystery, beginning with that of the desert spaces, a symbol of despairing souls, and the very close communion with Christ, taking the place of the remote multitude of men . . . . Anthony had before received visits of varying duration, although always temporary, and the presence now of these visiting monks only partially interfered with his opportunities for meditation in solitude. He could always escape to his cave whenever he wished to. But we must not anticipate. Anthony was an amazing man to his last hour. Due to the two monks' care of him, his austerity relaxed a little, but he seemed all the more easily to put himself in close touch with God's Presence, and his visionary ability became more pronounced. He walked more slowly, leaned more heavily upon his stout palm-wood staff, and slept sometimes when the afternoon sun blazed down on the mountain; but there was a new serenity in all his gestures. When he climbed the steep, rocky goat track which led to his cave, he breathed hard and stopped every now and then to gather strength. But he was not ashamed of his weakness, and he did not feel that it made him an unworthy monk. He feared God no longer.

All this trust in God brought him one day full recompense. An event occurred, and the three variations of it that we have are widely different, but they do not seem to surround the central facts with suspicion.

Anthony had just reached his ninetieth year. Either a Bedouin desert messenger or some visitors who had lost their way had told him of the presence in the mountains of an old hermit; or an angel had really told him: "Before you, came a man whose feet are too holy to tread the earth; it is in answer to his prayers that the Lord sends the rain and causes the Nile to rise above its banks at the appointed time." However this may have been, Anthony was sure that another hermit lived in the same desert and that he must make his acquaintance. He told the two monks, took up his staff and set forth according to the Coptic text, "with no guide but his thoughts." for he did not know definitely where to begin his search. It was blazing hot, and, if we are to believe Saint Jerome and the Coptic Life of Paul the Hermit, he had some painful encounters—with one of those beings that the learned call "hippocentaurs." then with one of those "that the gentiles call satyrs." Both times, naturally, it was the Devil, furious at finding his old enemy walking about the desert. He had assumed these disguises in order to give Anthony a good fright, but the Coptic *Synaxary*—with great reasonableness—ignores these occurrences in its account of

Paul, the Theban, and we imagine that they were pure mirage, or little touches put in to please the reader.

Evening came, then darkness. Anthony kept on walking (a good chance for the Devil to play tricks on him, but there is no textual evidence that he did). It was not till the next day, and perhaps at nightfall, that Anthony came upon a cave with an overhanging palm and a little wooden door closing off half of it. He threw some pebbles at the door, but the hermit whose meditations he had interrupted barricaded himself with a large stone. Thus Anthony was left outside, in much the same way that he had shut out Paul the Simple several years before.

This time the waiting was of shorter duration. Without even having to mention his own name, Anthony wheedled the shy hermit with gentle words and well-chosen quotations until he opened his door. They embraced, introduced themselves, and began at once to talk of religious matters. Anthony's host, Paul, was one hundred and thirteen years old, and he had been in the desert for a long time, at least sixty years; his clothes had long ago worn out and fallen from him, so that he was now wearing a tunic made of palm-leaves. He had no idea what was happening in the world; he did not know the present Emperor's name, what new heresies had sprung up, or about the victory of Christianity.

Anthony was in the midst of delivering a lecture to Paul when he saw a raven flying towards the cave; and we now find ourselves in the very midst of the miraculous. The bird flew into the cave, hovered a moment above the two men, dropped a loaf of bread, and flapped away. "And when the bird had gone," says the Coptic text, "they marveled at what had happened." We can easily believe this, but we must also understand the reason for Paul's marveling. The raven was an old friend of his and brought his food to him every day, namely half a loaf. Paul marveled that Christ could suddenly change his schedule to meet the needs of two men. Hermits were soldiers of Christ—he who denied that was a liar—and they had a remarkably efficient commissariat officer to look after them.

At this point in the story, Saint Jerome rises to the loftiness of his subject and his flowing style recalls certain fine passages in *Manon Lescaut* or *The Martyrs*. "They gave thanks to the Lord and sat down at the edge of the clear stream. Then they began to argue about breaking the loaf. Who should do it? And the argument lasted till evening. Paul claimed the privilege of host, while Anthony put forward that of his younger age. Finally they agreed that each one should take hold of an end of the loaf and pull, and that each should eat the piece that remained in his hand. This done, they bent over and drank a little from the stream, offering praises to God; then they watched and prayed the night through."

We are still in the realm of the miraculous. On that splendid night, two men whose combined ages totaled two centuries of living, a century and a half of asceticism, and about a century of life in the desert, gave, each to the other, an exclusive recital of psalms and an exhibit of endurance. And a close and fruitful friendship could easily have resulted, for the furtherance of monasticism; but as soon as the day broke and the faces of the hermits emerged from the darkness, Paul, as though he had been a little forgetful in not mentioning something of trifling importance, told his companion that he, Paul, the same Paul who had been fed the evening before by a raven, was at the point of death. Anthony groaned loudly despite his ninety years; though he had known Paul less than a day, he felt like a son about to lose his father. He besought Paul not to abandon him. Paul was calm and told Anthony not to shed tears for him. And would he go to Mount Qolzum and fetch the robe Athanasius, the Archbishop, had given him? For Paul wanted to be buried in it.

This was merely a pretext. Paul was a solitary old man who intended to die alone. Anthony had not slept for two nights and his ninety-year-old legs were stiff, but he set out for Mount Qolzum. The next day, on reaching his hermitage, he wasted no time in answering the brothers' questions but went inside, put the robe over his arm, and started back across the desert. Thus another day passed; a great weariness came over him and his hands gripped the staff in his anxiety lest Paul might die before his return. And the next morning, after walking all night, he had a vision: Paul, surrounded by angels, apostles, and prophets, going up into Heaven. And he was angry because it seemed to him disloyal of Paul to have failed him when his legs were so weary. He reached the cave at last; and, for an hour, he cherished a vain hope that Paul was asleep. At last he decided to clothe him in the beautiful robe and to chant suitable psalms. But, he thought, Paul must have a grave and there was no spade to dig it. Of course he could go back to the hermitage and get one, but the effort after so much walking already—almost four more days of it—was more than he could contemplate. So he concluded that he would stay where he was and die beside his brother.

But God, the God who, with the raven's help, had sent down the rations of bread, doubled to meet the needs of his soldiers— did not view the matter that way. Anthony had barely made his decision not to get the spade, when two magnificent lions rushed into the cave. "When he saw them," says the Coptic manuscript, "his hair stood on end." (If we take that literally, it would prove that baldness had not accompanied old age.) But the two lions, obviously of divine creation, threw them- selves at his feet, and he soon realized that their frightful roar- ing was in reality but weeping. They began to dig the earth with their claws, making a hole the length of a man, and when the grave was ready they licked Anthony's hands and feet with their rough tongues. He was so moved by their thought- fulness that he gave them a generous blessing; whereupon, as if he still felt that a certain caution was necessary, he said, "Off with you now," and the lions politely left the cave.

Alone, he buried his brother; and the following day he took the tunic of palm leaves which Paul had worn and went back to his hermitage, where he told the story of Paul's death to the two monks. Later, at Easter and at Whitsuntide, he reverently clothed himself in the tunic of palm leaves which had belonged to Paul.

Whatever the importance of the legendary parts of this account, there is the fact that Paul and Anthony must have met, and at a time when they were both very old. Saint Jerome has been accused by some of inventing the character of Paul the Hermit in order to take the credit for creating monasticism away from Anthony, whose exploits had been overpraised by Athanasius. "Many people," wrote Saint Jerome, " have wondered who was the first hermit to live in the desert. . . ." He challenges Elias and John the Baptist, discusses Anthony, and then continues peremptorily, "Paul of Thebes began it, but did not give it a name. . . ." Nevertheless, it is clear from his book that Paul of Thebes did not "begin" anything. He entrenched himself in the solitudes, and if an angel from the Lord had not told Anthony to go and look for him, Paul would very probably have died without ever seeing a human face again. During his life he was never an example to anyone.

Saint Jerome tried to use Paul the Hermit to strengthen his case against Anthony, making no real effort to discriminate in detail, but he did not invent Paul or his palm-leaf tunic. The two men really met, the classic desert heat blazed down on them, and they chanted psalms and shared a piece of bread. And even though (we shall certainly not insist on these details) the bread may not have been brought them directly from Heaven by a raven, or Paul's grave dug by two good-hearted lions, this astounding encounter was as great a joy to our aged Anthony as if it had been a gift straight from God. He was a humble man and he never dreamed of being ashamed at having believed himself the first one to come to those remote and solitary regions. All he thought about was that he had almost missed knowing his beloved brother Paul, but that God had been merciful. He felt now that the desert was beginning to be reconciled with Christ.

*   *   *

There is a monastery today close to Paul's cave. It stands about twelve miles, as a crow flies, from the monastery of Saint Anthony; but it is impossible to follow a straight line in going from one to the other. The mountain has to be skirted, and an extra sixteen hours of walking is required. Anthony was ninety when the meeting took place, and his walking speed was no longer that of young man. He had started off with no idea where he was going and doubtless covered more miles than we have indicated. At night he walked more slowly; he may even have stopped now and then. And it is likely that Saint Jerome did not exaggerate when he said that the journey took him almost two days each way.

Assuredly Anthony displayed magnificent resistance. And we have not the slightest doubt that, at least once a year, he crossed the desert to visit his spiritual children along the Nile. He stayed in harness. The approach of death did not increase his desire for leadership, or, as often occurs with very simple men, cause him to hang on in order to be certain of leaving his mark. But a strange quality became noticeable in him: his years of asceticism were bringing him rewards during his earthly existence. The eyes of his mind saw more clearly than before, and he dealt more easily with problems involving human souls and daily events. And he did not propose to confine the advantages of this new enlightenment to himself; he would let all monks profit by it.

In one of the groups organized for study, with Anthony present, he was heard to repeat the phrase: "I no longer fear God; I love Him," which had sounded so many times in the minds of all. And another time, the older ascetics crowded round him to find out what he considered to be the most effective virtue with which to combat the Devil, the one most likely to lead their hearts towards God's perfection. Darkness fell, and the discussion had continued into the night, before Anthony uttered a word. It was only after all the experts were exhausted that he made up his mind to speak. With professional subtlety, he paid tribute to the virtues already discussed, whose merits were beyond question. But it was experience, in the last analysis, which showed how, in certain circumstances, the practice of the virtues mentioned had done more harm than good. And why was this? Because they were practiced without the help of a very simple but indispensable one: discretion. The palm went to that virtue. *"Omnium namque virtutum genitrix et custos atque moderatrix discretio est.* Discretion is the mother, the protectress, and the regulator of all virtues. . . ."

If we can speak of a particular doctrine held by Anthony, though his praise of discretion cannot be dated, we believe this and his declaration of love for God constituted his swan song. Though it may possibly one day be established that the conference of the Fathers, on the subject of the chief Christian virtue, was held between the two visits to Alexandria, Anthony's declaration brings us face to face with a final result, with one of those truths reached by the soul after prolonged meditation, and never again altered, which shed a clear restful light upon old age.

What meaning shall we give to the word *discretion?* Not, we realize, the narrow contemporary sense, but a very broad significance, which the Abbé Jean Brémond calls the "knowledge of the practical, of opportunity. To be discreet is to know what virtue to make use of at a certain moment." And that is not easy, as again we realize; but long practice in meditative living—and who would dream of becoming a monk without it?—cures indecision. The discreet man does not make himself conspicuous, and he never boasts. Anthony's discretion, and afterwards, that of the desert Fathers, was somewhere between moderation and wisdom.

Anthony's apothegms, almost all of them relating to what may, up to a certain point, be called his public life—that long period after his leaving the fort and up to his death—performed the great service of demonstrating that the acquisition of discretion could not be managed in one day, but was the result of a protracted series of incidents and struggles.

Anthony was informed one day of the ill behavior of a nun. He took his staff and trudged off to rebuke her. On his way, Christ appeared to him, questioned him, and finally reproached him for his hardheartedness. Crestfallen, Anthony returned to his hermitage. In another vision, in Alexandria, he had been informed that he—the great monk—had not the religious stature of a certain harness maker. So he went to find the man, admitting easily that this could be so, and impelled by a pious curiosity.

"Explain to me how you live," he asked; and the question seemed absurd to the artisan.

"When I get up in the morning, I tell myself that I am the lowest of the low, and that the other people in the city will get into Heaven while I shall probably be left outside the gates. You see, I'm just an ordinary man. I start to work and keep repeating to myself, while working, that I am a good-for-nothing, and that the others are wonderful people. Then evening comes—and that's all, my friend."

Anthony raised his arms:

"That's all—you say! But it is amazing! Without leaving your house, you are getting closer and closer to Heaven. When I think that I myself, just as though I didn't know the value of discretion, have tied myself down to a whole life of solitude! I give you my word that, as an athlete of Christ, you are far ahead of me."

The seeds of all the virtues were present in Anthony as a child—even discretion, as was shown by his absolute obedience to his parents. Later on it can be said that discretion was the least of his worries. He was constantly looking for trouble;

always annoying the old man within him; setting against himself all the light brigades of Satan's army. Who was it who deprived himself of sleep, went two days without a crumb of bread, had showdowns with Asmodeus, Beelzebub, and all that crew? Anthony—always Anthony!

Must we speak of the difference between the adult and the old man? Are we in a position to say that the second disowned the first?

The incident of the harness maker in Alexandria must certainly not be taken literally. Once again the Fathers, in their good humor, have probably elaborated quite a simple occurrence. For instance, the harness maker would have thrown himself at Anthony's feet, protesting that he was unworthy to be near him. And Anthony, his modest soul slightly annoyed, would put things in their proper relation: an artisan of the city was just as good as the most austere of monks, if he possessed a humble heart.

Probably, for himself, Anthony continued to favor hardships, the "indiscretions" of his ascetic beginnings. "You need not do as much as I do," he always told others, thus stressing and agreeing with the moderation of Pachomius. But when he looked again at his past life, he did not consider that the young Anthony should have behaved in a less fanatical manner. He gave thanks to God for His continual guidance, and, very logically and naturally, for having reconciled his program of austerity towards himself with the ability to be the great Father of Monks, indulgent to all.

Anthony's holiness was sometimes upsetting to his questioners, but he was so humble in his ways that they were eventually at their ease with him. They even put puzzlers to him. Once when trying to help his two monk companions to avoid acedia, he chatted for a while with them and soon had them laughing. A hunter of gazelles and wild asses came in during one of these periods of relaxation, a rough customer who must have thought that they were behaving oddly for hermits.

"Put an arrow in your bow and draw it," said Anthony; and when the hunter had complied, "Draw it again."

"It is done."

"Again!"

"Not so fast! If I keep on bending the bow, it will break."

"It is the same with God's work," said Anthony with a smile. "If we push the monks too hard, they will wear themselves out, so we let them relax now and then."

The incident probably went the rounds of the monasteries. "He is a fine man," the young monks would whisper, and many of them thought, "Better than our Fathers here." A delegation was sent to old Anthony, and his gentle courteous manner further reassured the probationers.

"How can we be saved?" they asked, hoping he would say that they had exceeded themselves in asceticism.

Anthony bristled. "I am not an oracle. Read your Gospels and then you will know everything."

"No, no," they protested, "do not be too modest. We know how great your knowledge is. You are the father of all monks and you must give us a word of your own wisdom."

Anthony pretended stupidity. "Haven't you read, 'Whosoever shall smite thee on thy right cheek, turn to him the other also' ?"

The young monks hid their embarrassment behind ironical smiles, and one of them declared, with what he thought was unusual audacity: "You forget that we are not athletes of Christ. We cannot do what you ask."

"Well, don't do it," smiled Anthony. "Only, when someone smites you on the cheek, try to endure it."

"That would be impossible for us," they answered.

Anthony calmly turned to one of his monk companions. "These men are sick. Be good enough to stir them up a little milk pudding."

Athanasius says that when Anthony was a hundred years

old he inspected the monasteries along the Nile. Wherever he went, he told the brothers that he would not come again, that Providence had made known to him the near approach of death. Apparently he had had another "warning"; from it he emerged physically depleted, and it may have been more of a signal than a warning. But he was hale and hearty; he could walk for many hours; his eyesight was good; and his powers of reasoning were more lucid than ever. Nevertheless, he could not escape all the indignities of old age: when he knelt, his old bones cracked, and he needed help to get to his feet again.

> Behold, how good and how pleasant it is
> For brethren to dwell together. . . .

The anthem of the monks probably followed the founder of monasticism wherever that last triumphant round of visits took him. When monks and friends of Christ were alone together, the general situation of the Church, the confusion of the Arian intrigues, and the rough treatment of the Archbishop Athanasius, who had been well grounded in asceticism, could be deplored, but no less on that account was there good reason to sing joyful praises. Not because bad luck had to be faced with cheerfulness, but because their faith in God, upon which monasticism was founded, required it—and quite rightly so.

Occasionally, a goblet of wine was offered by the monks to their Father Anthony, as a mark of reverence. This conformed to the ascetic principle that only the sick and the aged might drink wine.

"Stay with us, good father," the brothers said, when he was about to take leave of them. They embraced him and wept because they did not want to let him go. Why must he return to Mount Qolzum? Why go back there to die in silence and alone, when he could draw his last breath here, where everyone loved him?

Saint Anthony of the Desert

Anthony escaped at last. Perhaps it would have satisfied an unavoidable human weakness in him, had he awaited death in one of those monasteries, but for several reasons which even his silence made clear, weakness was not a part of his program. He did not want to die here; such a death would have seemed to him too pampered—chanted psalms and softly treading monks —in comparison with death in the desert solitudes. It was true that he must die soon, and his body showed signs of weakening, but it had not failed him yet. There was no reason for him to retire to a monastery as though to a hospital.

He shared with Paul, and almost all the great hermits of the period, a grim determination to be self-sufficient and a nuisance to no one. The idea that his death might be the occasion for noisy ceremonial was repulsive to him. Death should be an act of simplicity, a small physical formality to be accomplished in silence: head turned to the wall and the soul escaping into Heaven with as few people as possible looking on. The death of Paul the Hermit had been a model for that kind of death.

Anthony was used to the desert and he was determined that his end should be like Paul's. He had no special wish to die at the foot of Mount Qolzum and be buried there, as Chateaubriand was later laid to rest with his head facing the open sea. His desires were not ostentatious; he merely wanted to end his days in the place where the meaning of life, so to speak, was so clearly exhibited. Let the welcoming sands have his bones; let his body return to that world of vegetable, animal, and mineral which must be reconciled with God.

Athanasius speaks of a final reason, though, to our sense, it does not deserve to be regarded as the principal one or to be taken with full seriousness. Anthony must have been fonder of Pispir than of any of the other monasteries which claimed him as founder, because it was placed where there were so many reminders of his conflicts, and perhaps too because it was the most prosperous and pious of them all. But no favoritism! He was silent on that score, thinking that if he were to die in a certain monastery it would be a disadvantage to the others; for the monks had their pettiness. "We have Father Anthony's tomb here." Of course there was nothing wrong in saying that; what of the man who was keeping the palm-leaf tunic that Paul the Hermit had worn? But would he really be buried? Or would his body receive the usual absurd and hateful reverence? "The Egyptians liked to wind the bodies of their pious dead in linen," says Athanasius, "especially those of their martyred saints. Instead of burying them, they laid them upon beds, keeping them at home and thinking thus to honor them." And he reminds his readers of the fact that Anthony had fought strenuously with the bishops about these customs, urging their agreement with him. The Catholic Church did not take a stand on this matter, but, since the bodies of patriarchs and prophets had at one time been buried in the usual way, especially the body of Christ, the custom of not concealing the dead seemed, quite naturally, to be tainted with paganism. But Anthony knew that the monks were not always to be trusted. For very pious motives, such as creating a reason for pilgrimages or obtaining from Heaven a series of miracles that would make Arianism ridiculous, they were capable of ignoring his last requests and exposing his body, like that of some strange creature, in a church. . . . No, the earth would take back its own. Anthony's body would disintegrate, as it was written; it would become one with the sands of the desert.

At long intervals, Athanasius uses expressions which show his clear understanding of his chief character: "He went to the mountain as if to his house." And then, when Anthony took leave of his monks and withdrew to the desert to die: "Like a man departing from a foreign land to return home. . . ." This phrase must be taken two ways: "home" meant both the solitudes and Heaven.

Anthony's instructions to the monks, as they are reported

to us by Athanasius, correspond in many ways to the biographer's own desires, for he was completely absorbed in his anti-Arian and anti-Meletian activities, and, without the least dishonesty, was using Anthony in his campaign. "Do not have any dealings with the Arians . . . or with the schismatic Meletians. . . ." Thus indeed Anthony should have spoken, and he must have warned against being disquieted by the temporary success of the heresies; but unless we are greatly mistaken, he laid the chief emphasis on asceticism, with repetitions, improbable stories, hammer blows alternating with counsels of great tenderness. "Feed my lambs, feed my sheep." It was by the practice of asceticism that one became an ascetic. A monk should say to himself every morning: "Today, I am going to die."

Accompanied by his two body servants, Anthony crossed the desert without mishap, and settled down again beside his mountain. Several months went by; and then, one morning, he woke up feeling infinitely weary. Dizziness and shortness of breath. . . . "Father Anthony, your time has come!" He summoned the two monks and told them that as they might see, he was going to die.

"Are your feet cold? Shall we bring you some bread and wine?" they asked automatically. He shook his head, and they fell to their knees. A great pride mingled with their grief: they would be the ones to witness Anthony's death!

"Speak to us, Father," they begged. "Do not leave us until you have given your final advice. When you are not here, we shall be like young birds fallen from the nest."

Anthony scolded them. How could they say such things when Christ was their best friend? Then with faltering voice he spoke a few sentences, formulating for the last time the duties of an ascetic: "Do not stop on your way. Keep your joy in God. Beware of heresies." And he commanded them:

"Let no one carry off my body to Egypt and put it in a house. Shroud it yourselves and hide it in the earth. No one but yourselves must know where my grave is." He stopped for a moment. Had he forgotten something? "Divide my clothes," he continued. "Give one skin, and the cloak I've been wearing, to Athanasius. It was new when he gave it to me, and I have worn it out. Give the other skin to Serapion, the bishop; and you can keep my camel's hair hood." Then he smiled feebly at them: "And now, my children, Anthony is on his way. He is not with you any longer."

The two monks bent over and kissed him. The smile was still upon his lips.

It would be unfitting to prolong the account of that peaceful death—so simple, and by no means unbeautiful. Anthony died as though he had done nothing else all his life, which, if we take from death all its artificial grief and sadness, is absolutely true. Death was merely a rendezvous with God. There was a stark simplicity about the scene. "He stretched out his feet, and, with a friendly glance at his companions, showing his pleasure at their presence, he lay for a moment with a look of joy on his face. Then he left them to join his Fathers."

The monks quickly followed Anthony's instructions, for there was always the danger of unexpected visitors. They buried his corpse carefully in a well-chosen spot, tramping the earth afterwards and scattering pebbles—in any case, concealing the location of the grave. And they never disclosed their secret.

In 391 or 392, Anthony's disciple, Macarius of Skete, died at the age of ninety-seven. During his last moments two saints appeared, in the traditional manner, to take him into God's presence. He recognized one of them as Saint Pachomius, the founder of monasteries as powerful as cathedrals. The other . . . "Don't you see who I am?" came the gentle question.

Macarius looked at him more carefully and then spoke: "I think you are my good Father Anthony." After which Macarius died.

*   *   *

Saint Anthony's Monastery on the Red Sea takes pride in possessing the mortal remains of its founder, eventually discovered at the foot of Mount Qolzum, but this does not prevent two French churches from also claiming to possess them.

Back of this situation is a tale as involved as an adventure story. In the sixth century, the Emperor Constantius had a daughter who was possessed by nine demons which resisted all exorcism and refused to leave the Princess until the body of the great Saint Anthony was brought to her room. With little hope, the Emperor sent a bishop to Egypt to bring back the body. Miraculously assisted by two leopards, the bishop was successful in finding it. The nine demons abandoned the Princess at top speed, and Constantius placed Anthony's remains in the Church of Saint Sophia.

Much later, a certain gentleman from the province of Dauphiné, named Jocelyn, returning from Palestine by way of Constantinople, charmed the Emperor Alexis Comnenus to such an extent that he offered Jocelyn any gift he cared to name. Jocelyn requested and obtained the body of Saint Anthony. He took it back to his estate at La Motte-Saint-Didier Then, later, two other gentlemen, who had been cured of erysipelas by praying to Saint Anthony, removed the remains to a Benedictine monastery in the village. At that point, events became complicated. The Benedictines had to make way for the Antonines, and the latter, if we are to believe their account, carried Anthony's body at night down to the River Isère, where they put it into a boat which was then pushed out into the current. The boat, it was said, grounded on a sand bar in the Rhone near Arles. At La Motte-Saint-Didier nothing was known of the body's removal.

Veterans' Peace

Thus Anthony's last wishes are said not to have been carried out. But though his actual remains may never have been found, and though, as we like to think, he may still be at rest in some unexplored desert cave, men keep on venerating these bones, which, with the modesty of a true Christian and a man of solitude, he was determined should mingle forever with the earth.

We might be tempted to speak here of a setback for Anthony, on a much higher plane. It is perhaps not fitting that we should put forward our own opinions, and, regarding our desires as actualities, declare that he would have severely disapproved of the Coptic schism. Furthermore, no matter how great the glory of his name, Anthony does not by any means represent the whole ancient Egyptian Church, which had so many thinkers and martyrs. Supposing that there was a break in the religious evolution of the country, Anthony had not been alone in his efforts to prevent this from occurring. Having said this, and since the name "Father of Monks" is largely justified—Anthony having played a major role in the development of monastic civilization—we can at least deplore the Egyptian decadence. What has become of Christ's athletes in Anthony's native land, which was so dear to his heart, and whose language was the only one he spoke? Where is all that pious exaltation? In the Wadi Natron, at Qolzum, at Pispir and elsewhere, there are a few sleepy monasteries, getting their scanty religious sustenance from dead traditions. And the once living flesh of Egypt, with its young hope, is no more today than a dusty curiosity for tourists to look at, of no stature compared to the monuments of past ages which a youthful Christianity scorned. Laughing at oblivion, these monuments now boldly command the admiration of everyone, including the Christians themselves.

A setback for Anthony? Yes, if we may speak of a setback for Christ because the Jews refused to acknowledge Him as

247

the Messiah and because He sent His disciples forth to preach
His Gospel to all nations. Anthony's message possessed a universal value, and what did not thrive in Egypt was to flourish
in the Western world.

We can say that up to a certain point, the message has been
"revised and corrected." Theologians have considered that,
during Anthony's lifetime, people were much more outspoken
in their expectation of the return of Christ to the earth; at
the time when monasticism had become well established and
there could be no hesitation as to building it on solid foundations—since the time of the Second Coming was uncertain—
what might be called the revolutionary excess of earlier years
no longer seemed essential. But this did not prevent the new
moderation from drawing inspiration not only from the example of Pachomius, but also from the great leitmotiv of the
aging Anthony: discretion and pure love.

Nor did this prevent the new moderation from being entirely relative, from depending upon a certain initial violence,
an early period of confusion. "If possible the monk must tell
his elders confidently the number of steps he takes, and how
many drops of water he drinks in his cell." The precision of
this apothegm of Anthony's runs counter to the preoccupa-
tions of our day and tempts us to smile a little. Modern Christians pride themselves on practicing a much broader type
of religion, one that is much more sociable and social. No
more flights into the desert; instead, the love of cities and
crowds. Yet contemporary monasticism does not object to the
spirit in which Anthony acted and spoke. Its discipline is
much more flexible, but it never fails to be explicit and to require much from the man who adopts it. Even if his solitude
remains an inward thing, it is, for him, indispensable; and the
dialogue between man and God, meditation and prayer, retain their insistent importance.

To assess the present position of Anthony, or to pronounce

upon the continuing value of his work and precepts, is beyond the scope of this study. But at the moment of leaving the monk, we come again to the question that was asked at the beginning of this book. Did Anthony, or did he not, provide a mere pretext for artists and men of letters? There is something to be said on both sides of this question. None of them has attempted to disengage the "historical" personality of Anthony from his encumbering legends, and almost all of them have striven to present him in one of his phases—the Anthony of the temptations peopled with visions of women and furious beasts, rather than the hero with the full sweep of his thinking and his unending conflicts, love casting out fear, and fanaticism yielding to discretion. But they have fully grasped and given us what there was in him of stiffness, abruptness, and immeasurable greatness. And we see the man who lived in a tomb, shut himself in an old fort for twenty years, and then disappeared into the desert with the joyous ease of a swimmer plunging into a limpid pool.

To picture him with a pig, as religious iconography does, is an excellent bit of fun and in no sense irreverent. Egyptian monks of the great epoch might not have cared to be painted with a pig, but, after all these centuries, Anthony takes on a singularly changeable aspect, naive and good-natured, and a certain amount of deception is justified. The pig has been explained as a symbol of lust; it is suggested that the corkscrew-tailed companion represents temptations overcome. This is possible, though there are many explanations. We shall speak of only one other, surely not valid, but of interest to Frenchmen. Anthony, according to this legend, once went to France, summoned there by a monarch whose son had been born with a pig's head and was therefore not well fitted to take his father's place when the time came. In front of the palace, Anthony spied a little blind pig to which, out of pity, he restored sight immediately. "I will pay you in kind for this," said the mother sow, beside herself with gratitude. And a few moments later, Anthony needed only to touch the Dauphin with the tips of his fingers to give him a human head.

Anthony of the Desert, Anthony of the Pig . . . it availed him nothing not to be a native of France, or, in his holy way, to be snobbish about his Egyptian nationality; mediaeval France claimed him immediately as an unfailing friend. And in a very few years he found himself the patron of gravediggers, gardeners, basket makers, glovers, shearers, weavers, butchers, confectioners, bell ringers, firemen, makers of Nevers china, and Reims gunsmiths, and a famous specialist, as well, in the curing of erysipelas. Is it difficult to imagine such enthusiasm. It seems strange for the land of the *fabliaux* [1] thus to involve itself with the man who of all men was most severe in the matter of privation, the man who cared nothing about rational living, the man who abandoned himself to fierce battles with the demonic hordes! But that point of view is oversimplified. We can no more interpret Mediaeval France in terms of the *fabliaux* than we can turn Anthony into a man of gloom. The pork butchers might joke about his pig; but there was about him a clear decisiveness and an air of being able, as it were, to produce a perfect piece of work at any moment, and these qualities appealed strongly to the artisan able, as it were, to produce a perfect piece of work at any crushed monsters that were more awful than the most terrifying gargoyles? Besides, he was a resourceful man, a stubborn fighter upon whose aid to call in the most desperate moments, and with all that, a man of extraordinary humility. It may not have been amusing for probationers to live with him in the desert, but nevertheless a great debt was owed him. And he

[1] In the pages of desert literature there appears a monk from Gaul who warmly defends the cause of his countrymen in the matter of food. "Your way," he says to a fellow monk, "is to miss no opportunity to accuse us of being gross eaters. But it would be cruel of you to force us Gauls to live like angels, and in any case I am sure the angels themselves eat for the pleasure of eating."

had made truly axiomatic and fundamental the principle, "A gloomy monk is a bad monk."

In this affection on the part of the Gallic people for Anthony of the Desert were mingled pity, a kind of sympathetic fun-poking, admiration, unavowed curiosity, and absolute confidence. It seems to have been a very understandable affection. The hermit of Mount Qolzum was one of man's greatest friends. An apothegm records: "Three monks made a habit of going to see the blessed man every year. During one of these visits, two of them questioned him about the things of the mind and the soul's salvation. The other monk was absolutely silent, asking no questions. After quite a time, Father Anthony said to him: 'You have been here so long, and you have asked me nothing?' Then the third monk spoke: 'All I need is to look at you, Father.' "

For centuries, the drifting sands of the desert have been piling up to obscure Anthony's existence from the historian, but an honest striving to draw close to it will soon be rewarded by the exquisite awareness of a vivid physical presence. Out of the dark past will emerge a true and living man. The mysterious waves of his prayers are still surging across the world, and those words uttered so long ago in silence and solitude have the power even now to stir to their very depths the souls of men with ears attuned.